HASR

FARM BUILDINGS OF THE WEALD
1450-1750
A wood/pasture region in south-east England
once dominated by small family farms

David and Barbara Martin

Farm Buildings of the Weald
© David & Barbara Martin

ISBN(10) 1-905223-24-2
ISBN(13) 978-1-905223-24-4

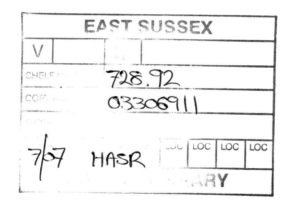
Typeset and produced 2006 by:

Marketing & Publications Ltd

Hill Farm
Castle Acre Road
Great Dunham
King's Lynn
Norfolk, PE32 2LP
Tel: 01760 755645
Fax: 01760 755316
Email: publishing@heritagemp.com
Website: www.heritagemp.com

CONTENTS

LIST OF ILLUSTRATIONS

PREFACE

This present volume is essentially a metamorphosis of a previous study entitled 'Old Farm Buildings in Eastern Sussex, 1450-1750', which first appeared in 1982 as Volume 3 of the privately published occasional series *Historic Buildings in Eastern Sussex*. The product of an intensive phase of fieldwork, this cheaply produced, limited edition volume sold out rapidly and was republished in similar format in 1992, but by 1995 this too had sold out.

Since then printing technology has moved on very rapidly. Whereas the limited budget available in both 1982 and 1992 meant that it was impractical to include anything more than a very limited number of black-and-white photographs, with the continued development of desk-top publishing and the advent of print-on-demand, such restraints have at last been lifted. For these reasons, when the opportunity arose to yet again reprint 'Old Farm Buildings' the decision was taken to develop the original text into a new publication which includes a greatly increased number of illustrations.

This course of action has allowed other improvements too. In analysing and presenting the results of the original surveys in 1982 we felt it essential that the buildings be considered not merely as examples of ancient architecture, but that they be placed within their overall agricultural context. It was the changing fortunes and techniques of agriculture which moulded their design, prompted their periods of alteration and extension and which finally rendered them obsolete. Obviously, as buildings archaeologists, we relied heavily upon the researches of local agricultural historians for much of the background information; in particular the articles by Brent, Chalklin, Cornwall and Searle were of great assistance. This was, however, supplemented by our own research, especially regarding the size of agricultural holdings, the quantity of land devoted to arable, and the analysis of early 18th-century inventories. Because of the constraints of space, a heavily summarized version of this research appeared in the original 1982 volume, whereas within this present publication that summary is replaced by the unabridged text, updated where considered necessary.

Regarding the buildings themselves, we have always been aware that the thematic, analytical approach adopted in the original text addressed the individual elements found in historic farm buildings, but failed to give a holistic view of individual structures. To address this shortcoming two additional chapters are included in which a series of case studies are presented. The first of these concentrates on medieval barns: the second deals with the two centuries up to 1750. It would perhaps at this point be worth mentioning something about the illustrations included within this volume. The aim throughout has been to give a clear visual impression of the points mentioned in the text, and for this reason perspective and architectural drawings have been included. Whereas the maps and architectural sketches are drawn to scale, it should be emphasized that the perspective illustrations are not and, furthermore, some details in this latter group have had to be omitted in the interests of clarity. For this reason any researcher wishing to make use of the information collected during on-site survey work should always refer to the detailed archive reports on each building. The archive is deposited in the East Sussex Record Office where the individual reports are held under the generic reference ESRO HBR/1.

Although the number of farm buildings surveyed by us since 1982 has not been anything like the quantity previously studied, these additional buildings have in some instances added considerably to knowledge. Furthermore, some of the buildings included within the original study have been revisited during conversion work, and this has resulted in a number of revisions to previously held views. Although no attempt has been made to modify the statistics used within the original analysis, where necessary the text has been fully revised to take these new discoveries into account and to amend previously held views.

It is our hope that the modifications listed above have enhanced the value of the original study and will encourage others to contribute similar studies, either into other agricultural regions or for later periods within the study area dealt with here. In this respect it should be emphasised that this publication is the result of detailed analysis into a small region of England and should be used to compare and contrast the buildings of other areas and periods. It will, hopefully, indicate the kinds of features which need to be considered, but should not be used as a pro-forma for the development and dating of similar buildings found elsewhere. At present there can be little doubt that the subject remains a woefully neglected aspect of our built heritage, an aspect which deserves much additional attention.

In carrying out our research into farm buildings we have accumulated many debts of gratitude for help and assistance freely given. We wish to express our gratitude to the owners and tenants of the agricultural buildings for so willingly allowing access to their properties, to Laurence Woodham, then county chairman of the National Farmers' Union for publicising to the local farmers the aims of our research, to Gwen Jones for her advise regarding oasthouses, and to the staff of the East Sussex Record Office for their invaluable and patient assistance throughout our research. Special thanks must go to Christopher Whittick, the late Margaret Whittick, and Don and Maureen Clark for their constructive criticism of the original text.

A large number of illustrations have been included within the volume. Most have been supplied from our own archive, but a few historical photographs are derived from other collections. Most notable amongst these are the scenes of local rural life taken by the pioneer photographer George Wood (Figures 2.14, 2.17, 2.18, 2.23, 2.29, 2.30, 2.31, 3.2 and 5.1). We are grateful to Hastings Museum and Art Gallery for allowing these scenes to be reproduced. Likewise, The National Trust are to be thanked for allowing reproduction of the exceptionally early photograph of 1854 showing the oasthouse at Newhouse, Bodiam (Figure 13.17). Sadly the sources of the old photographs included within Figures 1.9, 3.14, 4.6, 13.11 and 14.16 are anonymous, but the efforts of these early photographers are, nonetheless, warmly acknowledged. The plan of an ideal oasthouse as advocated by Reynold Scot (Figure 13.1) is reproduced from 'a Perfitte Platforme of a Hoppe Garden (1574).

David and Barbara Martin
April 2006

1   INTRODUCTION

Anyone who enjoys the countryside, whether interested in historic buildings or not, cannot fail to notice how an ancient farmhouse with its attendant cluster of traditional farm buildings enhances a view. The more elderly among us, however, will also have noticed how, of late, such views are becoming increasingly hard to find, for even where traditional farm buildings survive they have usually been converted into dwellings or - if still in agricultural use - they are dwarfed by functional concrete- or steel-framed structures which seem entirely alien to the countryside in which they are set. Yet, putting sentiment aside, it should always be remembered that farming is a large and important industry upon which we rely for much of our food. As such it is essential that, like other industries, it is run efficiently with modern machinery and convenient buildings.

Putting it bluntly, most traditional farm buildings have become both inconvenient to use and expensive to maintain and thus, in time-honoured tradition, are having to make way for their successors. Until the late 1980s this mostly meant demolition or abandonment. Many gems of vernacular architecture - prominent landscape features in their day - have been lost in this way. In many instances the loss has occurred silently without even a photograph having been taken. This should be considered a particular tragedy in the case of the High Weald of Kent and Sussex, for the area was exceptional in England for the number of surviving agricultural buildings which pre-dated the 'Agricultural Revolution'. Such a rich heritage should have been cherished, yet perhaps because such buildings were so 'common' locally they were for a long time ignored as a subject for serious study. It was not until the late 1960s that the recording of farm buildings in eastern Sussex got underway, and even then the rate of survey was initially very slow.

By 1977 so many local traditional farm buildings had been destroyed, and the rate of attrition was accelerating so fast that it was obvious that the speed of destruction was seriously outstripping the rate of survey. Thus, in 1978 an extensive but rapid superficial survey was undertaken in order to ascertain the extent of the problem. This was followed during the springs of 1979-1982 by a period of intensive recording intended to cover all surviving farm buildings which were considered to predate *c*1750. By 1982 all but twenty of the then known examples had been inspected, measured and interpreted. Permission to survey was withheld in only five of these

Figure 1.1
Farmhouse and medieval barn at Burgham, Etchingham. Neither building looks anything like it did when first built: the walls of both originally showed exposed timber framing whilst the barn, and probably the house, had a thatched roof covering. Yet, despite these changes, both buildings show features which help give the High Weald its unique local character. [From a slide]

Figure 1.2
The modern buildings which dominate the traditional buildings within this farmyard at
Home Farm, Vinehall Street, Whatlington could be located anywhere in England.
They do nothing to enhance the local character of the region. [From a slide]

Figure 1.3
Despite its present totally modern external appearance, this barn at Bunces, Penhurst
is a survivor. Embedded within it is the frame of a small timber-framed barn built in 1702.
It has been re-roofed and extended on three sides. For an interior view see Figure 7.14. [287/33]

Figure 1.4
The last remnants of a small, probably 17th-century
barn at Millers Farm, Ninfield. [From a slide]

20 cases: perhaps significantly all five were owned by persons not engaged in farming. In the remaining instances either the owner could not be located, or the building had already been converted into a dwelling.

The objective of this period of intensive survey work was to analyse and make sense of this rich source of data before it was lost forever. It was felt that these neglected buildings had the potential to much enhance the study of local vernacular architecture and, more important, our understanding of local agriculture in past times. The importance of agriculture to this country is beyond doubt, as indeed is the role it has played in our history. As an historical subject it has long been studied. Locally the theme is well represented by learned articles within the pages of *Sussex Archaeological Collections*. Yet, to our knowledge, not one of these articles mentions farm buildings, let alone makes use of them as an aid to the study of agriculture. It is not only agricultural historians who have ignored them; as will be obvious from the preceding paragraphs, buildings archaeologists too have till recently given them little attention. Many fully-illustrated, detailed reports exist on farmhouses, yet all too often the associated barns, of equal antiquity, are dismissed in a single paragraph. Even R T Mason in his pioneer work *Framed Buildings of the Weald* only found room in 99 pages of text for fourteen lines regarding barns. Of all the local researchers, only Stuart Rigold recognized the importance of the agricultural buildings: his article 'Some Major Kentish Timber Barns' which appeared in *Archaeologia Cantiana* **81** in 1966 will long stand as a masterpiece of its kind.

Since 1982 a few new studies have been published. In 1983 Lucy Caffyn presented a study of farm buildings in three mid Sussex parishes, whilst in 1990 the memorial volume to R T Mason included three chapters on barns.[1] Gwen Jones and John Bell brought

Figure 1.5
Medieval barn at Limden Farm, Ticehurst, under demolition on a foggy day in December 1975.
It was chance that the authors were passing, and thus it was possible to obtain a record before
the building disappeared: in many other instances no such opportunity presented itself. [163/26]

*Figure 1.6
Crownpost roof over
the barn at Limden
Farm, Ticehurst,
viewed during
demolition in 1975.
163/29]*

their work on Sussex and Kent Oasthouses to publication in 1992.[2] But it is worrying to relate that many farmyards are still being demolished or converted to new uses without any archaeological record being made. Given the general lack of interest in traditional farm buildings, it is of particular concern to observe that today it would be difficult to undertake a similar study to that presented within the pages of this volume. So many buildings were destroyed during the period immediately prior to the late 1980s that in many parts of the country the sample available for study is now too small to be representative of the buildings which once existed. As an indication as to the gravity of the situation, in 1992 the authors of this volume were commissioned to undertake a study to ascertain the fate of the 178 barns of pre-1750 date included within the detailed study carried out by us ten years earlier. Also included were 12 barns identified since that date, giving a total sample of 190 buildings.[3] The study found that in the interim about a fifth of that total has been destroyed: 32 barns (17% of the sample) had been demolished and a further four lay in total ruin. Amongst the casualties were some of the most stunning and important within the sample: some were of medieval date. In 1992 only 58% of the barns survived in an unconverted state: most of these stood either totally redundant or were little used and poorly maintained.

Back in 1982 it was still virtually impossible to obtain permission to convert barns into houses. It was only during the late 1980s that attitudes changed as those responsible for conserving our heritage realized that this course of action was the only means of preserving this important class of building. Undoubtedly it was as a result of this change that the number of barns lost since

they had been surveyed was not higher - already by 1992 almost a quarter of the sample had been converted. Since then the percentage has increased considerably, whereas, encouragingly, very few of the buildings which survived in 1992 have been demolished subsequently.

Allowing the conversion of farm buildings into dwellings has always been controversial, and to this day opinions remain divided. Yet it has always been the case that unless an alternative, economically-viable use can be found for a redundant building, it will disappear. Clearly where retention of an historical building in its original use is not an option, if that building is to survive conversion is the only choice available. Whether such conversion strips the building in question of its architectural and historical interest and diminishes the landscape in which it is set is another matter. The answer has much to do with the way in which the conversion is achieved, rather than the basic concept.

With regards to preserving the special architectural and historical interest of a building there are, in our opinion, a few golden rules. Most obvious of all - though it is all too often forgotten in favour of financial gain - the conversion must not be allowed to destroy historical fabric. In a timber-framed building that means the frame should be conserved to a high standard, repairing rather than replacing damaged timbers wherever possible. Where this proves impossible to achieve, decayed timbers should be replaced with accurate replicas cut from green timber. Although using secondhand material for such repairs may seem the best solution, such action is best compared to replacing the damaged pages of a manuscript with pages from a document of similar style, but having a different content.

Figure 1.7 (above)
Interior of medieval barn at
Chittinghurst, Wadhurst, prior to
conversion. [283/35]

Figure 1.8 (right)
The same view after conversion.
Inevitably, in order to make the
building habitable there has been
a considerable change to the
internal character of the building
in as much as it has lost its rustic,
utilitarian feel and internal walls
have been inserted. Even so,
apart from the unfortunate loss of
a section of wall framing over the
rear half-height wagon doors, the
medieval fabric has been retained
totally intact. Given that the
building was redundant, surely
conversion of this type has to be
better than the total loss of the
building! [from a slide]

Figure 1.9
A typical High Wealden farmyard scene in the late 19th century.
Although the farm buildings may survive to the present day, and perhaps - if very lucky - the traditional-style fences and gates too, the uses to which the spaces are put will have subtly changed over the years, modifying both the character and setting of the buildings. Such change is inevitable and cannot be avoided. However, with care the important elements of the setting can be retained, ensuring that the regional characteristics are maintained. [From a postcard]

Figure 1.10
Converted barn and farmhouse at Staces, Dallington. In this conversion the external character of the building has been maintained, as too has its traditional setting. [From a slide]

Such a repair may look fine to somebody who is illiterate, but to everybody else it makes complete nonsense of the story the document tells. The same is equally true of an historical building. Care is also necessary to ensure that important fittings (such as, for example, feeding racks) and, where relevant, intact original claddings are not swept away unless absolutely necessary. Unfortunately, some conversions have not been carried out to these high standards. In the worst instances the conversion has totally destroyed everything of historical significance.

If retention of original fabric is important, so too is the building's external character. On a number of occasions during our 1992 study we were appalled by the external appearance of some of the conversions we saw - a former rural idyll had become a tiny piece of suburbia set in the countryside. On the other hand, some conversions were very impressive, proving that success

in this respect is possible with care.

Although conversion work carried out over the past two decades has meant that much more of our built agricultural heritage has been preserved than would otherwise have been possible. It is none-the-less true that without an adequate pre-conversion record such buildings are of greatly reduced use for the purposes of historical research. Even in the case of a good conversion, where the date, original form, and subsequent evolution of the building can still be read within the exposed fabric, modern wall infilling means that many of the details essential in interpreting a building are hidden from view. Similarly, it is often impossible to retain some of the more ephemeral details of a building, even during the best conversion. It is for this reason that recording prior to conversion is so essential if we are to adequately understand our agricultural and architectural heritage.

2   THE AGRICULTURAL SCENE

TOPOGRAPHY OF THE REGION

The area chosen for study comprises the 250 square mile region at the eastern end of Sussex known as the Rape of Hastings. Apart from the recent alluvial silt deposits in the river valleys and delta marshlands around Rye and Pevensey, the Rape lies entirely within the geological area known as the High Weald, a region comprising a complex mixture of cold wet clays and relatively well-drained sands known as the Hastings Beds (*see* Figure 2.1).[1]

In general terms the variations in geology are reflected little in the local topography, the physical features of the region bearing little relationship to the underlying geological strata. In contrast, the physical features themselves have affected the way in which the land was colonized and used. In the north of the Rape, flowing west to east, is the River Rother, the largest of the rivers and one which, for a considerable length of its course, forms the north-eastern boundary of the Rape. As Figure 2.2 illustrates, to its south, and running diagonally across the region from Heathfield in the

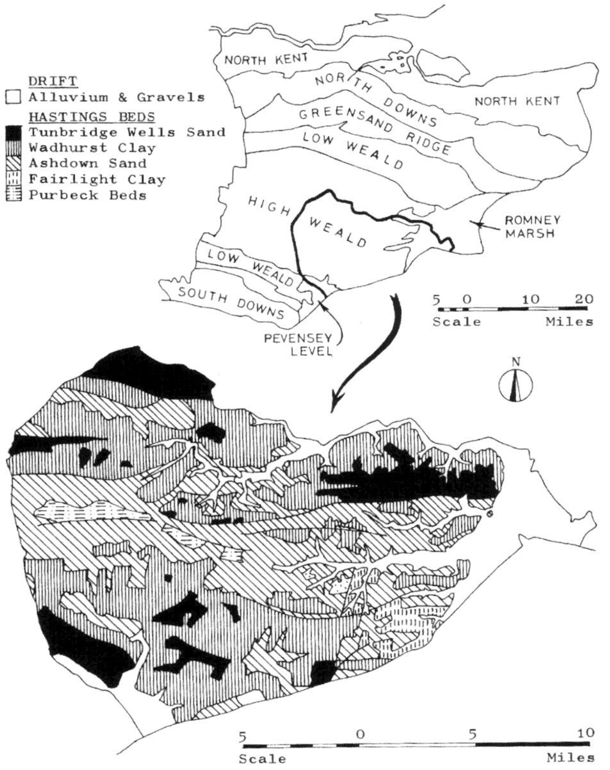

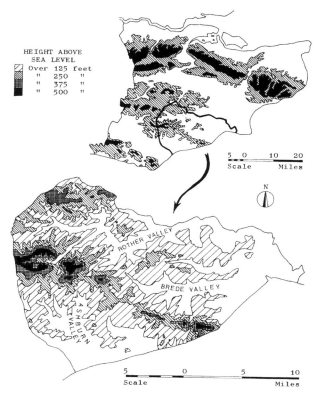

Figure 2.1
Above:- The principal geological regions of Kent and East Sussex.
Below:- Simplified geological plan of the Rape of Hastings.

Figure 2.2
Above:- The physical terrain of Kent and East Sussex.
Below:- The physical terrain of the Rape of Hastings.

Figure 2.3
Park Farm, Mountfield. A typical view of a valley in the High Weald showing the extent of woodland.

north west to Fairlight in the south, is the southern forest ridge, a narrow range of low hills which reaches less than 90 metres (300 feet) near Battle, but rises to 197 metres (646 feet) at Brightling in the north west and 176 metres (576 feet) near the coast at Fairlight. In many places the sides of the ridge are deeply cut by small streams set in steep-sided wooded gills.

Although the Rape in general is still heavily wooded, the woodland cover is particularly thick along the ridge itself. In addition, on the relatively bleak high ground at the ridge's western end were, until the late 18th century, considerable expanses of open roughland known locally as 'down' (*see* Figure 2.4). There appear to have been similar areas of open land on the equally-exposed high ground between Ore and Fairlight at the coastal end of the ridge, whilst 200 acres of 'down' in Catsfield Parish are known to have been enclosed soon after 1598.[2] On the whole, however, the open wasteland tended to be small in extent, especially when compared with the northern and western regions of the High Weald.

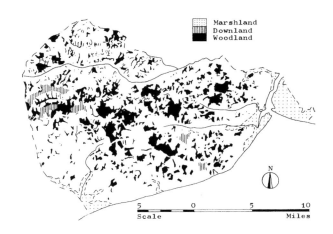

Marshland
Downland
Woodland

Figure 2.4
The known extent of marsh, down and woodland in the Rape of Hastings during the 17th century.

Figure 2.5
Hackwoods, Salehurst. A typical view indicating some of the characteristics of the High Weald landscape.

Figure 2.6
The High Weald landscape showing its wooded nature and ridges of high ground.

To the south west of the forest ridge is the watershed of the Cuckmere and Ashburn Rivers, an area of relatively low undulating land which, unlike the majority of the rape, is almost devoid of woodland. In contrast, the joint watershed of the Rother, Tillingham and Brede Rivers to the north east of the forest ridge incorporates many steep-sided slopes and here, away from the valley floors there are considerable expanses of woodland, particularly in the east of Ticehurst Parish and along the broad ridge which sweeps down eastwards from the main forest ridge and runs out towards Rye, on the edge of Romney Marsh.

Quality of the Land

Although the Weald contains a great deal of very poor ground, in the 18th century a correspondent reminded Young that some second-class arable soils did exist and that away from the upland core was much good land, rich loam and fertile clay, generally mixed with some sand capable of producing every kind of crop.[3] In particular the marshland around Pevensey and Rye was exceptionally rich, and by the 17th century most of these lands were either owned or rented for pasturage by the more wealthy farmers of the Wealden upland.[4] With such variations in land quality it is of some importance to ascertain which areas possessed poor ground, and which rich.

An analysis of the land tax returns for 1711 shows that the average ratable value of agricultural land per acre varied considerably from parish to parish. Udimore for example was assessed at approximately 9/1d per acre, but Catsfield only 3/7d per acre (*see* Figure 2.7).[5] In general terms the results of this analysis show a close

comparison with the Ministry of Agriculture's land classification published in 1964 (*see* Figure 2.8).[6] Figure 2.9 is a compilation based on these two sources. As can be seen, the best quality soils are located in the coastal marshlands around Pevensey and Rye (as would be expected), together with a belt of land adjacent to the Rye marshes, this latter being principally located within the parishes of Icklesham, Udimore and Iden in the east. The poorest lands are spread in a belt along the high ground of the southern forest ridge stretching from Fairlight cliffs in the south to Heathfield in the north west. By comparing Figure 2.9 with Figure 2.4 it will be

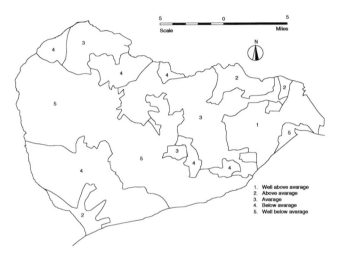

Figure 2.8
The quality of agricultural land in the
Rape of Hastings as assessed by the Ministry of
Agriculture and Fisheries in 1964.

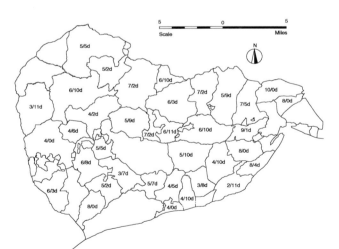

Figure 2.7
Ratable value of plainlands per acre in the
Rape of Hastings in the early 18th century
(Based upon the Land Tax Returns)

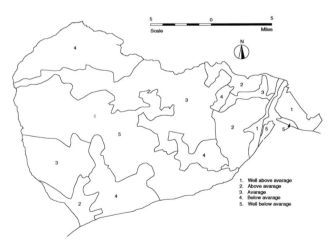

Figure 2.9
The quality of agricultural land in the
Rape of Hastings in the early 18th century
(based upon data shown in Figures 2.7 and 2.8)

noticed that the major tracts of woodland and open down were chiefly concentrated within this area.

The Size of Agricultural Holdings

From what little is known of the period preceding the Black Death it would appear that in the late 13th century the Wealden landscape comprised a scattering of relatively large, economically viable gentry properties intermingled with a mass of small peasant holdings of up to thirty acres in extent, the majority probably capable of supporting their occupants only at subsistence level. There appear to have been very few properties which could be described as of medium size (*viz.* 50-150 acres of plainland).

There are indications that as a result of depopulation during the 14th century, by the early 1400s many peasant holdings were becoming increasingly derelict, whilst others were being merged. Most amalgamations at this time appear to have been of a minor nature, though a few of the more ambitious men were able to accumulate holdings of reasonable acreage. Such was John Gunn of Sedlescombe. During the late 14th century he took advantage of the break up of Battle Abbey's Marley demesne to form a holding in excess of 50 acres. His well-built hall house survives. Both Gunn, and his neighbour Robert Hammond, however, appear to have been exceptional.[7]

The picture pieced together by Eleonor Searle regarding Telham Borough south of Battle illustrates well the trends found throughout the Rape as a whole. She has shown how, as a result of the upheavals and catastrophes of the 14th and early 15th centuries, the number of holdings within that borough was reduced

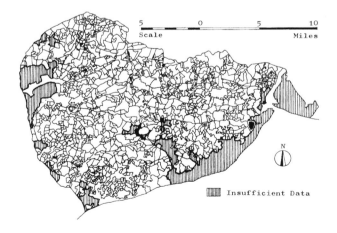

Figure 2.10
The distribution of farms
in the Rape of Hastings
in the 17th century.

from thirty in 1252 to twenty by 1433. This was accompanied by a corresponding increase in the size of the properties, though only one tenant was successful in accumulating a holding of more than 30 acres. Although previously occupied entirely by peasants owing labour service to their lord, by the mid 15th century several of the Telham properties were being acquired by Battle burgesses, by members of the lesser gentry, and by the more ambitious of peasant 'foreigners', all holding at an annual quit-rent.[8]

This trend, once started, continued. The second half of the 15th century saw a revival in the land market as an increasing number of people bought up available property with a view to enlarging their holdings. Thus, when a survey was made of Battle Manor in 1569, only six houses and one cottage remained within Telham Borough, by which date three of the farms comprised over 70 acres each.[9] Although this is but one instance, every indication suggests a similar, though perhaps less marked situation occurring throughout the Rape.

In a few instances major landowners were disposing of some property during the late 14th and early 15th centuries, though the overall demesne acreage probably remained relatively stable during the period *c*1300-1500.[10] However, despite this apparent stability, major changes were taking place on these holdings, changes brought about by a general abandonment of direct farming in favour of leasing out. Due to the size of many of the properties, it was common, perhaps even usual, for them to be divided up into smaller, more easily leasable units. It was probably during this period that the demesne lands of Dixter and Wigsell (amongst others) were divided to form Great and Little Dixter and Great and High Wigsell.

A rash of manorial surveys made during the mid 16th century allow for the first time a more confident appraisal of farm sizes to be made. Not surprising in view of what has already been said, the surveys depict a wider spread of acreages than that indicated by earlier sources. To generalize, ignoring smallholdings of less than 15 acres, by this date as many as one in three farms comprised between 50 and 150 plainland acres. Small farms of 15-50 acres, however, were still the most numerous, apparently making up just over half the total. Only one farm in ten appears to have exceeded 150 acres, whilst farms possessing more than 250 acres of plainland were very rare. These statistics are an overall assessment. A glance at Figure 2.10 will show that the mix of farm sizes was not even throughout the Rape as a whole. Some areas (particularly the better quality lands along the valley bottoms and the poor soils on the wooded ridges) were dominated by large holdings, whilst other areas show a multiplicity of small farms.

In contrast to the high level of amalgamation encountered during the late 14th, 15th and possibly the early 16th centuries, case studies coupled with statistical analysis suggest that during the 200 years from the middle years of the 16th century through to the middle of the 18th century little change occurred in the balance of farm sizes (*see* the data for *c*1711 in Figure 2.11). This is not to say that there was complete stability, merely that the number of farms being merged was in balance with the number being sub-divided into smaller units. It is also true that during the initial years of this period some increase in the amount of land devoted to agriculture was occurring, as indicated by the reclamation of marshland near Rye, the disparking of Battle Great Park, the enclosure of downland in Catsfield Parish, and the clearance of woodland to form Billingham Farm, Udimore.[11] Major reclamation of this type, however, appears to have been rare compared with that undertaken within the weald further to the north and west, areas which in any case possessed more extensive wasteland. In contrast, improvements in the quality of existing agricultural land were commonplace (*see* below).

The halt in farm amalgamation during the second half of the 16th century was probably largely brought about by a rapid increase in population, an increase sufficient to create a wider demand for land. That the trend in farm engrossment, although arrested, was not reversed is important, for as a result an increasing proportion of the rural population was forced to occupy landless holdings. It is no coincidence that during the period *c*1580-1650 many widows and poor persons were being forced to erect cottages upon small narrow strips of wayside waste. Such cottages were virtually unknown in the mid 16th century, yet it is estimated that a hundred years later at least one in seven of the rural population within Hastings Rape were housed in them.[12]

A second peak in wayside grants occurred during the late 18th and 19th centuries; yet another period of rapid population growth. However, unlike its predecessor, this phase was accompanied by a further burst of farm amalgamations, an activity which was still taking place when the tithe award surveys were compiled in *c*1840. These show that at that time about one in three farms exceeded 100 acres in extent, compared with only one in five (or less) during the period *c*1570-1720. Significantly, the overall number of agricultural holdings had fallen by between a quarter and one-third, though as

figure 2.11 demonstrates, two-fifths of all farms still possessed less than 50 acres of plainland. This spate of amalgamations was accompanied by an increase in arable farming (*see* below). When the amount of land devoted to arable was again reduced during the late 19th century, farms began once more to be divided into smaller units.[14] Since then, however, automation, coupled with a very marked decrease in the number of people employed in agriculture has largely removed the small farm from the wealden scene. Those which remain are principally used as amenity land.

Up to this point we have been considering individual farms, each with its own house and buildings and each in single occupation and ownership. However, this approach gives an over-simplified picture. For instance, a manorial rental of 1664 states that Samuel Sampson of Bexhill not only occupied a messuage, barn and 60 acres of land owned by Daniel Sole, but also another messuage, barn and 100 acres in the ownership of William Vinall, gentleman.[15] Likewise, during the early 17th century John Everenden, gentleman, not only farmed his own lands called Beech in Sedlescombe, where he lived, together with another farm with house and buildings called Killingham, but he also leased for his own use a house, buildings and lands called Chittlebirch in Sedlescombe, as well as marshland near Winchelsea.[16] During the same period John Roberts, gentleman, worked two detached farms in Ticehurst called Boarzell and Dalehill, both of which he owned and both of which possessed a house with associated farm buildings.[17] These are typical examples. Other men merely leased extra land, perhaps a field or two, in order to supplement their acreage. Some groupings, once formed, became permanent - as indeed was the case with those lands occupied by Samuel Sampson - though in most cases the associations were short term. All the Everenden and Roberts farms, for instance, were once more in separate occupancy by the second half of the 17th century.

Unfortunately there is no way of checking how common such multiple units were during the 16th and 17th centuries, though the land tax returns of the early 18th century do allow an assessment to be made for that period. Indeed, the 1711 returns indicate that such units were by that date common: a little over a quarter of all farmers held more than one farm, or worked extra lands in addition to their farm (*see* Figure 2.12). Obviously, if such groupings are taken into account, the balance in the size of the agricultural units shifts from that previously stated. Indeed, the number of farming units in excess of 150 acres almost doubles to *c*18% of the total, whilst conversely, units of 50 acres or less fall from *c*55% to *c*45% of the total.

In most cases the existence of grouped holdings probably had little effect on farm buildings. Case studies

| DATE | PERCENTAGE OF | | | | NUMBER OF HOLDINGS IN SAMPLE |
	SMALL 15-49a	MEDIUM 50-99a	100-149a	LARGE 150+a	
c1711	55%	25%	9%	11%	319
c1840	44%	21%	15%	20%	217

Figure 2.11
Size of holdings in a sample of seven parishes,
c1711 and c1840.[13]

NUMBER OF HOLDINGS MAKING UP FARMING UNIT	NO. OF FARMING UNITS OF			TOTAL
	c15-49a	c50-149a	c150+a	
ONE	98	61	24	183
TWO	13	22	9	44
THREE OR MORE	2	10	12	24
TOTAL	113	93	45	251
TOTAL AS %	45%	37%	18%	100%

Figure 2.12
Details of holdings making up single
farming units in 1711.
(Sample of seven parishes).[18]

suggest that only rarely at this date did such associations result in the destruction of either houses, barns or outbuildings. Usually demolition was avoided by the lessor writing dilapidation clauses into the lease. A typical example of such is found in 1739 when Thomas Frewen, esquire, leased a house, barn, oasthouse and 32 acres of land called Broad Oak Farm, in Brede to Francis Bourne of Reysons Farm, Brede on condition that he 'cause some person of credit and reputation to dwell and inhabit in the demised messuage called Broad Oak . . . . and not suffer the same to stand empty'.[19] Some destruction of both farmhouses and barns must occasionally have occurred, especially in those instances where the association of two farms became permanent. Many surplus farmhouses, however, were no doubt occupied by labourers, and it was probably not uncommon to find such dwellings divided into multiple occupancy in order to house more than one labouring family.

The Distribution of Arable and Pasture

Agricultural historians agree that the Weald - in common with most woodland landscapes - was primarily a cattle fatstock region, though a certain amount of arable has always existed.[20] But how much land was devoted to arable, and was the ratio influenced by chronology? The answer to both these questions will have affected the size and design of agricultural buildings.

As in England as a whole, there is ample evidence within the Weald of massive depopulation during the 14th century, though whether this was any greater than elsewhere is at present impossible to ascertain.[21] Certainly within the area around Battle the population was decreasing prior to the Black Death and continued to do so afterwards. The final phase of major desertion appears to have occurred after c1380, and may have continued into the early 15th century.[22] This was possibly a result of migration away from the poor soils of the Weald to richer agricultural land: a tendency

recognized elsewhere in England.[23] What is certainly true is that both the urban and rural areas of the Rape of Hastings were far less heavily populated during the early 15th century than they had been in c1300.

In consequence, the demand for both food and land was substantially reduced. Around Battle during the early 15th century, and probably before, there is abundant evidence of increasing dereliction, a picture probably common throughout the Rape as a whole.[24] Much former arable land was reverting to bush and scrub, whilst it was probably no accident that the lords of Bexhill and Herstmonceux Manors chose this period to enlarge their hunting parks.[25] Such parks were not the sole preserve of the gentry, for there are records of Battle burgesses purchasing tenements in the Telham area, south of the town, solely for recreational purposes.[26]

When in the mid 15th century the land market finally began to revive, the vacant properties were not being taken for arable, as they had been in the past, but for cattle pasture and, above all, for their standing timber.[27] The Abbot of Battle urged his new tenants to 'cut down any trees, except in the ridges and hedges, in order to make the land ploughable', though once the land was cleared of its valuable timber few tenants appear to have converted it back to arable. The Abbot's views were again echoed in 1526 when the lessee of a tenement which had been arable in the 14th century was required to prepare one field for ploughing within ten years, and to render ready for the plough any other land from which he took timber.[28]

Such remarks should not be interpreted as an attempt at returning former arable lands to permanent cultivation, for the reduced level of population did not warrant exhausting the soils, as had been done during the late 13th century. By returning the land to a ploughable condition, however, the tenants could cultivate it for short periods in order to restore the pasture to good condition. There is ample evidence of convertible husbandry of this kind being adopted within the Weald: indeed most Wealden upland required long periods of rest between relatively short cultivated sequences if it was to maintain its fertility. As an example of this, on the major demesne farm of Barnhorne in Bexhill many of the upland fields during the late 14th and early 15th centuries were used as pasture for more than eight years in ten, whilst even the high quality upland fields were cropped for three to five years and then left for a similar period to recover.[29] An equally low level of cultivation is evident on the demesne of Bexhill Manor during the same period, where, although there were 100 acres of arable land, only 48 acres were sown in 1388.[30]

The available data for the mid 16th century suggests little or no increase in crop production in the interim. Indeed, with a stable, or even reduced level of population there would have been no need for it. Figure 2.13 summarizes a land-usage assessment of the parishes of Iden and Playden made in 1568. The assessment lists only 13 acres as arable out of a total of 1,256 upland acres (excluding woodland). No less than 723 acres were classified as pasture, and a further 260 acres as rough ground. The latter was presumably derelict and semi-derelict land synonymous with the 'bushy ground' and 'furzy fields' found in surveys of the period. There are a number of extant surveys dating from the 1560s covering farms of all sizes spread throughout the Rape.[31] Only very rarely do they mention arable. Pasture land was the norm. Even so, crops were obviously grown, and most holdings possessed a barn in which to store and process them. It would appear that very few fields were cropped with sufficient regularity to warrant the classification 'arable'. In 1559/60 even the pasture land on the demesne of Ore Manor was so poor as to be valued on a par with the wood and roughland, meadowland alone being singled out for a higher assessment.[32]

Despite the apparent low level of tillage, the port books of Rye for the period 1581-84 indicate that the rural population could normally grow sufficient wheat and oats for its own needs, leaving a surplus of oats for export. In a good year even the port itself could largely be provisioned with wheat.[33] However, by this date the arable/pasture ratio may already have been changing, for there is considerable evidence for a 'revolution' in Wealden agriculture during the period 1580-1620.

Stimulated by inflated foodstuff prices, the cultivated acreage was significantly extended during this period, and some previously non-agricultural land was brought into cultivation.[34] Furthermore, under the same stimulus, many Wealden improvers were placing new emphasis on the application of lime and chalk, a procedure which 'grew so greatly in extent, frequency and volume, that it became effectively revolutionary'.[35] The reason for so much labour being expended on such improvements appears to have been the more frequent tillage of the land, for in many instances the fields were now cropped at sufficiently regular intervals to be classified as arable rather than pasture. Whereas survey references to arable had previously been rare, from *c*1580 onwards it was the norm to find some fields so described on most farms. The valuation of a Burwash farm in 1585, for example, describes about a third of the 122¼ plainland acres as arable.[36] This figure is comparable with that given for six farms in Crowham Manor, Westfield in the early 17th century.[37] Statistics for the Kentish Weald during the same period indicate a similar percentage of land classified as arable.[38] Whilst during the 17th century as a whole the relative proportion of land classified as arable, meadow and pasture within the Kentish Weald probably changed little, exceptionally

PARISH	ARABLE	MEADOW	PASTURE	ROUGH GROUND	MARSHLAND	WOODLAND	TOTAL
PLAYDEN	13	84	251	125	275	-	748
IDEN	-	176	472	135	409	199	1391
TOTAL	13	260	723	260	684	199	2139

Figure 2.13
Land usage within the parishes
of Playden and Iden, 1568.[39]

high corn prices might for short periods have increased the amount of land tilled.[40] An analysis of the available data suggests that this statement also holds true for the area of the Sussex Weald here under discussion.

Despite the increased regularity with which the fields were cropped, the level of tillage remained low. Even those fields considered arable still required long rest periods, despite regular liming and marling. It was at least in part to prevent unscrupulous tenants from exhausting the land that many leases incorporated penalty clauses limiting the acreage put to the plough. The ploughing of some fields was often specifically prohibited, failure to comply resulting in the imposition of very heavy penalties. During the 17th and early 18th centuries the limit on tillage appears usually to have been set at about a fifth of the total plainland acreage, a level which seems largely to have been adhered to.

The mid to late 18th century and 19th century will next be considered. Surveys made of the Pelham Estate in 1761 and of the Icklesham and Wickham Estates in 1767 show no marked change in the arable/pasture ratio from that calculated for the region in the 17th century. However, comments added to the schedule relating to the Icklesham and Wickham Estates a short time afterwards, suggest that the arable potential of certain pasture lands was by that date being considered.[41]

Perhaps significantly, about half the plainlands upon Sempstead Farm, Ewhurst were in 1784 stated as arable, compared with about a third for farms in the same area earlier in the century.[42] Even so, the 1801 crop returns for Sussex, if accurate, show no marked increase in the percentage of cultivated land over that of the early 18th century, though contemporary notes made regarding the returns suggest that the sown acreage was indeed rising. Certainly by this date the proportions of the various crops being cultivated had changed, for whereas oats (chiefly grown as an animal foodstuff) had previously been predominant, there was now a much more even balance between oats and wheat.[43] By *c*1840 between two-thirds and three-quarters of the farmlands within the Rape were classified as arable, regardless of the size of the holding.[44] It should, of course, be borne

Figure 2.14

*Ketchingham Farm,
Etchingham in about
1900 showing the well
maintained hedges.
[456/15A]*

in mind that the annual cultivated acreage would have been considerably lower, for account has to be taken of those fields lying fallow. Even so, such a high level of cultivation had almost certainly not occurred locally since before the Black Death.

Due to its poor soils, the Weald has never been suited to high levels of tillage. It is therefore perhaps not surprising that, with the advent of the railways and of cheap bulk haulage, the Wealden arable acreage again fell back to its former low levels. Figures relating to Sussex as a whole show a swing from 62% arable in 1867, to just 38% by 1905.[45]

From the foregoing it will be noted that, until modern times, the increase and decrease in the percentage of land devoted to arable broadly reflects the variations in the level of the local population. Fields were pushed to high productivity (at least in Wealden terms) during periods of either high population or national emergency, but returned to extended periods of rest during other periods.

THE FIELDS

Although many fields are today being thrown together to form more economic units, the Weald is still, none-the-less, a region of small enclosures, most of which probably date back to the initial woodland clearances. Analysis of field sizes during the 17th and early 18th centuries show that many fields were of no more than one or two acres in extent, whilst on farms of less than 50 acres the vast majority did not exceed five acres. Larger fields were more common on the major holdings, though as indicated by Figure 2.15, even on farms of more than 150 acres approximately half the

enclosures were of less than six acres in size. Mid 16th-century surveys suggest a similar situation at that period too.[46]

It is worth mentioning that not only were the fields small, but in addition they were normally surrounded by exceptionally broad hedges which probably often included large numbers of mature trees. In 1567 the hedgerow timber on some of the Robertsbridge manorial tenements was thought worthy of specific mention.[47] Such thick hedgerows, with their shade-casting trees, greatly hampered arable farming, a feature noted by Short with regards to the Ashburnham Estate in the 19th century.[48]

Despite the likely existence of many hedgerow trees, the shade-casting nature of the hedges themselves should not be overstated. Today many hedges tend to be unkept with the bushes within them growing tall. This is unlikely to have been the case on most farms in the past, for prior to the advent of cheap wire the hedges had to be well maintained in order to serve their primary function

SIZE OF HOLDINGS (ACRES)	NO. OF FARMS	TOTAL NO. OF FIELDS	NO. OF FIELDS (Size in Acres)				TOTAL ACREAGE	AV. FIELD SIZE
			0-4a	5a	6-9a	10+a		
15-49a	37	341	279	33	26	3	1138½	3.3a
50-99a	18	286	178	46	47	15	1227¾	4.3a
100-149a	3	79	46	11	16	6	397½	5.0a
150+a	3	101	41	9	32	19	647	6.4a

Figure 2.15
*Analysis of field sizes on farms over 15 acres
during the period from the early 17th century
to the early 18th century.[49]*

Name of Farmer	Parish	IN ACRES						TYPES OF PULSES PRESENT	NO. OF CROP TYPES
		WHEAT	BARLEY	OATS	RYE	PULSES	TOTAL		
J. Martin	Ewhurst	3	-	1	-	-	4	-	2
W. Newson	Peasmarsh	3	-	4½	-	1½	9	1	3
M. Benden	Udimore	4	3	4	-	22	13	1	4
H. Richardson	Brede	-	-	18	-	9	27	3	4
W. Petter	Peasmarsh	10	12	-	-	10	32	2	4
W. Harman	Ewhurst	13½	2	17	-	4½	37	1	4
W. Patteson	Peasmarsh	9	2	14	-	13½	38½	2	5
R. Friend	Iden	12	17	15	-	14	58	2	5
		54½	36	73½	-	54½	218½		

Figure 2.16
A sample of eight early 18th-century inventories showing the variety of crops grown on individual farms.[50]

as stock-proof barriers There remains ample evidence within the surviving mature hedges to indicate that many were layered - that is, the stems of the bushes were cut partially through and bent over nearly horizontal along the hedge, in which position they continued to grow. Further, it should be borne in mind that the brishings from the hedges were a valuable source of fuel - a further incentive to regular maintenance.

THE CROPS

Grains and Pulses

Wheat, barley, oats, peas, beans and tares were all commonly grown in the Weald throughout the medieval and post-medieval period, though prior to the late 18th century it was oats which dominated.[51] On Marley Farm, Battle, in the mid 14th century oats accounted for almost 60% of the sown acreage, a figure higher even than for most farms during the 17th and early 18th centuries (Figure 2.16).[52] The crop was grown primarily as animal fodder, as too were the pulses (peas, beans and tares) and, occasionally, rye.[53] The combined total of the fodder crops throughout the period here under consideration appears never to have dropped substantially below 60% of the total sown acreage, a figure which well illustrates the importance placed on fatstock. It should be stressed that the early 18th-century statistics for the extreme eastern end of Sussex show a much more even balance between oats and pulses than found in the Kentish Weald during the 17th century, though it is unclear as to whether this is a quirk of the region or represents a genuine switch from oats to a mixture of oats and pulses as animal fodder.

Wheat (for flour) and barley (for malt) represent the principal local cereals grown for human consumption. Both were cultivated in much lesser quantities than on the Kentish North Downs or within northern Kent, where the number of plainland acres devoted to such crops was three times that within the Weald.[54] Barley was, in general, not suited to the stiff clays of the Weald, a factor illustrated by its complete absence at Marley Farm, Battle in the 14th century and its virtual absence in the 17th-century Kentish Weald.[55] Larger acreages were, however, grown in the more fertile 'grade-2' lands in Iden, Peasmarsh, Udimore and Icklesham in the extreme east of the rape (*see* Figure 2.9). During the early 18th century William Petter and Richard Friend, for instance, devoted about a third of their extensive sown acreages to barley on their farms within the parishes of Peasmarsh and Iden.[56] Wheat on the other hand was consistently grown throughout the study area, being absent from only one farm in a sample of 48 early 18th-century Rape of Hastings inventories which mention crops.[57] The acreages were not large, though apparently usually sufficient to serve the needs of the local rural population.[58] Small farms probably grew only sufficient for their needs, leaving the larger units to produce surplus for the local market.[59]

It should be noted that it was usual for a farm to cultivate from two to five different types of crop in any one year. As Figure 2.16 illustrates, in general terms the higher the sown acreage the greater was the variety.

Hay

Although most farms would have harvested hay, there is no way of assessing the acreage involved. As depicted in the scene shown in Figure 3.2, the crop was stored externally in ricks (known locally at that time as stacks). The number of ricks on individual farms varied from one to as many as ten. The ricks were cut into as required, and there are several references in inventories

Figure 2.17
A photograph of a local farm in c1900
showing harvesting cereal crops in the
traditional manner. [456/4A]

Figure 2.18
Cider making out in the open air on a
local farm in c1900. [456/17A]

to cores (*ie* partially used stacks). Only small quantities were brought in and stored under cover within the cattle stalls and stables, ready for use.[60]

Other Crops

Apart from cereals and pulses, small plots were usually set aside for the cultivation of fruit, hops, herbs and vegetables. At least three-quarters of the farms possessed an orchard for the cultivation of apples, pears, cherries and plums.[61] Such orchards were usually incorporated into the farmstead complex (*see* Chapter 3). Most were very small, only very occasionally exceeding one-and-a-half acres and usually under three-quarters of an acre. It is extremely rare to find reference to more than one orchard on a single farm. Clearly there was no great local commercial interest in fruit, though the enterprise was sufficient in a few rare instances to warrant the construction of an apple mill for the manufacture of cider.[62] Probably one of the largest such mills was that recorded at Robertsbridge Abbey in 1567. It was described as a mill house 'covered with straw, standing over the river, wherein are one wheatmill, one maltmill, one apple mill, and over the same, one fair gardyner (storehouse) to lay and keep corn in'.[63] Probably of much smaller size was the 'mill house to grind apples' recorded on the 60¼ acre Rowley Farm, Ticehurst in 1618.[64] As Figure 2.18 shows, on at least some local farms the crop was processed out in the open.

Introduced into Kent from Flanders in the second quarter of the 16th century, hops became firmly established in that county during the 1560s and 70s.[65] The earliest known reference to their presence in Eastern Sussex is in 1581 at Mayfield.[66] By 1597 William Hopkinson, clerk, had converted a relatively large medieval hall house in Northbridge, Salehurst, into a hop house, suggesting that by the end of the 16th century the crop was well established within Salehurst Parish.[67] However, despite reference to a hop house in Rye in 1585, during the late 1580s hops were still being imported into that town, a situation which had been reversed by at least 1613/14.[68] Exports were made through Hastings by 1638/39, if not before.[69] By the mid 17th century their local cultivation was extensive, a quarter of the hop acreage for the south east of England being claimed by Sussex by that date.[70] By then Salehurst Parish, with its readily available labour force at Robertsbridge, had already established itself as the local centre, a situation well illustrated by the numerous references to hops found within the pages of parson John Lord's tithe book. It remained so at least until the early 19th century.[71] An analysis of early 18th-century probate inventories throughout Hastings Rape indicates that by the early 1700s about a third of the farms cultivated hops. As might be expected, most of the hop interests were concentrated on the medium-sized and large farms. Only roughly one in six of the inventories for holdings of less than *c*50 acres makes any mention of the crop.

The hop gardens of the 17th and early 18th centuries were often little larger in size than the local orchards, only rarely exceeding 2¾ acres.[72] However, unlike fruit, hops formed an important part of the local agricultural economy. Average gross profits ranged from between £10 and £15 per acre.[73] The 15 bags of hops grown in Stephen Ketchle's 7¼ acres of hop ground at Billingham Farm, Udimore, in *c*1719 were valued at £130, virtually double the combined value of his other crops, and about the same as the total value of his livestock.[74] Although the rewards could be high, so were the cultivation costs, whilst both poor and ruined harvests were not infrequent.[75] To give an indication of the costs, an acre of hops alone would contain approximately 10,000 bines rooted in a thousand hills and supported by 3,000-4,000 poles.[76] The initial capital outlay was enormous, whilst, in addition, the poles (cut from trees of between ten and fifteen-years growth) needed replacing every three to four years.[77] It was estimated that between three and four acres of hops could give full-time employment for a man throughout the year (except at the hay and corn harvests) whilst considerable additional labour was required during the hop harvest itself.[78] After the harvest the hops required drying. This was initially carried out in a makeshift manner, but by the mid 17th century purpose-built oasthouses were normally used: yet another massive capital outlay!

In considering crops, gardens should not be ignored, for although their produce would have been of little commercial worth, they were of great importance in feeding the household. As with orchards, the existence of a garden is not always recorded in contemporary documents, though this is probably due more to their small size than to their absence.[79] The crops would have included hemp, flax, carrots, cabbages, onions, peas, parsnips, turnips and asparagus.[80] Occasionally a separate plot was set aside for the cultivation of hemp, and probably flax.[81] The gardens were often located a little distance away from the house, though set within the confines of the farmstead itself. There would, in addition, usually have been a small plot for herbs - sometimes, if sufficiently large, called a 'herber' or harbour.[82] For convenience this was more often set adjacent to the house.

LIVESTOCK

Cattle

The cattle herd was undoubted the most important element of Wealden farming. Indeed, as has been shown, much of the crop cultivation was geared to the production of animal foodstuffs. An analysis of 64 early 18th-century probate inventories of farms over *c*15 acres in the north-east of Hastings Rape shows only five (all of relatively small size) without a herd, whilst six of the small-holdings of less than 15 acres possessed one or two cows, some with calves.[83] Broadly speaking, the herd sizes varied with the acreage of the farm, holdings of less than 50 acres possessing herds of between 1 and 12 head, whilst the largest recorded in the sample are those on two farms of over 200 acres with 77 animals each. Most herds on farms ranging from 50-99 acres possessed between 10 and 32 head. All these totals included young beasts (*see* Figure 2.19).

The Weald was principally a fatstock region, though cows, necessary for breeding purposes, also supplied most, if not all the region's dairying needs.[84] A proportion of the fatstock was granted a stay of execution

SIZE OF HOLDING IN ACRES	NO. OF FARMS	NO. OF FARMS POSSESSING HERD SIZES OF						SIZE RANGE OF HERDS
		0	1-5	6-20	21-35	36-50	51-100	
c15-49a	25	5	5	15	-	-	-	1-12
c50-99a	17	-	-	5	11	1	-	8-32
c100-199a	18	-	-	1	7	8	2	9-62
c200+a	4	-	-	-	-	-	4	57-77
TOTAL	64	5	5	21	18	9	6	

Figure 2.19
Analysis of herd sizes in 64 early 18th-century probate inventories relating to an area in the north-east of Hastings Rape.[85]

in return for working in the teams as draught animals.

The heifers were usually put to the bull from the age of three, the bull's services in most instances apparently being 'hired' from a neighbouring farmer, for probate inventories suggest that only about one in five farms possessed such an animal.[86] Not surprisingly, these were mainly found on the larger holdings, being rare on farms of less than 100 acres. The bull's working life commenced at 3-4 years and usually lasted until 12-15 years old. It was recommended that he should never be utilized as a draught animal, and would do best if kept housed in a stall.[87]

Once the calves were born they were usually allowed to suckle for a full year, though weaning could begin after three weeks, taking one teat away at a time by milking it dry.[88] The first stage of slaughtering began early, for many calves were fattened and killed to provide veal. Thomas Roberts of Boarzell, Ticehurst, for instance, had one calf killed for his own needs at intervals of approximately two weeks between 1567 and 1576.[89] Mascall, writing in the late 16th century recommended that when the cattle were put out from the farmstead in the spring, those calves required for slaughter should be kept in the cattle house by day as this resulted in faster fattening.[90]

Animals which escaped early slaughter were usually safe until maturity when those not required for breeding and draught purposes were fattened for the butcher's knife. Wealden bullocks were said to be amongst the biggest and best in the country, though runts (poor small animals of both sexes) were amongst those slaughtered at this time.[91] Even this did not mark the end of the fatstock chain, for at the end of their working life both the cows and the draught animals were withdrawn and fattened. Only the bull was likely to have escaped the meat market, and even this is uncertain.

It would be wrong to give the impression that all Wealden farms conformed to a standard pattern as regards their cattle herds. Of those farms analysed, two

SIZE OF HOLDING (ACRES)	AVERAGE YOUNG ANIMALS PER COW
c15-49a	1.3
c50-99a	2.2
c100-199a	3.3
c200+a	4.2

Figure 2.20
Proportion of young animals of 0-3 years
per cow in a sample of 64 early 18th-century
probate inventories. (Sample as in Figure 2.19).

SIZE OF HOLDING	NO. OF FARMS	NO. OF FARMS POSSESSING			
		COWS	OXEN & STEERS	BULLS	YOUNG ANIMALS
c15-49 acres	25	19	4	-	16
c50-99 acres	17	17	15	1	17
c100-199 acres	18	18	17	7	18
c200+ acres	4	4	4	3	4
	64	58	40	11	55

Figure 2.21
An analysis of the animals making up the cattle
herds in a sample of 64 early 18th-century
probate inventories. (Sample as in Figure 2.19).

Inventory No. ESRO W/INV	Approx. Acreage	No. of Working Animals			Total Herd Size
		Steers	Oxen	Size of Team	
1791	33	-	6	6	11
1157	51	2	-	2	15
28	53	-	2	2	21
1476	116	4	-	4	16
2221	116	-	4	4	19
2352	122	-	6	6	28
2433	178	2	-	2	50
826	184	-	6	6	62
794	210	-	16	16	57
353	215	-	12	12	60
963	319	-	8	8	77

Figure 2.22
Details of working oxen and steers, where specified.
(Sample as in Figure 2.19).

stand out very noticeably as being atypical in that they possessed above average dairying interests.[92] Both, perhaps significantly, were located on grade-2 lands situated close to the town of Rye (*see* Figure 2.9). Even so, both herds also had clear fatstock interests. On others farms too there are noticeable variations which, broadly speaking, were influenced by the size of holding. Those herds comprising less than five animals invariably consisted of milk cows with their calves, and thus supplied the dairy needs of the household, whilst at the same time producing calves for sale as leanstock.[93] In the late 16th century Mascall advised men with little pasture to sell their calves in order to allow sufficient milk for the household. He did, however, suggest that

they should rear sufficient for their own replacement needs.[94] Rearing and fattening tended to be a speciality of the larger farms, and their herds were regularly increased by the buying-in of stock from outside the county, as well as purchasing leanstock from the smaller local holdings.[95] To judge from the herds analysed in Figure 2.20, the differences in cow to young-beast ratio between the small-holdings and the sizable farms seems to have been very marked.

A noticeable feature of the small farms would have been the almost complete absence of draught animals: oxen and steers are listed on only four of the twenty-five farms analysed in this size range, and on only one of these are the animals specifically described as working beasts. In contrast, as Figure 2.21 demonstrates, draught animals are absent from only two of the *c*50-99 acre farms, and from one *c*100-199-acre holding. Presumably the cost of maintaining a working team was not warranted on a holding with little arable acreage and thus little demand for such animals. As with the services of the bull, on these smaller farms it is

Figure 2.23
Local team of draught
oxen, c1900. [456/9A]

Inventory No. ESRO W/INV.	Approx. Acreage	Animals Fattening				Mature Animals in Herd
		Cows	Steers	Oxen	Total	
2281	34	1	-	-	1	6
2575	51	-	-	2	2	8
1157	51	1	-	-	1	6
972	76	2	2	-	4	4
1314	107	2	-	-	2	8
2221	116	-	-	2	2	11
2352	122	-	-	2	2	14
1155	150	-	-	2	2	17
2433	178	1	-	-	1	19
826	184	-	-	2	2	19
353	215	4	2	2	8	11
963	250+	-	-	4	4	18

NOTE: The inventories were appraised during
the following months:-
1155 = January; 2221 = March; 963 = April;
972 = May; 2352 = June; 2433 = September;
353 & 2575 = October; 826 & 2281 = November.

Figure 2.24
Details of mature animals specifically listed
as fattening

assumed that a team was either borrowed or hired from a neighbour as required.

It is noticeable that occasionally a small-holder atypically possessed a team of draught animals.[96] Brent cites a case in 1634 where a Salehurst small-holder kept six oxen 'employed in carriages by the highway'.[97] It should not be surprising to find carriers (with minor farming interests) in a region requiring heavy haulage in attendance on the iron and timber industries.

Although, as Figure 2.22 illustrates, oxen were the principal draught animals used locally, references to working steers are not uncommon. Some teams were a mixture of both oxen and steers.[98] Many inventories do not specify which were draught animals and which were being fattened, though where they do the teams can be seen to have varied from 2 to 16 animals, though most comprise either two, four, or six (*see* Figures 2.22 and 2.24). Normally two animals at a time were removed from the team for fattening, though occasionally four were withdrawn.

Horses

By the early 18th century almost all farms possessed at least one mature horse (the exception being a few low-acreage small-holdings). However, as Figure 2.25 shows, on farms of less than 150 acres totals in excess of three mature animals appear to have been

Size of Holding	No. of Farms	No. of Mature Horses per Farm					Range	
		0	1	2	3	4+	Excl. Colts	Incl. Colts
c15-49 acres	25	5	14	3	3	-	0-3	0-4
c50-99 acres	17	-	10	5	2	-	1-3	1-4
c100-149 acres	11	-	-	3	6	2	2-6	2-6
c150-199 acres	7	-	-	1	1	5	2-8	3-13
c200+ acres	4	-	-	-	-	4	6-7	9-18
	64	5	24	12	12	11		

Figure 2.25
Horses listed in 64 early 18th-century farming
inventories. (Sample as for Figure 2.19)

very rare.

From the references to saddles, side saddles and pillions it is clear that most of the horses were used for riding and carrying, though reference to horse harnesses are sometimes encountered.[99] Because of their greater speed, horses were particularly suited to harrowing, and a few inventories do specifically mention horse harrows.[100] In two of the inventories analysed specific reference is made to road horses, and in one of these eight animals are so described.[101]

In Dorset it has been noted that there was a nearly three-fold increase in the number of persons owning horses between the late 16th and mid 17th centuries, and it may be that the same applied to the Weald of Sussex.[102] Unfortunately there are no surviving late 16th-century inventories for East Sussex, and thus this possibility cannot be explored.

Sheep

Despite the predominantly heavy wet clays of the region, sheep flocks were usually present on farms in excess of 50 acres, and appear also to have been kept on a little under half of those below that size. However,

Size of Holding (acres)	No. of Farms	No. of Farms Possessing Flock Sizes of								Size Range of Flocks
		0	1-5	6-20	21-35	36-50	51-100	100-150	150+	
c15-49 a.	25	14	2	4	4	1	-	-	-	0-40
c50-99 a.	17	3	-	5	5	3	1	-	-	0-56
c100-199 a.	18	4	-	2	2	1	6	3	-	0-143
c200+ a.	4	-	-	-	-	-	-	1	3	131-1170
	64	21	2	11	11	5	7	4	3	

Figure 2.26
Sheep - Flock sizes as listed in 64
early 18th-century farming inventories
(Sample as for Figure 2.19)

Size of Holding	No. of Farms	No. of Farms Possessing Herds of					Size Range of Herd
		0	1-5	6-10	11-20	21+	
c15-49 acres	25	3	16	4	2	-	0-16
c50-99 acres	17	-	9	8	-	-	2-10
c100-199 acres	18	-	6	5	7	-	1-15
c200+ acres	4	-	-	-	2	2	13-103
	64	3	31	17	11	2	0-103

Figure 2.27
Swine - Sizes of herds listed in 64
early 18th-century farming inventories.
(Sample as for Figure 2.19)

with only one notable exception (Edward Wilmshurst of Playden with 1170 sheep and lambs) all flocks on the 64 farms analysed were of less than 275 head, whilst only seven exceeded 100 animals.[103] Over a third possessed between six and thirty-five head, but a further third had none whatsoever (*see* Figure 2.26). The average flock size on the farms (excluding Wilmshurst) calculates at 49 animals, not atypical of other parts of the Weald.[104] It should be borne in mid that several Wealden parishes in eastern Sussex included limited marshland pasture along the river valleys, and this was extensive around Rye on the edge of Romney Marsh, and on the fringes of Pevensey Level. Romney Marsh and Pevensey Level were the principal sheep-rearing areas of the region and it is therefore perhaps not surprising to find that Wilmshurst's holding, with its exceptionally large flock, included much marshland.[105] Some upland farmers took in marsh sheep for over-wintering.

Apart from temporary folds formed out of hurdles, sheep required no shelter, and thus had little influence on farm buildings. Only one instance of a sheephouse is known (*see* Chapter 14). Even so, the fleeces did need to be stored, either in the barn or the farmhouse.

Swine

The number of swine present on early 18th-century farms in the region is indicated by Figure 2.27. Not surprisingly, few farms lacked swine, whilst by the early 18th century many of those over 50 acres possessed more than 11 animals, though herds in excess of 20 head were rare. Probably most farmsteads incorporated pigsties, though due to their insignificance, references to them are not found in either manorial surveys, deeds or estate maps of the period. Certainly entries concerning either their construction and repair costs are found in account books of the period.[106]

Poultry

Inventories rarely give details of the fowl present on farms, though where such information is given the flocks appear to have comprised a mixture of geese, ducks, chicken, and, in one instance, 'gulls' (Sussex dialect for goslings).[107] Mascall writing in the early 1580s refers to poultry houses as if they were then common in Sussex, though as with pigsties they were too insignificant to be mentioned in surveys *etc*.[108] Occasional references to them are found in account books.[109]

HUSBANDRY TACKLE [110]

All farms would have owned quantities of small equipment, a typical list being that found on the *c*40 acre farm of Nehemiah Bayden of Udimore in 1724.[111] In his barn and oasthouse he housed 'two yokes, two sieves, some forks, six sacks, one tovet, a schawl, a scuppett and flail, two saddles, one bridle, one pair of hampers, two horse harnesses, one gallon, one basket, one old malt mill, one oast hair, one old chest, two old spades and one shovel'. Out doors, in addition to his heavy tackle (*viz*. wagon, cart, harrow and plough) he had 'a parcel of old iron, one old scythe, three old sneads, one old saw, one bucket and two well ropes, and one old grindstone'.[112]

Size of Holding	No. of Farms	Wagons and Carts					Harrows				Ploughs			Rollers	Bodges	Timber Tugs	No Heavy Tackle Whatsoever
		0	1	2-3	4-5	6+	0	1	2	3+	0	1	2				
c15-49 acres	24	12	5	7	-	-	15	4	5	2	19	4	1	1	-	-	11
c50-99 acres	12	2	6	4	-	-	5	3	1	3	4	8	-	1	-	1	1
c100-199 acres	13	-	1	4	6	2	2	1	3	7	2	6	5	5	2	2	-
c200+ acres	2	-	-	-	-	2	-	-	-	2	-	-	2	1	-	-	-
	51	41	12	15	6	4	22	8	7	14	25	18	8	8	2	3	12

Figure 2.28
Heavy tackle on individual farms, abstracted from a selection of early 18th-century
probate inventories relating to the north-east of Hastings Rape.[113]

Figure 2.29
Moving a plough, c1900. [456/5A]

Figure 2.30
Wagon drawn by a team of oxen, c1900, outside
Pepperingeye Farm, Battle. [456/22A]

Figure 2.31
A field scene taken c1900 showing a cart
drawn by a donkey. Donkeys and mules are
noticeably absent from the early 18th-century
probate inventories. [456/13A]

It was the heavy tackle which represented the highest capital outlay. An analysis of such items on a sample of 51 early 18th-century farms shows wagons, carts, harrows and ploughs to have been the most common items. Ploughs were absent from half the farms, though this, at least in some cases, may have been due to their inclusion under the blanket term 'other husbandry tackle'. Some farmers probably hired or borrowed ploughs from their neighbours, especially where the holding lacked draught animals. A high percentage of small farms possessed neither carts, wagons nor harrows. As Figure 2.28 illustrates, no farm of less than *c*99 acres is recorded within the sample as having more than three wagons and carts, though more than this figure was relatively common on the larger farms. John French of Iden possessed two wagons, four carts on wheels and three cart bodies without wheels.[114] Such references to carts and wagons without wheels are not uncommon, whilst spare wheels are sometimes mentioned. Harrows, some referred to as horse harrows, are another item often found in multiples, and there are occasional references to rollers, water bodges and timber haulage vehicles. Only on the larger farms, with their greater quantity of heavy tackle, do wagon sheds appear to have existed, though even on these holding such buildings were rare until the early or mid 18th century. Small tool-sheds, on the other hand, are likely to have been present on many holdings.

The general range of implements appears to have varied little from medieval times. If the accounts of the cellarer of Battle Abbey can be taken as a guide, it would appear that the wealthy 15th-century landowners possessed as many wagons and carts as did their early 18th-century counterparts.[115] Likewise, if an inventory of a farm of between 20 and 33 acres in Hooe taken in 1455 is typical, it would appear that the same also applied to the small-holder, for the husbandry tackle on the farm is listed as 'two wagons with iron tyes, four yokes with iron chappes and bolts and equipment, one hanging, two ploughs with their apparatus, two plough shares, two coulters, two harrows with iron teeth and their equipment, one basket, one hay fork, one dunk fork, one flail, one spade, one 'marra', one axe, one hatchet, one iron bill for hedges, one hammer, one auger, one wimble, one stone and one grindstone'.[116]

THE FARMERS

Tenure

Reference has already been made to the safeguards written into leases to prevent deterioration of the

Approx. Size of Holdings Excl. Woodland	Gentry Estates No. of Holdings in		Other Holdings No. of Holdings in			Total
	Owner occupation	Tenanted	Owner occupation	Tenanted	Unknown	
c15-49 acres	-	13	32	73	8	123
c50-99 acres	1	16	9	18	-	44
c100-149 acres	1	8	5	13	-	27
c150+ acres	1	15	--	2	-	18
Total	3	52	46	106	8	215
	55 (26%)		106 (74%)			

Figure 2.32
An analysis of the owners and occupiers of 215 holdings in the adjacent parishes of Beckley, Brede, Ewhurst, Northiam, Sedlescombe and Whatlington during the early 18th century, based on the Land Tax returns and the Ewhurst Poor Book.[117]

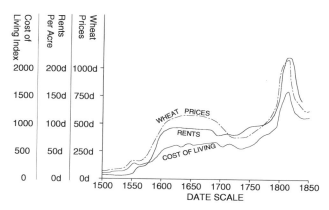

Figure 2.33
Comparison of local rents with wheat prices and the cost of living index.[121]

buildings, but of course not all farms were leased out: some were in owner-occupation. An analysis of the early 18th-century land tax returns for the six adjacent parishes of Beckley, Brede, Ewhurst, Northiam, Sedlescombe and Whatlington (in which both owners and occupiers are stated) is shown in Figure 2.32. This indicates that at that date approximately three-quarters of the 215 farms in these parishes were tenanted, the larger-acreage holdings in particular being far more prone to be leased out. About one in four farms were located on reasonably large gentry estates, though this was probably above average for the region as a whole. Although estates had always existed, without doubt the late 16th and 17th centuries saw a considerable buying-in of property by the gentry classes, both to enlarge existing estates and to form new ones. Some of these newly-acquired farms were merged with others in order to form larger units, though it was usual at this time to retain most at their former acreage.

The existence of gentry estates should not be seen as the sole reason for tenanted farms, though undoubtedly the expansionist tendencies of the more affluent classes must have increased the proportion of holdings out on lease. Even so, in 1711 about two-thirds of the farms not located upon gentry estates were tenanted, as opposed to being in owner-occupation. Other sources indicate that the leasing out of lands had been common since at least the 16th century, and probably before.[118] It should, however, be borne in mind that tighter manorial control during the early periods may on some manors have limited the amount of letting, for the leasing out of copyhold property was often 'controlled' by the issuing of licences.

The leases themselves varied: tenancies for life, for a specific number of years, and for an unspecified term determined at the will of the owner and tenant, existed locally. As tenancy-at-will usually took the form

of a verbal agreement, it is today difficult to assess how common this form of tenancy was. Perhaps significantly, in 1567 all but four of the Robertsbridge demesne farms were held in this way, as was also the case with all but two of those on Etchingham Manor in 1597, and all but four of the fourteen local farms on the Pelham Estate in 1761.[119] During the early 19th century many of the tenants on Ashburnham Estate held by verbal agreement.[120]

Unless for life, most of the written agreements were for terms ranging from seven to 21 years. The annual rent (always clearly stipulated) varied considerably from farm to farm, even where the leases are dated the same year, the sum payable being a reflection of both the quality of the land and demand for the farm. Prospective tenants often tendered for a lease. Inflation also had its effect on rents. Figure 2.33 charts the relationship of local rents to wheat prices and the cost of living. As the graph illustrates, for long periods the general rise in rents closely mirrored the increase in the cost of living. There were, however, three critical periods during which this appears not to have been the case, and these are here thought to be of sufficient significance to warrant more detailed discussion.

During the 15th century and first decades of the 16th century both prices and rents remained stable.[122] Throughout the second half of the 15th century most Battle Abbey rents were constant at between 6d and 8d per acre, whilst some lands were available at rents as low as 3d.[123] Likewise, in 1517/18 the three farms forming the demesne of Pashley Manor, Ticehurst, were leased out at rents of between 8d and 10d per acre of plainland.[124] After c1510 prices generally began to rise, the cost of living by 1550 being approximately double that in 1510. Surprisingly, there appears to have been no corresponding increase in Wealden rents, the demesne lands of Robertsbridge Abbey still being leased out at 6¾d to 7¼d per plainland acre during the period

1530-1553, whilst in 1530 and 1540 Gatecourt, Northiam, and Great Bainden, Mayfield, were rented at figures as low as 3½d and 4d respectively.[125] Such figures imply a general lack of demand for Wealden farms and a correspondingly depressed level of agricultural activity, a factor largely confirmed by other sources (*see* above).

Between 1550 and 1557 a major rise in prices occurred and in this instance the increase was reflected in Wealden rents. Thus, at Robertsbridge the demesne farmlands let between 1555 and 1567 were fetching between 1/5d and 2/1¼d per acre.[126] Sir Richard Sackville's estates in the parishes of Ore, Guestling, Westfield and Fairlight were being leased at values varying from 11d for the semi-derelict demesne farm of Guestling Manor, to 2/7d for the demesne of Frenchcourt in Fairlight.[127] On Ore Manor, he was leasing out his 87 acres of meadow at 3/4d per acre and his 534¾ acres of pasture, wood and rough at 1/4d.[128] Methersham Farm in Beckley, leased out by the Sidney family in 1553 for 21 years at 1/4d per acre, was in 1567 valued at 2/2d, clearly reflecting how rents were by this date rising.[129] Even Great Bainden in Mayfield, let for 21 years at just 4d per acre in 1540, was granted out in 1577 at 1/7¼d, almost five times its 1540 rent.[130]

After another period of relative stability, the 1590s and 1600s once again saw the cost of living rising. Rent however, appear to have continued to rise throughout the 1570s and 80s, for already by 1585 the plainlands on one Burwash farm had topped the 5/- mark, with a valuation of 5/5d per acre.[131] Even Great Bainden, which fetched 1/7¼d per acre in 1577, was in 1598 let at 3/8d.[132] In like manner, in 1597 the demesne lands of Etchingham Manor were leased out at figures ranging from 3/9½d to 6/5¼d per acre.[133] By the 1620s and 30s rents of between 6/- and 9/- were common. In 1626 Park Farm, Salehurst was held at 8/3d, and Udiam, Ewhurst at 8/5d per acre. Figures in excess of 10/- per acre were not unknown.[134]

In comparison with the cost of living, which rose between five and seven-fold between 1510 and 1630, rents (after remaining relatively stable until *c*1550) had by *c*1630 risen to between 10 and 16 times their *c*1550 level, the greater proportion of which increase appears to have occurred after *c*1570.[135] Taking just two specific instances, the rent of Udiam Farm can be illustrated to have risen to 14 times its 1553 level by 1626, whilst by as early as 1598 that of Great Bainden had reached 11 times its 1540 level and by 1651 14½ times its 1540 level.

The very fact that owners were able to increase rents so dramatically without catastrophic effect clearly indicates an agricultural revolution giving rise to more efficient and profitable farming. During a boom period of this nature both owners and tenants invested heavily in improvements. Those undertaken by the tenants were mostly with regards to the quality of the land (*see* above), whilst the owners' attentions were chiefly directed towards building stock. Many farmhouses show clear evidence of having been rebuilt or, more often, remodelled during this period. More importantly, a heavier emphasis on cereals and pulses necessitated the provision of increased crop storage facilities. High profits would have encouraged many owners to replace their small barns by larger, more modern buildings.

After the boom, both rents and inflation tended to level off. The very fact that rents were not reduced implies no lack of tenants, and it may be no coincidence that at Bodiam in 1626 the prospective tenants were willing to undertake the construction of houses and barns.[136]

The final period of discrepancy between rents and the cost of living occurred in the 1690s when rents actually fell during a period of inflation. The chief cause was a run of exceptionally bad harvests which left the tenants unable to pay their rents, and prospective tenants reluctant to take on farms unless sufficient incentives were given.[137] Leases falling in during this period were often renewed at a lower rent, and although the situation did improve after *c*1700, for the next forty years the landlords were only able to maintain rents at a value lower in real terms than previously.[138]

Relative Status and the Farming Labour Force

What people called themselves and their neighbours can, in some circumstances, not only indicate their occupations, but also give a clue as to their status. In agriculture the yeoman and husbandman were the two principal classes (excluding the gentry and farm labourers). The yeoman were the more wealthy and respected of the two. As more and more people aspired to the ranks of yeoman the status of that class became increasingly debased. Thus, whereas during the first half of the 16th century all but the most wealthy of farmers were content to be styled husbandman, by the early 18th century even relatively poor small-holders were in many instances regarded as yeomen, and the more wealthy yeomen were styled gentry. Husbandmen by this time included landless labourers skilled in the art of husbandry. In addition, a new relatively wealthy class of 'farmers' and 'graziers' had by now appeared.[139]

The acreage capable of supporting a family without the aid of an alternative source of income is not known: the figure must have varied considerably depending upon such factors as the size of family, the standard of living acceptable to that family, the quality of the land, and the economic conditions prevailing at the time. Many small-holders supplemented their income to a greater or lesser extent either by plying a craft or trade,

PROPERTY	ACRES	LAND TAX RATE	HEAD OF HOUSEHOLD	OCCUPATION / RANK	TENANT or OWNER-OCCUPIER	'ADULT' HOUSEHOLD: WIFE	CHILDREN	PARENT	RELATION	FARM SERVANT	TRADE SERVANT	HOUSE SERVANT	LODGER	TOTAL ADULTS
OVER 150 ACRES														
Lower Standard Hill	403	£65	John Noakes	Yeoman	T	✓				3			1	6
Moorhall Place	227	£38	John Plummer	Gentleman	T	✓			1	2				5
Upper Standard Hill	190	£42	Bart Walker	Yeoman	T	✓				1				3
Pashley	163	£43	John Soane	Yeoman	O				2	2				5
100-149 ACRES														
Ingrams	120	£33	Hen Lasher	Gentleman	O	✓				1				3
Messens	120	£18+	Thos Blackman. jnr	Yeoman	T	✓				1				3
50-99 ACRES														
Hollis Street	94	£23	Rich Sampson	Mercer	O	✓				1		1		4
Hole Farm	65	£20	Thos Blackman. snr	Yeoman	T/O	✓	1			1				4
Thorne	65	£14	Jos Blackman	Yeoman	T			1						2
15-49 ACRES														
Tanhouse	46	£15	Walt Osborne	Tanner	T		2				1			4
Church Farm	44	£12	Will Markwick	Yeoman	T	✓								2
The Stock	c.40	£11	Step Cooper	Carpenter	T/O	✓								2
Combe Hill	42	£14	John Easton	Bullock Leech	T	✓				1			1	4
@ Hollis Street	30	£5	Will Brook	Wheelwright	O		1							2
Bunt Barns	30	£9	John Morris	Yeoman	T	✓								2
Combe Mill	25	£11	John Mepham	Miller	T/O	✓								2
Church House	21	£6	Nat Mills	Schoolmaster	T	✓							2	4
Millers Farm	20	£7	Rich Gander	Tailor	T	✓								2
Macks	19	£6	John Hull	Weaver	O	✓							1	3
Waites Land	15	£6	John Vigor	Butcher	O	✓	1				1			4
5-14 ACRES														
@ Lunsford Cross	14	£6	Thos Bray	Weaver	T	✓					1		1	4
Martins Farm	12	£7	Will Easton	Tanner (retired)	T	✓								2
@ Ninfield Street	9	£4	Will Boadle	Glover	O				1					2
Brickhill Land	?	£4	John Harris	Labourer	?			1						2
UNDER 5 ACRES														
@ Lower Street	3	£3	John Vigor	Shoemaker	T	✓	1							3
@ Lower Street	3	£2	John Wesbrook	Tailor	O	✓	2							4
?	?	£2	Jas Roberts	Carpenter	O									1
@ Ninfield Street	?	£2	Thos Coleman	Carpenter	O									1
@ Ninfield Street	4	£2	Thos Harris	Butcher	O									1
@ Hooe Common	1	£2	Phil Bates	Labourer	T									1
A wayside cottage	¼	£1	Robt Friend	Carpenter	O									1
	?	£1	Rich Frankwell	Labourer	T	✓								2
	¼	£1	Robt Grant	Tailor	T									1
Buttfield House	½	-	Elias Sinnock	Mercer	T	✓								2
@ Hollis Street	2	-	Thos Seldon	Labourer	T	✓								2
	?	-	Hen Elliot	Collier	?	✓								2
Blacksmiths Arms	?	¼	Thos Taylor	Sheepshearer	O	✓								2
	?	-	Will Weeks	Labourer	?	✓								2
	?	-	Phil Philcox	Brickmaker	?									1
	?	-	Edwd Hunt	Hopman	?	✓								2
	?	-	Will Langridge	Butcher	?									1
@ Hollis Street	?	-	Edwd Merrick	Labourer	T	✓								2

Figure 2.34
Adult occupants of Ninfield Parish in 1702, indicating the occupation of the head of the household and relationship to the head of the household of the other members.[141]
T/O = Tenant of some land, owner-occupier of other lands

or by working in one of the many jobs allied to the Wealden timber and iron industries. Others hired out their agricultural skills to more wealthy neighbours. For many men such occupations were probably primary, their small-holdings supplying food for the family and perhaps a meagre source of income.[140]

Bearing in mind the Wealden bias toward non-labour-intensive animal husbandry, many medium-sized holdings would probably have supported a family with little or no need for external income. Conversely, the hiring-in of labour, except during busy periods, would probably have been relatively rare on these medium-sized holdings, much of the work having been undertaken by family labour.

Only very rarely are we able to obtain a reliable picture as to the typical number of adult members making up a family, and even where this is possible it is extremely rare that the principal occupations of the various members of the household is known. Such an instance is Ninfield Parish in 1702 where the compiler of a Poll Tax return fortuitously supplied this information. The return is even more valuable on account of the fact that the households listed can be correlated with the Land Tax return for the same year. An analysis of the title deeds and other documentary sources for the parish has allowed the locations of virtually all the households to be identified geographically, together with a reliable indication of the acreage of land attached to each holding. The combined data from these sources is summarized in Figure 2.34.

Ninfield was in many respects a typical parish, though there were some anomalies. In 1702 there were some 42 households of which about half - a higher than average number - were supported by holdings of less than 15 acres. Most of these were landless or near-landless cottages - 18 households had less than 4 acres to support them. Most of these landless properties were occupied by craftsmen and tradesmen: a shoemaker, a mercer, two tailors, two butchers three carpenters, a brickmaker and a collier. Five others were the homes of labourers (not all of whom were necessarily agricultural labourers) whilst in addition there was a sheepshearer and a hopman. As figure 2.34 shows, the occupations listed for those living on the small-holdings of 5-14 acres were very similar in make up to those occupying landless properties.

The picture painted by the Ninfield 'farms' of over 15 acres is typical of that suggested from other sources relating to the other parishes within the study area. At the head of the agricultural hierarchy were the large-acreage farms of over 150 acres; farms upon which both the small-holder and labourer would have relied most heavily for additional employment. In Ninfield these farms accounted for 20% of the holdings in excess of 15 acres, which percentage, as Figure 2.12 suggests, appears to have been average for the region. It is, however, worth stressing that one of these farms - the 403-acre Lower Standard Hill (now Luxford House) - was at that time one of the largest holdings in the entire study area. Not surprisingly, all four of these large farms employed full-time staff who lived within the main house, or perhaps in some instances within an associated outbuilding. Live-in agricultural employees are also listed on the two holdings of 100-149 acres, as well as two of the three farms of 50-99 acres. However, on the small-holdings of 15-49 acres - which it should be remembered accounted for 55% of all the 'farms' - only John Easton the 'bullock leech' (or vet) employed a live-in farm worker. Within the 1702 return these live-in workers are consistently termed 'husbandmen' rather than agricultural labourers. Most appear to have been young, and a number are found farming their own local holdings later in the 18th century.

As is to be expected within an area bias towards non-labour-intensive cattle fatstock, the number of live-in farm workers on individual farms was low - Lower Standard Hill employed three such men, whilst both Pashley and Moorhall Place each had two, and a further six farms employed one each.

All holdings of any size would have needed to hire-in some labour at busy times of the year and even on the large farms most labour appears to have been hired on a casual basis, as and when needed. Thus, in 1646 John Everenden of Sedlescombe, a wealthy yeoman sufficiently respected locally to be described as 'gentleman', hired nine named casual workers at various times throughout the year for grubbing, ditching, hedging, mowing and reaping. All the engagements were of a short-term nature.[142] Similarly, Laurence Noakes, who worked the 30-acre small-holding called Brown Oak in Brightling, was hired by the local rector, John Lord, to undertake sundry carrying duties with his ox-team and wagon, as well as hedging, ditching and labouring upon the glebe.[143]

Although casual employment of this kind would have been essential in keeping many of the smaller farms viable, by no means all of those occupying these smaller farms would have hired out their services to local neighbours as farm workers. For a considerable number of men within the study area their small-holdings were subsidiary to their principal non-agricultural occupations. As the occupations of the Ninfield parishioners listed in 1702 reminds us, although properties of 15-49 acres may have accounted for more than half the 'farms' in the area, in at least some parishes the majority of those occupying these small farms were not engaged primarily in agriculture. Only three of the eleven Ninfield occupiers of small-holdings of 15-49 acres were primarily involved in farming. For the others (listed as a tanner, carpenter, wheelwright, miller, schoolmaster, tailor, weaver and a butcher) their non-agricultural occupations would no doubt have provided their main source of income. If Ninfield is typical in this respect, perhaps it was the landless and near-landless who carried out most of the casual work on the larger holdings!

Although the Ninfield data reminds us that many, if not most of the small-holders in the area were dual-economists, to imply that dual economy was the sole preserve of the small-holder would be wrong. As an example, most gentlemen farmers possessed alternative sources of income, not least being their interest in property and in the timber and iron industries. Although the tanner and principal butcher in Ninfield ran relatively small farms, capital-intensive industries such as these were often run in association with medium to large holdings, whilst their proprietors were by necessity men of some local wealth. One of the nine holdings of over 50 acres in Ninfield was occupied in 1702 by a wealthy mercer who also had interests in distilling, whilst two of the others were gentlemen. Despite the fact that the practice of dual economy on large holdings should not be ignored, it is none-the-less true that the majority of families occupying these larger holdings appear to have been farmers whose other interests - if they had any - were of secondary importance to them.

3   THE FARMSTEAD

LAYOUT AND COMPONENTS

The farm buildings and their attendant yards, closes, orchards and gardens form the farmstead. Only rarely can we obtain an overall picture of a farmstead, though often we are misled into assuming that we can. For instance, many estate maps show the farm buildings set within or on the edge of a single enclosure. A typical example from a 1618 map of Hammerden Manor is Bines Farm, Ticehurst, shown in Figure 3.1.[1] In addition to the farmstead enclosure with its house and barn, a further ten parcels made up the 33¾ acre farm. In the relevant entry in the detailed survey which accompanies the map the property is described as a messuage, barn, croft, orchard, garden and ten pieces of land.[2] Thus, although the farmstead is depicted in the map as a single plot of 1½ acres, the survey makes clear that it comprised a croft, orchard and garden. This situation is general

throughout the survey. An analysis of the entries for all the bondhold farms on this extensive manor shows the farmsteads to have ranged in size from around ½ acre up to 4¼ acres: the majority were between ¾ and 1¾ acres. Apart from the buildings themselves, the farmsteads comprised between one and four enclosures averaging half an acre each. Crofts were present on virtually all farmsteads in the sample, whilst orchards and gardens were less commonly listed, being recorded on about three-quarters and a little under two-thirds of the holdings respectively. Four included two crofts and a further two possessed two orchards. This in general can be taken as the norm, other manorial and estate surveys showing a similar situation.

Even this, however, is not the whole picture. A glebe terrier of Bodiam Vicarage made in 1675 gives a holding typical of those described above, having a house, barn, orchard, close and garden comprising c1 acre in extent. Yet forty years earlier, in 1635, another more detailed account of the same farmstead describes it as comprising 'one dwelling house containing three bays of buildings, one barn with one stall and stable at the north end of the said barn, one garden, one orchard, one small court before the door, one small close between the said court and barn for the feeding and watering of beasts, and one little back close for laying of wood and faggots, the which said parcels of ground, together with the little croft called the vicarage croft, containing 1¼ acres'.[3] The 1675 description can therefore be shown to have omitted three small enclosed areas considered too small to be worthy of inclusion. Surveys containing this amount of detail are rare, especially as in this instance the use of the various plots is stated, thus giving a vivid picture of the workings of a farmstead at this period. The general rule in the making of surveys appears to have been to mention anything thought sufficiently large or important, and to ignore all else. Many orchards, gardens and small yards must have been ignored in this way.

By the early 18th century some surveyors were beginning to portray the farmsteads accurately, and it is upon the maps they produced that we must rely for a

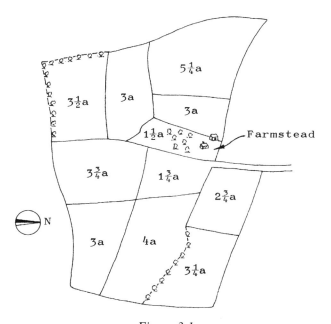

Figure 3.1
Bines Farm, Ticehurst, as depicted on the Hammerden manorial map dated 1618.

Figure 3.2
A traditional farmstead scene showing
working oxen in the stack yard or forstall.

clear picture. A selection, redrawn to a standard scale is shown in Figures 3.3 to 3.9.[4] Unfortunately they relate principally to the larger farms, though the complex of small enclosures which they indicate is in keeping with the description of Bodiam vicarage. Formal farmsteads in which the buildings are shown clustered around a yard are, as far as can be told, unknown at this period. The most formal arrangements are those where the house and barn are set close together, as in the 39-acre Broad Oak Farm, Brede, shown in Figure 3.3, or the 268-acre Kitchenham Farm, Ashburnham, illustrated in Figure 3.6. The layout depicted for Broad Oak is particularly common on the smaller holdings. In many instances, however, there is no clear relationship between the house and its barn or other farm buildings, which appear to

have been constructed where space allowed.

Ignoring those dual-economy farms within the villages and small townships, most farmsteads appear to have been located near one edge of the farmlands, either by the side of a road, or, where the lands did not abut a road, at the end of a clearly defined farm track. The house and buildings on Peens Farm, Penhurst, however, were approached across the fields, there being no enclosed access road, a situation also found at Conster Manor, Brede (*see* Figure 3.5). It was usual for the house to be located within the farmstead. Even some large mansions, where one would expect the farmyard to be set a little distance away, had the house and barn set side by side. This situation is recognizable at Great Dixter, Northiam, where the large medieval barn is located close to the parlour of the mansion. At Conster Manor, shown in Figure 3.5, however, the buildings are a little distance away, as is also the situation at the formerly moated Great Wigsell, Salehurst, and to a lesser extent at the moated mansion at Ashburnham Place (rebuilt 1665; *see* Figure 3.7). In all three instances, although the farm buildings were thus separated from the house, they were not hidden from view, but instead were passed by visitors approaching the house. Indeed, at Ashburnham Place visitors were directed around the barn in order to gain access to the courtyard in front of the mansion. These examples are essentially medieval in origin, though the same features are recognizable at the 17th-century Brickwall, Northiam, and at the 1591 Iwood Place, Warbleton (rebuilt), both of which had their farm buildings set across a public road but clearly visible to visitors.

All farmyards incorporated either an un-enclosed area called a 'forstall' or alternatively a 'close' set aside for what can best be described as 'general purpose' usage

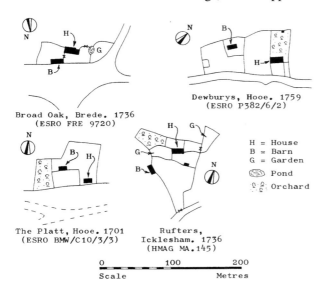

Figure 3.3
A selection of farmstead layouts (farms of 15-49 acres)
based on early/mid 18th-century estate maps.

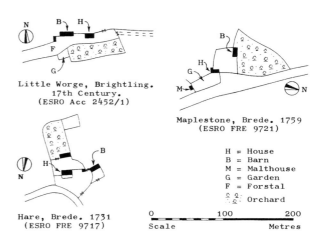

Figure 3.4
A selection of farmstead layouts (farms of 50-99 acres)
based on 17th- and early/mid 18th-century estate maps.

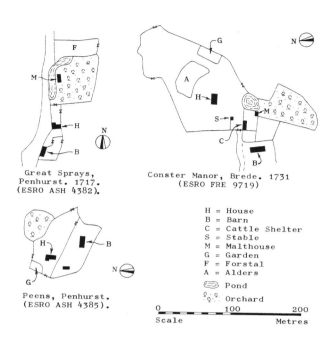

Figure 3.5
A selection of farmstead layouts (farms of 100-149 acres)
based on early/mid 18th-century estate maps.

such as the storage of wood, faggots, hurdles, hop poles, carts, ploughs and, of course, the hay ricks. At Bodiam vicarage one of the enclosures is listed as 'a little close at the back of the house for the laying of wood and faggots'.[5] Although many houses possessed a back yard, others abutted direct onto a field or orchard. A glance at Figures 3.3 to 3.9 will show that the vegetable gardens were normally set away from the house, the house instead often being approached through a small front close.

A few barns had tiny yard-like closes attached to them, though as often as not they were either freestanding within a field or alternatively set against a boundary with a field or road on one side and a general-purpose close on the other. Formal yards edged by ranges of shelter sheds have in most instances been added to one or more sides of the barns since. It has been noticed that, for some reason not clear to the authors, oasthouses were not infrequently located within or on the edge of an orchard. Another popular location was near the rear of the house. This latter location may be influenced by the gradual taking over of a detached kitchen, first for malt manufacture and finally for hop drying.

How often the small closes of the farmstead were

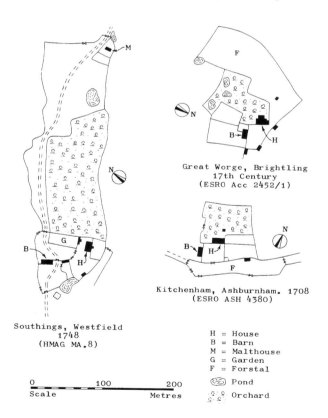

Figure 3.6
A selection of farmstead layouts (farms of 150-299 acres)
based on 17th- and early/mid 18th-century estate maps.

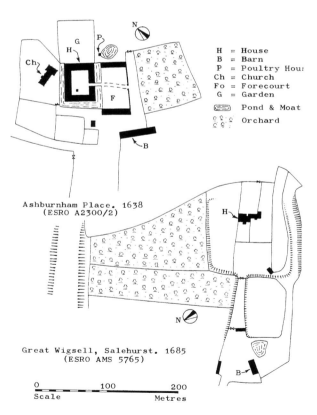

Figure 3.7
Farm buildings associated with two major mansions.
Based upon 17th-century estate maps.

muddy enclosures (as opposed to grassed areas) is unknown, though one suspects that the smaller closes, especially those kept for 'feeding and watering beasts' as at Bodiam in 1635, would have been of this type. Indeed, this is largely confirmed by a particularly detailed survey of two estates in Icklesham Parish made in 1767.[6] In addition to clearly indicating gardens, orchards, ponds and all buildings (including small sheds and the like) the surveyor used colour to depict the state of those areas which, in most maps and surveys, would merely have been classified as closes and crofts. Thus those used as pasture he coloured green, whilst those containing bare earth, metalling or rough land were shaded brown. The farmsteads included in the survey are shown in Figure 3.8, in which the green enclosures are marked as closes and the brown as yards. Most farmstead plans show a pond for the watering of beasts, and even where these are not depicted this was probably due to their small size rather than their absence.

It will be noted that none of the mid 18th-century farms included in Figure 3.8 are of 'planned' type with formal yards surrounded by buildings. This is not only the case with these farms, but also with those on Herrings Estate, Dallington in 1793/4.[7] Even as late as the 1830s and 1840s many farms depicted in the tithe

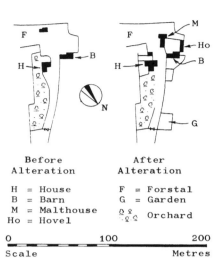

Figure 3.9
Haselden, Dallington, c1765 and 1830,
based upon ESRO ASH 4391

Figure 3.10
Toll Farm, Warbleton showing traditional
rail-fenced cattle yards. [109/11]

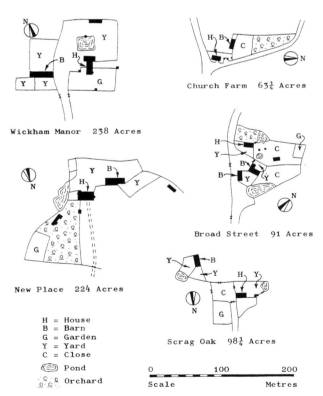

Figure 3.8
The layouts of five farmsteads in Icklesham
Parish, 1767, based on ESRO AMS 5788/1.

Figure 3.11
Beestons, Warbleton. A typical traditional muddy
farmyard. The flat-roofed building in the centre
once had a half-hipped pitched roof. [865/14]

maps were still completely informal in their layout, though some more formal layouts had by this date begun to appear, especially on the estates and larger farms where a few purpose-rebuilt farmsteads are found. One such reconstruction occurred between *c*1765 and 1830 at Kitchenham Farm on the Ashburnham Estate. Most improvements, however, appear to have been achieved by adapting and adding to the existing buildings. A relatively early example of this type of a modification is to be found in the second half of the 18th century at Haselden Farm, Dallington where the adjustments are indicated on an estate map of the period (*see* Figure 3.9). Apparently a copy of an earlier plan upgraded in a contemporary hand, the map depicts a new yard surrounded by a pre-existing barn and newly constructed hovel and oasthouse. Today only the oasthouse survives.

BUILDINGS ON THE FARMSTEAD

Being the largest and most dominant, barns are the structures which most readily come to mind when farm buildings are mentioned, yet other types of agricultural building existed in the past, as indeed they do today. For example, poultry houses, pigsties and the like were probably absent from few farmsteads through, being very small, all but the most detailed of documentary sources omit them. For this reason, these minor structures are excluded from this assessment of the buildings present upon farmsteads. Conveyances, leases and other similar documents are, in the main, inconsistent in their degree of detail regarding the buildings present on individual holdings, whilst many manorial and estate surveys ignore all but the barns and largest farm buildings. Bearing this in mind, in analysing the local farmsteads only those surveys which give 'full' details have been used. A summary of the details from these sources is shown in Figure 3.12.

As might be expected, in general terms there is a tendency for the larger farms to have possessed the greatest number of buildings. Considering first those farms in excess of 150 acres, it was usual, even by the

Size of Farm (acres)	No. of farm Buildings on each farm (in addition to the farmhouse)						Total No. of Farms
	0	1	2	3	4	5	
15 - 49	5	32	7	-	-	-	44
50 - 99	2	8	6	5	-	-	21
100 +	-	2	3	3	1	2	11

Figure 3.12
Table showing the number of farm buildings in a sample of 76 farmsteads during a period between the mid 16th century and the early 18th century.[8]

middle of the 16th century, for such holdings to possess more than one farm building, though at that date more than three appear to have been rare. Next to the ever-present barn it was the stable (whether for riding or draught animals is not known) which appears to have occurred with most regularity, though a second barn, cattle shelters and even oasthouses (for malt) are all encountered during the second half of the 16th century. In 1567 the 330½-acre Abbey Farm, Salehurst (the former site of a Cistercian monastery) possessed two barns, a combined oxstall, stable and hayloft, and an oasthouse, in addition to other non-agricultural buildings, including a triple mill and extensive stables for riding horses.[9] It should, however, be borne in mind that the abbey was not only a site with numerous buildings and building materials awaiting reuse, but also one of the few large-acreage farms in the area. Even on holdings of this size such a variety of buildings cannot be assumed to have been the norm. This point is well illustrated by the equally large *c*370 acre Pebsham Farm, Bexhill, which in 1590 possessed nothing more than a great barn with an attached lean-to stable.[10]

Little change in this general picture appears to have occurred until the late 18th century, though oasthouses (for both malt and hops) became increasingly common during the 17th century. The wagon shelter, until this time a very rare building, also became more popular during the first half of the 18th century, such buildings being mentioned in several early 18th-century inventories. However, wagon shelters were still comparatively rare even in the mid 18th century.

A similar pattern to that found on large farms is recognizable on the medium-sized holding of 50 to 149 acres, though prior to the late 18th century something like two-thirds possessed two or fewer farm buildings (inclusive of barns) and only very rarely (even in the early 18th century) did the total exceed three. One such exception was the 148½-acre Church Farm, Etchingham, which by 1597 possessed a four-bay barn, oasthouse, a five-room cattle shelter, a small stable, and 'one other little house'.[11] More typical, however, was the adjacent 145-acre Park Lodge Farm which at that date incorporated nothing more than a three-bay barn and stable.[12] Even during the early 18th century about a third of the medium-size farms possessed nothing more than a barn; indeed such an arrangement appears to have existed on roughly half the holdings of 50-99 acres. As with the large farms, however, from the late 17th century onwards oasthouses were becoming increasingly common, being present on roughly half the farms of 50 to 149 acres by the early 18th century.

In dealing with the final group, (the small farms of 15-49 acres) it should be borne in mind that prior to the late 18th century this size of holding accounted for around half the overall total. Until the mid 18th century

Name of Farm	Acreage in 1830	Description of Newly Constructed Buildings
Lakehurst, Dallington	26	2 Lodges and a Wagon Lodge
The Swan, Dallington	44¼	Wagon Lodge
Cinderhill, Ashburnham	87	Lean-to Cattle Lodge
Herrings, Dallington	140½	2 Hovels
Slivericks, Ashburnham	169	3 Lodges and a Wagon Lodge
Lattendens, Ashburnham	248¾	Oast and Lean-to Wagon Lodge

Figure 3.13
Details of buildings constructed upon six
farms on Herrings Estate, Dallington,
between 1793 and 1830.

Figure 3.14
Farmhouse and collection of thatched traditional farm
buildings at Lower Stonelink, Fairlight, c1900. [387/34]

Figure 3.15
Parkhill, Burwash. A typical local farmstead scene
with buildings flanking the farm track. The view
is taken from outside the farm house. [192/7]

about three-quarters possessed nothing more than a barn, whilst a further fifth had only two farm buildings, or, in very rare instances, three. A few possessed none whatsoever. One 25¾-acre Etchingham holding in 1597 was somewhat exceptional in that it incorporated a 'little house for calves', but no barn.[13] Where buildings other than a barn existed, these usually took the form of stables or cattle shelters, though from the late 17th century onwards a few oasthouses were constructed. Oasthouses, however, were not nearly as common on these holdings as on the medium and large farms, being present on about 1 in 6 small farms during the early 18th century.

It should not be assumed that those farms (of whatever size) which possessed only a barn did not incorporate provision for stabling or cattle housing, though undoubtedly this must have been the case in some instances. Many barns had a dual or even multiple function, for in addition to housing the unthreshed crops they also contained stabling, stalls and the like, a feature more fully discussed below (*see* Chapter 6). From the early 18th century (if not before) oasthouses also sometimes incorporated cartsheds, stables and granaries.

The above deals only with the years up to the mid 18th century, though bearing in mind the major changes which occurred between *c*1770 and *c*1850, it is necessary to give the modifications of this period brief consideration. This was a time of much building activity, for as the acreage devoted to hops and cereal crops increased, so barns and oasthouses were commonly either reconstructed or modified (*see* Chapters 4 and 13). At the same time new stables and implement sheds were supplied to house the extra draught animals and equipment required to work the land. The greatest increase, however, was in the number of buildings erected to shelter cattle, which during this period were kept in stalls and stock yards (served by shelter sheds) in greater numbers and for longer periods than ever before.

This general increase in the number of buildings is well illustrated on Ashburnham Estate where, by 1830,

farmsteads incorporating only one farm building were virtually unknown except on small-holdings of less than 50 acres. Medium-sized holdings often possessed four separate farm buildings, whilst numbers ranging from 5 to 10 were commonplace in the farmsteads on holdings exceeding 150 acres.[14] These statistics exclude attached ranges stretching out either from the end of a barn or at right angles to it, a favourite location for enclosed cattle sheds and open-fronted lodges during the period of the agricultural revolution, though virtually unknown locally prior to the late 18th century.

Six farms included in the 1830 Ashburnham Estate survey also appear in an equally detailed survey of Herrings Estate made in 1793. All show some building works to have been undertaken between these dates (*see* Figure 3.13).[15]

4   BARNS: SURVIVAL AND CONSTRUCTION DATES

THE LEVEL OF SURVIVAL

In the analysis of any type of building it is important to ascertain, even if only approximately, how common such buildings once were and what proportion survives. With barns these statistics can only be estimations and this should always be borne in mind. However, based upon a detailed reconstruction of 17th- and early 18th-century farm boundaries (for which *see* Figure 2.10) and farmstead sites (for which *see* Figure 4.1) coupled with an analysis of the 1711 land tax returns, it appears that during the early 18th century the Rape of Hastings contained around 1250 barns, 1140 and 1530 being extreme totals. Figure 4.2 shows the 198 barns of mid 18th-century date and earlier as known to survive in 1982, though, allowing for a few which escaped detection during the survey (due to re-roofing or major extension works) the real total is known to be a little higher.[1] From these statistics, it therefore appears that between 13% and 18% of the barns which existed within the rape in *c*1750 were still standing at the time the study was carried out between 1967 and 1982.[2] A similar number of barns survived which had been rebuilt in traditional style upon the sites of earlier barns during the late 18th and 19th centuries. Those constructed on virgin sites during the same period are ignored in the figures quoted in this chapter. On the remaining 65-73% of 'historic' barn sites no traditional barns now survive, either of historic or late 18th-/19th-century date. This destruction has largely been due to redundancy caused by an increase in the amalgamation of farms in recent years and the use of mobile threshing machines introduced during the second half of the 19th century.

If not used for the storage of sundry goods and equipment, those barns which escaped destruction became hay or straw stores, though (due to their design) double handling of the crop was necessary, something which has been overcome in modern buildings. Bearing this in mind, coupled with the fact that, if maintained, a well-built 15th-century barn will survive in as good a condition as a late 18th- or 19th-century example, in theory the level of destruction in modern times should be broadly similar regardless of the building's date of construction. However, it should be borne in mind that farm amalgamations were common during the late 18th and early/mid 19th centuries and, as already pointed out, such amalgamations have accelerated considerably since then. Although this appears only rarely to have caused

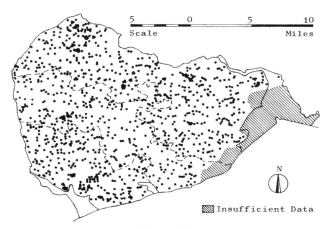

Figure 4.1
Probable historic barn sites
as known in 1982

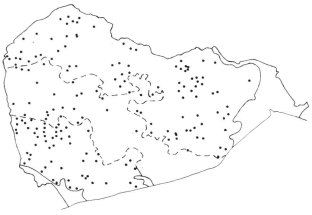

Figure 4.2
Surviving historic barns (Mid 18th century and earlier) as known in 1982

33

the immediate destruction of barns, it did, none-the-less, leave many isolated from the main farmstead. Such isolated buildings would only rarely - if ever - have been subjected to late 18th- and 19th-century reconstruction and were probably often at least semi-redundant and thus poorly maintained. These would have been the first to be left to decay and let fall when barns became less used. Thus, those barns which had become isolated from the main farmyards are likely to have been subject to an increased risk of destruction with a resultant overstating of the impact of the extent of reconstruction after 1750. Even so, that a major rebuild did occur during this late period is beyond question (*see* Figure 4.5).

It is worth stressing that the rates of survival are not consistent throughout the parishes of the rape. In some parishes, such as Bodiam and Catsfield, very few barns of any age remain, whilst in others survival of either historic, or late-18th and 19th-century barns, or both, is good. There are many reasons for these variations: the intensity of farm engrossment during the 19th century, the policies of individual estates (*ie* conservative or progressive), the quality of the land, and the variable effects of modern farming being the more obvious. The high survival in one parish is sufficiently exceptional to warrant special note. In 1982 Warbleton had an overall survival rate of between 1 in 2 and 2 in 3 barns, equalled by only two other parishes within the study area. More important still, in 1982 between 34% and 46% of the early 18th-century sites still possess barns of pre-1750 date. This amounted in all to 25 surviving historic barns. During the 17th and early 18th centuries Warbleton appears to have been a parish of average wealth - it was certainly not rich. It does, however, seem to have had an above average number of medium-sized farms. The reason for such a high survival of historic barns appears, in this instance, to have been due more to the conservatism of the landowners during the late 18th, 19th and 20th centuries (at least partially reflected in the low level of farm amalgamations) than to an exceptionally high number of well-built barns constructed between the 15th and mid 18th centuries.

BARNS WITHIN NUCLEATED SETTLEMENTS

'Urban' barns constructed within the towns and larger village centres were once common, but by the early 19th century were already rare. They appear once to have been particularly common in the larger villages of the area, settlements which in documents boast the title 'town'. These villages are still very rich in houses predating the late 16th and early 17th centuries, and appear to have obtained their wealth by the adoption of a dual economy of trade and agriculture. The largest of the settlements was Robertsbridge with 51 dwellings in 1567. Of these, fifteen possessed barns, of which eleven

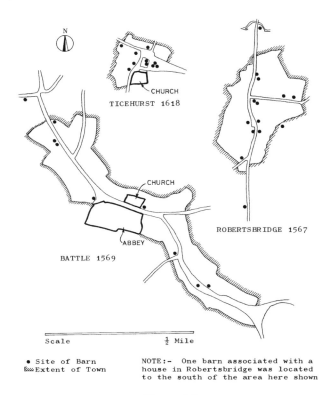

Figure 4.3
Urban barns

were located within the town itself.[3] The much smaller 'town' of Ticehurst boasted about 23 houses in 1618, no less than 10 of which had a barn (*see* Figure 4.3).[4] Although the documentation is much poorer for Burwash 'town', it too had several barns. Indeed, of the four 'rural townships' within Hastings Rape, only Sedlescombe, a settlement of 18 houses, appears to have had little agricultural interest - in the mid 16th century it had within it a maximum of two barns.[5]

The true towns - Battle, Hastings, Rye and Winchelsea - also possessed their barns, but they were apparently few in number and were mostly located on the outskirts. In 1569 a barn existed adjacent the church of Battle, and another attached to the Almonry (now the Pilgrims Rest) near the Abbey gateway, though, as Figure 4.3 indicates, the remaining seven were situated in the sparsely populated southern and northern outskirts. Almost all the Battle examples still existed in 1652.[6] In Robertsbridge (and probably the other rural townships as well) agricultural interests were decidedly on the wane by the late 17th and early 18th centuries. By 1840 Robertsbridge possessed just two (or possibly three) barns. Today only one early 18th-century example survives. Until the 1980s Burwash retained two early 17th-century barns, though that at Square Farm, on the periphery, has since been demolished. That at Mount House, right in the centre of the village, still survives. In Ticehurst none now remain.

DATING THE SURVIVING BUILDINGS

Those historic barns which survive vary considerably in age, the earliest being of 15th-century (or, in one instance, perhaps even 14th-century) date. Before any analysis could be attempted it was necessary to approximately date each building, and as the remainder of the section on barns depends upon this, it is worth describing in some detail the method used.

At the time when the study was carried out the use of tree-ring dating was much less used than it is today and was beyond the meagre finances available. Because of this, other methods which relied upon changing styles had to be used. The first step in the procedure was to date the buildings by impression derived from the authors' experience gained whilst carrying out over 750 surveys of local houses and barns. This was followed by a more systematic attempt to categorise four basic chronological groups using three features with broad chronological characteristics. These three features may be summarized as follows:-

a) The existence of a crownpost or related roof type, a method of construction which is widely accepted as having been largely superseded by side-purlin construction by *c*1530, though a few local examples were thought likely to have lingered through to the mid 16th century.

b) In walls which are daub-infilled, the braces may either be exposed to view externally or internally. Compliance with changing fashion resulted in the general abandonment of externally exposed bracing during the late 16th century and the omission of bracing altogether from most houses constructed after the opening years of the 17th century. Internally-exposed bracing was used occasionally in houses during the late 16th century and the beginning of the 17th century, but persisted in barns throughout the 17th century and even into the early 1700s.

c) By the close of the 17th century, and more particularly during the 18th century, thick straight bracing (which increasingly approached square section) took over from the earlier, more plank-like wall braces. Within this study these thick braces are called raking struts in order to differentiate them from the earlier form.

Obviously there must have been relatively long transitional periods during which some buildings incorporated the older methods of construction. Thus, using this method of sorting, these will be misdated. Other buildings, especially those with neither crownpost roofs nor raking struts, but with fully-weatherboarded wall, had to be omitted from this initial sort.

The crude chronological sequence obtained using this procedure was regarded as sufficiently accurate to establish and confirm other constructional trends, especially with regard to the various features found in clasped-side-purlin roof construction. Some features were shown to have been related to carpenters' preference, being affected little (if at all) by chronology. The results of this analysis, which produced no major surprises, were then utilized to analyse those barns with weatherboarded walls, and again the features relating to the development of wall framing in these buildings were largely as predicted. Thus, armed with a series of systematically-reasoned developmental sequences, the authors then tentatively established a date-range for each building, due consideration being made for the tendency of traditions to linger - some more than others. The allocated date-ranges were deliberately placed on the generous side, thus the authors are reasonably confident that, in all but a few exceptions, the true date of each building falls within the allotted date-range. The effect of this was, admittedly, to give many buildings a range of 50-80 years, whilst in a little under a quarter of the sample the range exceeded even this. In fact, thirteen buildings were at this stage omitted from the sample of surveys used in subsequent analysis, these buildings being considered not capable of being dated to within acceptable limits. A mid-date was then calculated from the allocated date-range for each building. As a control sample, the six barns for which firm dates are known, together with a slightly larger sample of buildings roughly datable from non-architectural evidence, were included in the above analysis. The date-ranges of all buildings were allocated by reference to charts of information which identified each building only by its survey number, thus maintaining an anonymity which was essential if unbiased results were to be achieved.

As can be seen in Figure 4.4, of the six dated buildings in three instances the mid date of the allotted range is very close to the true date; in a fourth it is within 20 years; in the remaining two the variation rises to 30 and 33 years respectively. In every instance, however, the true date did fall within the allotted date-range, and this was also the case with the buildings roughly datable

Name of Farm	Allotted Date Range	Mid Date in Range	Date of Erection
Trulilows, Wartling	1500 - 1580	1540	c1523
Parsonage, Salehurst	1530 - 1580	1555	1550
Bunces, Penhurst	1670 - 1730	1700	1702
High Holmstead, Warbleton	1690 - 1780	1735	1728
Marley, Battle	1650 - 1750	1700	1730
Pebsham, Bexhill	1670 - 1750	1710	1743

Figure 4.4
Calculated dates of barns for which the construction date is known.[7]

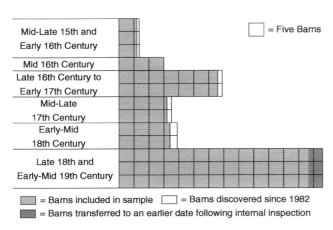

= Five Barns

Mid-Late 15th and Early 16th Century

Mid 16th Century

Late 16th Century to Early 17th Century

Mid-Late 17th Century

Early-Mid 18th Century

Late 18th and Early-Mid 19th Century

= Barns included in sample ☐ = Barns discovered since 1982

= Barns transferred to an earlier date following internal inspection

Figure 4.5
The sample of barns. Periods of construction.

by non-architectural evidence.

Using the calculated mid date, each building was next placed within one of five period zones - before 1530, 1530-1570, 1570-1635, 1635-1700, and 1700-1765. Although shorter periods would have been desirable, it was felt that they could not be justified having due regard for the length of some of the date-ranges. Having placed each building into its period, the results were compared with those obtained earlier based on what is here described as 'experience'. Encouragingly, in the vast majority of instances both methods placed the buildings in the same period. Where they did not, the evidence was re-examined and the building allocated accordingly. A summary of the results is given in Figure 4.5, which also includes approximate figures for the late 18th and early/mid 19th centuries based on blanket-survey work. The chart has been updated to show the barns surveyed since 1982 - the barns included in the original sample are indicated in grey, those surveyed since 1982 are shown in white. As will be noted, the additional data does not substantially alter the earlier results. For this reason, the stastistical data from the original sample published in 1982 has been retained in all subsequent chapters within this study.

Although it is accepted that such methods of dating as described above can only ever be regarded as a poor substitute for the true date of each building, in the absence of more reliable information such as obtained from an extensive programme of tree-ring dating, they are essential if a better knowledge of our past is to be

Figure 4.6
A non survivor. Rare internal photograph of c1900 showing the interior of an unidentified barn in Catsfield (perhaps at Church Farm). Apparently two aisled structures set at right angles in 'T' plan. The photograph serves as a reminder that barns of all sizes and ages have been lost in relatively recent times.

obtained. Inevitable some errors exist, but it is sincerely believed that the calculated construction dates used within this study have been given a sufficient margin of error as to minimize any inaccuracies to a level which will in no major way effect the conclusions given in the present volume.

DATES OF CONSTRUCTION

As Figure 4.5 illustrates, the data suggests that few barns survive within the study area from before *c*1530, after which the figures begin to improve, showing a rise in survival during the mid 16th century, and a major peak in the late 16th and early 17th centuries, after which the totals fall back markedly until the effects of the 'agricultural revolution' caused yet another burst of rebuilds during the late 18th and early 19th centuries.

By adding a second element, that of farm size, to the data upon which the analysis of barn construction dates is based, it is possible to draw further deductions. Seventeenth- and early eighteenth-century farm acreages are currently known for 109 of the barns included within the sample, whilst the storage capacity (measured to tiebeam level and excluding lofted ends) can be calculated for 137 of the barns. These figures are shown in Figures 4.7 and 4.8. Furthermore, as has been discussed in Chapter 2, it is known, even if only approximately, how many farms of each size existed. By comparing these statistics it seems clear that barns on farms of less than 50 acres have survived only poorly: indeed, a survival rate approaching a quarter of that on farms in excess of 150 acres, and half that on farms of 50-149 acres appears to be no great exaggeration. With regards to the small farms, it is further apparent that virtually no barns survive from before *c*1570, though they do survive at a consistent level from that date onwards.

Whatever form the barns of smaller farmers took before this date, they were clearly not regarded as acceptable for extension during the rebuild period. Indeed, prior to the mid 16th century this appears to have been the case on many farms, regardless of their size. If the barns had been built to a standard as high as that found from the late 16th century onwards, then many (if not the majority) would surely have been retained, though modified and extended in order to accommodate the additional quantity of crops needed to be stored and processed. It is probably no coincidence that well over half of the barns which do survive from this early period were modified during the period *c*1570-1635. In some of these examples the additional crops were accommodated by the removal of floors and partitions, whilst others were extended by a bay, or even two. On four farms a second barn was constructed to take the extra produce.

In contrast to the surviving early barns, only two

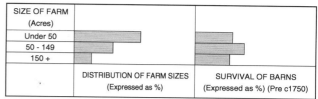

Figure 4.7
Chart showing the comparison between the distribution of farm sizes and the survival of 'historic' barns upon farms of varying acreages.

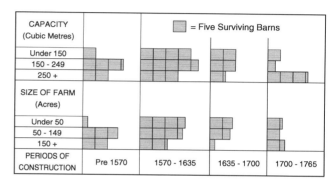

Figure 4.8
Barns within the sample showing the comparison between crop storage capacity and farm acreages, arranged by period of construction.

of the fourteen mid 16th-century examples were extended during the next 150 years, a fact which implies that by this date some barns were already being reconstructed for reasons which were later to cause the mass rebuilding of barns locally during the late 16th and early 17th centuries. That is, some of the farmers who were rebuilding their barns during the middle years of the century were doing so because they were already increasing their arable acreage. At least seven of the twelve barns not subsequently extended are associated with well-built houses of about this period, a feature which perhaps suggests that these farms were in the owner-occupation of progressive men who were quicker than most in taking advantage of rising wheat prices. Indeed, this may also be true for some of the barns constructed during the early years of the 16th century, especially those which lack subsequent extensions.

Just as the boom period which caused the bulge in barn reconstructions in late Elizabethan and early Stuart times appears to have been foreseen and capitalized upon by the more far-sighted farmers, the same appears to have been true of the second wave of reconstructions brought about by the 'agricultural revolution' and the high arable acreages of the decades around 1800. As in the mid 16th century, from the 1740s onwards both population and food prices were rising, albeit slowly at first. The recognizable increase in the number of large barns constructed during the mid 18th century must surely be due to a major increase in arable acreages by those farmers sufficiently bold to take advantage of the rising demand for food stuffs. The mid 16th-century barn at Pebsham, Bexhill, is a good example in that it was considerably extended in 1743, though the overall acreage of the farm is known to have remained virtually static. Also of mid 18th-century date is the barn at Great Knelle, Beckley (for which *see* Figures 5.7 and 5.8) which, although the largest surviving historic barn within the Rape of Hastings, was by 1800 considered too small and was thus extended.

5　BARNS: LAYOUT AND DESIGN
CROP STORAGE AND PROCESSING

CROP STORAGE AND PROCESSING

Although many Wealden barns had secondary functions *(see* below) it was for the storage and processing of unthreshed crops that they were principally constructed.

At harvest time, after the cereals and pulses had been cut, they were carted in from the fields, the wagons entering through tall double doors which gave access to a combined wagon bay and threshing area (known as the 'midstrey'). The wagons were here unloaded and the crops stacked in open storage bays, usually one or more on either side. Despite three to five different cereals and pulses being cultivated in any one year on many farms, prior to the late 18th century the entire crop was usually housed under cover: external corn ricks were constructed only very occasionally within the rape at this period.[1]

How full the bays were filled can only be guessed. George Ewart Evans describes how in East Anglia during the 18th and 19th centuries the crops were tightly packed by riding or leading a quiet old horse around on them, the horse only being taken down when there was insufficient room below the roof slope for the operation to continue.[2] It is not clear whether this practice, known as 'riding the goaf', was carried out locally, or, even if it was, whether

such a method was in use prior to the increase in arable acreage which occurred during the second half of the 18th and early 19th centuries. All that can usefully be added is that hipped ends - the most regularly used of local roof terminals - would have made high-level storage difficult, and the use of a horse at high level in many instances impossible. During the 18th century the use of both half-hipped and gabled terminals increased very considerably in popularity *(see* Chapter 10) thus giving greater headroom at roof level and perhaps indicating that by this date barns were being more fully packed.

It is also worth mentioning that where cattle feeding racks were included within the barn these considerably reduced the floor area available for crop storage, whilst open lofts, thought to have been used principally for the storage of hay and straw, may in some instances have been utilized for the housing of unthreshed crops. Both of these features are more fully discussed below.

Throughout the worst of the winter weather the harvest was threshed within the shelter of the barn. A flavour of the process is captured by the late 19th-century photograph reproduced in Figure 5.1, though it should be borne in mind that in this shot staged for the

Figure 5.1
Hand threshing with a flail in the closing years of the 19th century. Note the sacking hanging across the barn on the left separating the threshing floor from the unthreshed crops, the two spare flails hanging over the sacking, the sieve, and the sacks of grain waiting to be taken away for storage. Threshed straw is lying on the threshing floor behind the farmer. The wagon doors at the rear are closed for the camera in order to prevent flare from the daylight.

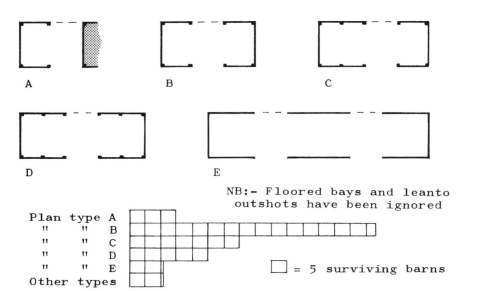

Figure 5.2
The five basic plan types found
in local barns showing their
relative level of survival

A   B   C

D   E

NB:- Floored bays and leanto
outshots have been ignored

Plan type A
  "   "   B
  "   "   C
  "   "   D
  "   "   E
Other types

☐ = 5 surviving barns

camera the rear external doorways are closed in order to prevent flare from the daylight outside. Hand threshing was a long and laborious task. For this a wooden flail was used, the flail being brought down rhythmically onto a small quantity of crops laid on the threshing floor within the midstrey. Care needed to be taken to ensure that the straw was struck just below the ears so as to shake the grain out without bruising it. Pulses were similarly processed. Depending upon available space, the straw residue would either be stored within the barn itself, or in small external stacks in readiness for taking to the cattle for conversion to manure.

It is often assumed that the less tall doorway in the rear wall of the midstrey was incorporated principally to allow the empty wagons to pass out of the barn during harvesting, though as is more fully discussed below, in many instances this was impossible. The rear doorway's principal function was to obtain a through draught during the processing operations, both the front and rear sets being pinned back as required to obtain an air current capable of clearing the air of resultant dust whilst the grain and chaff were being sieved. The crop was then winnowed by casting the mixed grain and chaff high into the air in order to separate out the chaff. It was during this process that the through draught was particularly important, the air current being relied upon to blow the chaff clear of the heavier grains which fell back to the threshing floor for collection. The cleaned grain was then measured off by the half bushel for storage in sacks.

Early 18th-century probate inventories commonly list crops at various stages of processing, some being unthreshed, others threshed but awaiting sieving and winnowing, and still others sacked ready for storage. Reference to unthreshed crops as late in the season as March are by no means rare, whilst occasionally this was still the case as late as May or June, though - bearing in

Figure 5.3
Interior of barn at Tilement Farm, Warbleton.
A typical small three-bay barn built in the
late 16th century, incorporating a single-bay
storage area on either side of its midstrey. [275/33]

Capacity (Cubic Metres)	Number of barns of each plan type (For plan types see Figure 5.2)						Total
	A	B	C	D	E	Others	
Under 100	9	2	-	-	-	-	11
100 - 199	4	48	3	1	-	6	62
200 - 299	-	21	21	5	-	2	49
300 - 399	-	2	6	12	2	2	24
400 - 499	-	1	-	5	1	1	8
500 +	-	-	2	2	8	-	12
Unknown	2	4	-	-	-	-	9
Total	15	78	35	25	11	11	175

Figure 5.4
Comparison of plan types with the
capacity of open storage bays
(measured up to tiebeam level; lofts excluded)

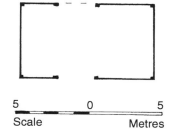

Figure 5.5 (Right)
Plan of barn at
Attwoods, Warbleton
(Initial phase - c1625)

5   0   5
Scale   Metres

Figure 5.6
Late 17th-century barn at Grovelye, Warbleton,
showing a two-bay crop storage area, viewed
across the midstrey. [278/14]

mind that this information is derived from probate inventories - this may, at least in part, be due to illness.

Although of little value and therefore often not specifically referred to, the work tools of the barn are, none the less, occasionally listed in inventories. For instance, the particularly detailed inventory of George Baker of Kingsley Hill, Warbleton, taken in 1727 lists a wire scry and three sieves for screening threshed but un-cleaned crops, a half bushel measure, a handle-less wooden shovel called a 'shaul', and another called a 'scuppett' for handling the threshed crops, and a seed cord used for carrying seed during sowing. Many barns also housed a ladder.[3]

THE STORAGE BAYS

The size and layout of a barn was largely governed by the quantity of unthreshed crops to be stored within it. Bearing in mind that throughout the period under discussion approximately half the farms appear to have been of less than 50 acres (*see* Chapter 2) it is perhaps not surprising that barns incorporating but one or two open storage bays accounted for about half the surviving examples, whilst very few incorporated more than four. Figure 5.2 illustrates the five basic plan types found within the rape of Hastings, by far the most common form being that comprising a single open storage bay on either side of the midstrey. This arrangement alone

accounted for about two-fifths of the surviving barns, more than double that of any other design.

The storage capacity of a single plan type varied depending upon the length, width and height of the bays, though in most the variation was not large. Indeed, as Figure 5.4 shows, the choice of design was principally governed by the storage capacity required. However, the type of crops to be stored may also have had some bearing. For instance, as most barns possessed only two storage areas, and some only one, inevitably two or more crops must have been stored together. It may have been that wheat, a cereal largely used for human consumption, was stacked separately. Alternatively, the pulses, which by the early 18th century accounted for about a quarter of the harvest, may have been segregated. There is no way of knowing which was the case, though the common use of unequal bay lengths in barns possessing only two storage bays implies that the designer often had a clear indication of the intended use of each storage area. Such disparity is found in about two-fifths of the barns of this design. As an example, the barn at Attwoods, Warbleton shown in Figure 5.5 had storage areas with capacities of 56 and 88 cubic metres when first built. This feature is

Figure 5.7
The mid 18th-century aisled barn at Great Knelle, Beckley viewed from the north, as in 1979. [282/12A]

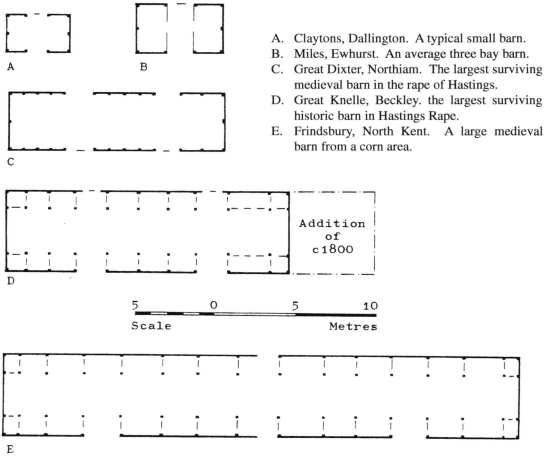

A. Claytons, Dallington. A typical small barn.
B. Miles, Ewhurst. An average three bay barn.
C. Great Dixter, Northiam. The largest surviving medieval barn in the rape of Hastings.
D. Great Knelle, Beckley. the largest surviving historic barn in Hastings Rape.
E. Frindsbury, North Kent. A large medieval barn from a corn area.

Figure 5.8
The plans of five barns illustrating their comparitive size

found less commonly in barns possessing a pair of two-bay storage areas, though in buildings of this capacity the same effect could be produced by designing the barn so that it had two storage bays on one side of the midstrey but only one on the other (type 'C' in Figures 5.2 and 5.4) and this appears commonly to have been the case. In many such barns the capacity of the two-bay storage area was considerably less than double that of the opposing single-bay area, again suggesting that the designer had specific storage capacities in mind.

Due to the difficulties incurred in stacking crops into areas of excessive length, three adjoining storage

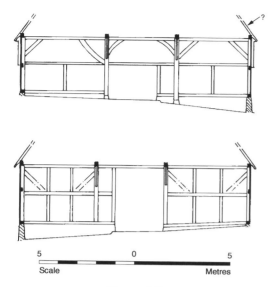

Figure 5.9
Longitudinal sections through the barn at Crouchers,
Crowhurst, showing sloping floor. Note the angled
soleplate in the lower illustration.

bays served by a single midstrey were avoided, except in specialized circumstances. Thus, where large storage capacities were required most farmers chose a barn served by two midstreys. Such a design not only eased handling problems, but was also useful in providing two entries and two threshing floors, thereby allowing unloading and threshing operations to be greatly speeded up.

Eleven of the 175 buildings within the sample for which the plan types are known do not conform to any of the standard designs. These either possessed two storage bays on one side of the midstrey but none on the other (8 examples) or had three to one side, but only two, or in one instance one on the other (3 examples). This group of eleven buildings represent the only plan forms not to be found at every date throughout the study period, the earliest surviving example being datable to the late 16th or early 17th century. At least eight of the eleven were designed principally as specialized cattle barns, and it seems likely that this asymmetrical plan form was developed primarily for specialized use of this type (*see* The Specialized 'Cattle Barn' below).

The largest surviving barn within the rape, a mid 18th-century aisled barn at Great Knelle, Beckley, had a storage capacity when built of 1360 cubic metres, over 26 times that of the smallest, which was capable of storing only 53 cubic metres of crops.[4] Even Great Knelle, however, is relatively small in comparison to some buildings in the grain growing regions of England. The major aisled barn at Frindsbury in North Kent is almost twice the size of Great Knelle (Figure 5.8).

Only rarely was any attempt made at levelling the earthen floor of a storage bay, even when the barn was built upon relatively steeply sloping ground. Several examples have been recorded where the floor falls by over a metre throughout the length of the barn. In one instance, at Crouchers, Crowhurst, the frame was purposely constructed to take the slope into account, the cill of one bay being set on a cant (Figure 5.9).

AISLED BARNS

Although the rape of Hastings is primarily a region of small unaisled barns, aisling of one form or another is found in about a quarter of the surviving examples. The feature is, however, regional, being common along the coastal fringe where aisled barns outnumber unaisled by two to one, whereas of the 90 barns surveyed in the north of the rape only four

Figure 5.10
Early 18th century
barn at Hancox,
Whatlington. For
the High Weald
this is a large
barn. [290/15]

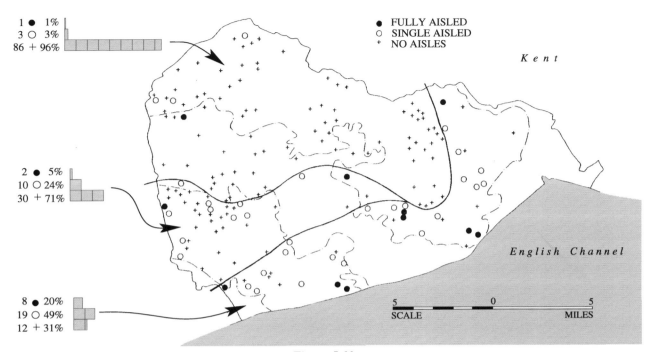

Figure 5.11
The distribution of surviving aisled barns in the Rape of Hastings (15th to mid 18th century).
[Sample of buildings as recorded up to 1982]

Figure 5.12
West elevation of the small mid/late 17th century fully-aisled North Barn at Downoak Farm, Westfield. This barn has a single-bay crop storage area on either side of its midstrey, with a return aisle at its northern (righthand) end and a lean-to cattle shelter at its southern (lefthand) downhill end. [319/15]

incorporate aisling (Figure 5.11). Between the two regions, especially immediately to the south of the forest ridge in the area around Warbleton, is a zone in which aisled barns, although not rare, are not common either. Insufficient work has as yet been undertaken to determine an accurate distribution pattern of aisling in the south east of England as a whole and, until it is, it would be rash to suggest the reasons for the inconsistent adoption of the design. Suffice it to say that although the use of aisling is often attributed chiefly to corn growing regions, at present there are no obvious indications of

bias toward arable farming along the coastal fringe of East Sussex.

Most of the aisled barns within the rape of Hastings are not large. Those incorporating but two storage bays - one on either side of the midstrey - are the norm and account for nearly half the surviving examples. They outnumber any other aisled type by two to one. Indeed, the distribution of plan types in aisled structures is very similar to that found in unaisled barns. Furthermore, few are fully aisled, the majority having only a single aisle running along the rear of the building.

Figure 5.13
Mid 16th-century aisled barn at Beestons,
Warbleton showing end storage bay incorporating
side and end aisles. [310/21]

Figure 5.14
Restricted wagon doorway at Kingsdown,
Heathfield. [334/22]

Figure 5.15
Side wall of barn at Froghole, Mayfield
(early 17th century) showing inset post to
restricted wagon entrance. [383/9]

Of the 47 aisled barns and extensions for which the layouts are known, in six instances the buildings were initially unaisled, single aisles having been added during the late 17th and 18th centuries. At the same period two single-aisled structures were extended and converted to fully-aisled type.

Ten barns possess a return aisle at one end, a feature most commonly found in the earlier buildings. Examples are shown in Figures 5.12 and 5.13.

THE MIDSTREY

In the majority of surviving barns the main doors range from 2.80 metres to 3.40 metres (9ft 2ins - 11ft 2ins) in width and have a height from the threshing floor of between 3.00 metres and 4.00 metres (9ft 10ins - 13ft 2ins). This range gives ample room for the passage of fully-laden wagons without undue waste of space. The barn of about 1730 at Stonelands, Warbleton, possesses easily the most narrow main entrance. Measuring only 2.00 metres (6ft 7ins) between the jambs, it would have been difficult, if not impossible, for a standard wagon to enter. Surprisingly it is one of only ten barns within the sample where the main door is narrower than the bay containing the midstrey, the width being restricted on one side by a heavy intermediate post. Examples of this arrangement are shown in Figures 5.14 and 5.15. Those buildings which possess restricted openings range in date from medieval times through to the end of the study period.

Most main doorways extend up to the eaves, though in nine of the tallest barns the doorhead was dropped to a lower level. An example is shown in

Figure 5.16
Separate plate at head of main wagon doorway
at Batsford, Warbleton (15th century). [524/35]

Figure 5.16. About a third of the full-height openings incorporate double plates giving additional strength to this otherwise unsupported length of wallplate.

In ten or possibly twelve barns a second full-height doorway was incorporated at the rear of the building, a design which appears to have been more common before the late 16th-/early 17th-century 'great rebuild' period than after. The majority of rear doors, however, were low, over three-quarters of those surveyed being between 1.50 metres to 2.50 metres (4ft 11ins to 8ft 2ins) in height with a few still smaller, especially in those buildings which incorporate an aisle or lean-to. In two such buildings with low eaves a taller opening was achieved by setting the doorhead slightly above wallplate level and sweeping the roofline over it. Other doorways were similarly adjusted later.

As with some main doors, 15 barns incorporated rear openings of reduced width, and in four of these they were less than half the width of the opposing opening. The timber cillbeams were continuous across the base of all four of the small doors, a feature also found in four of the standard half-height openings. Continuous cills were perhaps once more common than is now realized, for when neatly cut away the evidence is virtually undetectable. Clearly, where a continuous cill existed it was impossible for wagons to be drawn through the building, and in these instances all wheeled traffic must have been reversed in. Indeed, this must also have been the case in many other local barns, for about a third incorporate a drop beyond their rear doors. The drop at Wick Farm, Udimore, measures at least 2.00 metres (6ft 6ins). In most instances the barns could have been resited if through passage for wagons had been an important consideration.

Of the doors themselves, no surviving examples within the rape of Hastings appear to be of any great antiquity, though they may closely follow the design of their predecessors. Unless serving a narrow rear doorway, they are always arranged in pairs and open

Figure 5.17
Restored door of probably late 17th-century date at
Tickerage, Framfield. The boards are modern
replacements and the brace is an addition. Note the
projecting ends to the ledges. [From a slide]

outwards, being hung from iron rides driven securely into the external faces of the door jambs. The doors to the full-height openings are often two leaves in height, giving a total of four leaves per opening. The hinges themselves are usually fixed to horizontal ledges jointed into a heavy-section stile located against the door jamb. The ledges support the vertical planks making up the door. In the surviving later doors at least one, often two diagonally-set braces rise from the stile to the ledges to give rigidity, though the rare surviving, probably late 17th-century door shown in Figure 5.17 from the neighbouring rape of Pevensey is absent of bracing, begging the question as to how common such arrangements once were.

As in the example shown in Figure 5.17, in many instances the ledges of one door protrude beyond the closing edge, acting as a buffer for the opposing door when closed, though in some instances the same effect is achieved by splay-cutting the ends of the ledges. Both doors close against a horizontal rail which is usually fixed into position by inserting one end into a mortice cut into the jamb, and the opposing end into a drop notch in

Figure 5.18
Base of wagon doorway
showing grooved post against
jamb used to secure
removable boards, called a
'lift'. Note also the end of the
threshing floor with the
supporting joists beneath.
[From a slide]

the opposing jamb. An alternative method is for the locking bar to slot into 'L'-shaped iron brackets which project from the internal face of the doors. In both arrangements the rail incorporates an iron staple which, when correctly positioned, protrudes through a hole cut into one of the doors so that a wooden wedge can be dropped in as a fastening.

Many door jambs have a grooved post nailed to their base in order to receive a set of removable horizontal boards called a lift. As figure 5.18 illustrates, when in position, these blocked the lower portion of the doorway so as to act as a deterrent against livestock and fowls entering the barn and prevented bouncing grain from escaping during flailing. There is no way of dating the surviving grooved posts, and thus it may be that the feature represents a later innovation. Certainly the low boarded walls found along the sides of some threshing floors were rare locally until the mid 18th century (*see* below) and the removable lifts across the doorways may be additions of similar date.

Wagon porches are found in some of the large early medieval English barns and were relatively common in many parts of England from that time onwards. A wagon porch can best be described as an extension of the midstrey beyond the side walls of a barn (for an example *see* Figure 5.19). Apart from giving protection to the threshing floor during inclement weather, they allowed laden wagons to shelter whilst others were being unloaded. Perhaps because of the small arable acreages of Wealden farms, they were never popular within the rape of Hastings. Indeed, only two wagon porches predating the early 18th century are known within the rape (Great Bigknowle, Heathfield and New Place, Icklesham) though there may have been another incorporated into the fully-aisled 16th-century barn at Pebsham, Bexhill. Of the 17 locally recorded examples, eleven represent 18th-century additions to earlier buildings. With the possible exception of that at New Place, all (whether contemporary or not) are located in elevations which incorporated either an aisle or lean-to outshut from the outset and should be seen as a method of obtaining full-height doorways in such circumstances. An alternative to this method was to recess the full-height doorway back between the projecting outshuts.

An essential element of any traditional crop-processing barn was the threshing floor. This comprised a level platform set across the barn between the opposing doorways. It should be regarded as the work floor of

Figure 5.19
Barn at New Place,
Icklesham showing
original wagon porch
flanked by lean-to
outshuts. In this
instance the outshuts
may represent later
additions. [327/9]

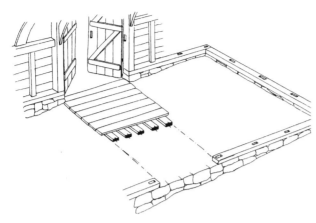

Figure 5.20
Details of a typical local threshing floor showing thick boards supported by heavy joists.

Figure 5.21
Threshing floor at Batsford, Warbleton with the boards removed, showing fixing pegs. [524/34]

Figure 5.22
'Cornhole' at Wick Farm, Udimore.

these combined factory/warehouses, and apart from withstanding heavy traffic, it had also to be sufficiently sturdy to withstand the incessant pounding of the wooden flail. Within the Weald these floors are of timber and comprise heavy wooden planks (probably never less than 40 mm thick and usually in excess of 50 mm) laid across the threshing floor on four or five heavy wooden bearers or joists similar in cross section to railway sleepers (*see* Figure 5.20). In some instances, such as the threshing floor at Batsford in Warbleton shown in Figure 5.21, the boards are fixed to the joists by large-diameter wooden pegs. As the floors of some barns slope, there is in some instances either a bank or drop between the threshing floor and that of the adjacent storage areas.

From the early 17th century onwards a few large local barns which incorporate either an aisle or side lean-to have a small room set within the outshut. These were divided from the remainder of the building by boarded walls fixed to studwork. The example shown in Figure 5.22 is that at Wick Farm, Udimore: it probably dates from the early 17th century, though it could have been inserted later. These small 'rooms' usually possessed a ceiling and were in all instances accessible from the midstrey. In Staffordshire they are called 'cornholes'. Their purpose was to house the mixed grain and chaff after flail-threshing until sufficient had accumulated to sieve and winnow.[5] A similar use for the Wealden examples seems likely. Only seven, possibly nine, contemporary 'cornholes' have to date been recorded within the study area, though five or six others were added to earlier buildings, probably during the late 18th or early 19th centuries. One of these, that at Toll Farm, Warbleton, is set within the body of an unaisled building and is the only known local example of its type.

6   BARNS: LAYOUT AND DESIGN
ANCILLARY USES

Although barns were primarily geared to the storage and processing of cereal crops and pulses, it is also true than many fulfilled a dual or even multiple function, incorporating as they do clear evidence of former rooms and lofts. There are two basic ways in which ancillary agricultural functions could be accommodated. An area of one or occasionally two bays was in some instances divided off within the main body of the barn, whilst in others the specialized functions were housed within lean-to outshuts constructed against the side and/or end walls of the building. Specialized bays (as opposed to lean-to outshuts) usually, but not always, incorporated a first floor, thus forming an upper room or loft. There are buildings which show evidence of having possessed both specialized bays and outshuts at the same period, though these appear to have been rare.

Figure 6.1 (above)
Very few first floors remain, most having been removed when the floored bay was converted to crop storage. This medieval example at Chittinghurst, Wadhurst is typical. Note the redundant window with shutter runner. The daub in the end wall is comb decorated [284/4A].

Figure 6.2 (right)
Mortices for removed crossbeam and rail in the barn at Mount House, Burwash (Early 17th C). The floored area was to the right. [354/5]

Figure 6.3 (below)
View into lean-to cattle house from crop storage bay, Hancox, Whatlington (Early 18th C). In most cases the dividing wall has been removed so as to increase space for crop storage.

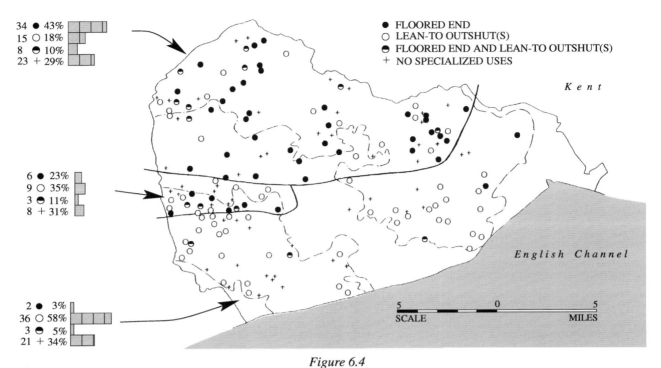

Figure 6.4

The distribution of surviving barns in the Rape of Hastings with rooms or lean-to outshuts (15th to mid 18th century).
[Sample of buildings as recorded up to 1982 - the number of lean-to outshuts is likely to be an under-estimate (see text)]

Barns incorporating specialized bays are found relatively commonly throughout the entire study period, whereas lean-to outshuts appear to have been more rare during the early period. However, this impression could be misleading as lean-to outshut are structurally weak and, as a result, are prone to demolition or reconstruction. It is often very difficult to know whether a late lean-to outshut represents an addition or the reconstruction of a predecessor. In 1982 only four barns predating *c*1570 had been recognized as having incorporated an early lean-to outshut, and in three of these the lean-to was associated with a specialized bay. Of these four known examples, two (Limden, Ticehurst and Chittinghurst, Wadhurst) were of medieval date - this represented just over 10% of the medieval barns within the sample.

The lean-to at Limden was evidenced by mortices only and may have been 'the outlett of a barn' demolished by William Oxenbridge under licence of the lord of Hammerden Manor in 1558.[1] Similarly, the outshut at Chittinghurst no longer exists.

Recording undertaken since 1982 (some during building works) has identified a further four demolished/ rebuilt medieval lean-to outshuts (Burgham, Etchingham; Great Dixter, Northiam; Mill Farm, Salehurst; and Great Buckhurst, Westfield) tripling the previously known total of medieval examples and increasing the number of medieval barns incorporating lean-to outshuts to over a quarter of the sample.[2] This fact serves to illustrate how

easily such ephemeral structures can be missed. Despite this, it remains likely that from *c*1570 onwards outshuts became more commonly used.

THE DISTRIBUTION OF BARNS POSSESSING EVIDENCE OF ANCILLARY USES (Figure 6.4)

In about two-thirds to three-quarters of all surviving barns constructed prior to *c*1750 there is recognizable evidence of the former existence of rooms and lofts associated with some activity other than the storage and processing of cereals and pulses. Some of these features are contemporary with the buildings in which they occur, whilst others represent alterations made prior to the mid 18th century. Such a high level of specialized activity had not always been the case throughout the rape, for in those buildings which survive from before the late 16th- and early 17th-century great rebuild, the majority show no signs of having housed specialized functions. Although the sample for this period is very small and includes no examples from small farms, it is noticeable that those which incorporate specialized uses are concentrated towards the north of the rape, an area in which upper floors existed in half the early extant barns. Of the eleven surviving barns surveyed prior to 1982 from the south of the region and for which the plan types are known only one, a major mid 16th-century aisled barn with an end lean-to outshut (for which *see* Figure 6.5) incorporates any form of ancillary function. Since 1982 a barn at Great Buckhurst, Westfield (late 15th or early 16th century) has been recorded: it shows evidence of a former side lean-to cattle shelter and a divided-off end bay. Because of its much altered external appearance, this barn was missed during the main phase of survey work carried out within the rape.

By the close of the rebuild period rooms and lofts had become more common: by *c*1635 about half the surviving barns incorporated secondary activities. Multi-purpose barns were, however, still noticeably concentrated towards the north of the region where such features existed in two-thirds of the surviving buildings, compared with a little under a third in the south. Of perhaps greater significance, in the north the use of specialized bays (usually lofted over) continued to be the most common form, whereas such types were virtually unknown in the surviving buildings of the south, the secondary activities in this region were mainly housed within lean-to outshuts. It is from this period that there are for the first time large number of barns surviving from small farms. An analysis of both barn and farm sizes indicates that the features noted above are not concentrated in either buildings or farms of any one size, but appear to be relatively evenly distributed across the whole spectrum.

By the close of the study period the same regional bias still existed between the use of specialized bays in the north and lean-to outshuts in the south. However, there was by this time only a slight difference between the north and south with regards the percentage of barns which included ancillary activities, though, in surviving buildings at least, multi-purpose barns were still less common in the south than in the north. By this date they accounted for about two-thirds of all the extant barns within the rape.

The regional variations noted above are sufficiently marked to be sure that they are not the result of chance survival, though it should be borne in mind that the number of barns incorporating early lean-to

outshuts could be significantly under estimated due to their ephemeral nature. It should be noted that a lean-to outshut is similar in general appearance to an aisle, whilst in terms of construction the only variation is that an aisle has an open arcade between it and the main body of the building, whereas a lean-to outshut is divided from it by a wall. It is, therefore, probably relevant that the use of aisles in barns is also largely confined to the south of the rape (*compare* Figures 5.11 and 6.4) and thus the more common use of lean-to outshuts in this area may be the result of regional variation. Whether these regional characteristics were caused by an as yet unrecognized difference in agricultural bias, or were rooted in local tradition is unclear. Indeed, until detailed work is undertaken in neighbouring regions it is not even known whether the variations noted within Hastings Rape form part of an overall pattern, or are merely an isolated local phenomena.

THE ANCILLARY USES

Although there cannot be said to be a wealth of documentary evidence as to the secondary uses to which the barns were put, there is, nonetheless, sufficient to give a fair indication of the most common activities. These can, in short, be summarized as the housing of animals. In 1597, for instance, Etchingham Parsonage possessed a barn of three bays with a stall in the end.[3] The 17th-century glebe terriers give several other examples, such as the 'barn with a stall' at Ticehurst Parsonage, the 'barn with one stable joined thereto at the north end' at Ashburnham Vicarage, and the barns at Dallington and Bodiam Vicarages, both of which incorporated stables and stalls at their end. The terrier of 1615 for Playden Parsonage mentions 'a barn and stable all under one roof.[4] There are other sources too, such as a lease of the demesne of Pebsham Manor at Bexhill made in 1590 where the west end of the great barn was in one occupation, whilst the east end, with its stable attached, was leased to another tenant.[5] This barn

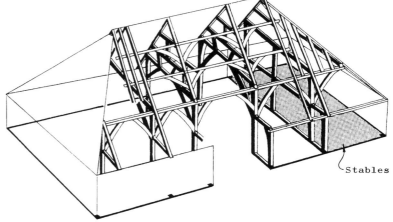

Figure 6.5
Mid 16th-century aisled barn at Pebsham, Bexhill. The remains of the end lean-to stable were incorporated into a crop storage bay when the barn was extended in 1743.

Stables

51

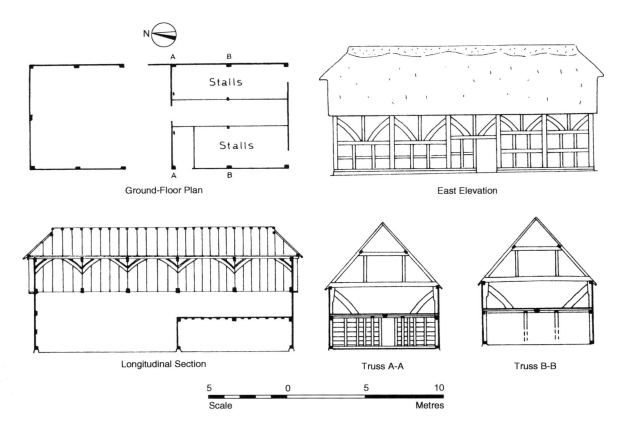

Ground-Floor Plan

East Elevation

Longitudinal Section

Truss A-A

Truss B-B

Figure 6.6
Wenbans, Wadhurst (late 16th century)

survived until 1985 and, as Figure 6.5 illustrates, the form of the lean-to stable was still identifiable within the structure. There are references to lean-to stables and cow stalls integrated into barns in an account of the Herrings Estate, Dallington made in 1793/4.[6]

It should be noted that the documentary sources continually refer to both stables and stalls. Despite modern connotations, the distinction may not be so much between horses and cattle, as between draught animals and those required for either fatstock or dairy purposes. Thus many of the stables referred to could have housed draught oxen rather than horses, for, as already discussed (*see* Chapter 2) until the late 18th century oxen were the principal draught animals used in East Sussex.

ANIMAL SHELTERS IN SPECIALIZED BAYS

Despite the documentary references, there is rarely any surviving architectural evidence to suggest the way in which the specialized bays were utilized; indeed some were certainly intended for purposes other than the shelter of animals (*see* below). In a few instances, however, sufficient survives to show how the lower rooms were arranged. The layout of Wenbans, Wadhurst is shown in Figure 6.6. This building is without doubt

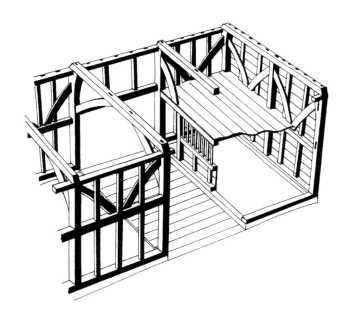

Figure 6.7
Cattle shelter and loft at Lea Bank, Whatlington
(Late 16th or early 17th century)

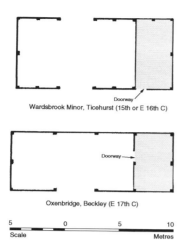

Wardsbrook Minor, Ticehurst (15th or E 16th C)

Doorway

Doorway →

Oxenbridge, Beckley (E 17th C)

5   0   5   10
Scale   Metres

Figure 6.8
First-floor plans showing the location of doorways
leading to the lofts.

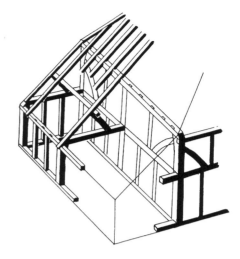

Figure 6.9
A typical end lean-to shelter shed

one of the finest surviving examples within the group of barns here under consideration, being a prestigious structure with half-hipped terminals and overhanging verges. Its southern bays retain clear evidence for the former existence of two unequal-depth rows of stalls, the animals being arranged facing towards a central feeding passage. In one corner was a loose-box. As the feeding passage was accessible from the main body of the barn, it seems likely that the first-floor loft was utilized for the storage of small quantities of hay, as is known to have been the case in the oxstalls and stables at the Abbey Mansion, Robertsbridge, described in 1567.[7]

The Maunser family, who owned Wenbans, are known to have had interests in the local ironworks and it has been suggested that the barn may have housed ox-teams used for the heavy-haulage requirements of that industry.

Another similar but smaller arrangement exists at Lea Bank, Whatlington (Figure 6.7). In this instance the animals faced the midstrey, from which they were fed by means of a slatted rack, an arrangement which also existed at Thornden, Ashburnham (where the stalls were never lofted over) and probably in at least three other barns. As at Wenbans, the loft area at Lea Bank was open to the midstrey/threshing floor of the barn: a typical feature, though by no means invariable. In the medieval barns at Wardsbrook minor, Ticehurst and Great Wigsell, Salehurst, for example, the lofted ends were separated from the midstrey by an open storage bay, from which it was divided by a partition. In these instances the lofts were accessible via an external doorway, though in a similar example at Oxenbridge, Beckley (Figure 6.8) the door leading to the loft was curiously located within the internal partition, which must have made access difficult when the storage bays were in use.

LEAN-TO ANIMAL SHELTERS (Figure 6.9)

Because of their structural vulnerability many of the early lean-to outshuts have been rebuilt. As a result, it is sometimes difficult to ascertain whether a late outshut attached to an earlier building represents the rebuild of a predecessor or a genuine addition. For this reason, the number of early barns which incorporated an outshut is likely to be understated in the record. Even so, although examples are known associated with some of the earliest surviving barns, outshuts appear not to have become common until the late 16th century. Those attached to one end of a barn, giving accommodation to between four and eight animals, were by far the most popular throughout the study period, though a single side lean-to, or the combination of an end and side lean-to are forms also encountered relatively frequently. On the other hand, only two examples are known of a pair of contemporary opposing end lean-to outshuts, and five where a side outshut is continued around and across both ends of the barn. Three of the latter type are the result of extensions made to existing barns already possessing outshuts.

At Crockers, Northiam, and Moat Farm, Salehurst (both late 17th-century) the lean-to outshuts represent open-fronted shelter sheds, and that at Moat Farm is fitted with a built-in feeding rack. Such open-fronted lean-to sheds became very common during the late 18th and 19th centuries, though apart from a few possible instances where the side walls have since been rebuilt and the evidence thus destroyed, those at Moat and Crockers are the only examples which predate the late 18th century.

Enclosed lean-to cattle shelters were, without known exception, always accessible via their own external doorway, there being no interconnection between them and the main body of the barn. They were located down hill from the main crop-storage area in order to avoid the possibility of waste products from the animals tainting the stored crops.

THE SPECIALIZED 'CATTLE BARN'

Although it has been shown that many barns incorporated some degree of cattle housing, in eight instances layouts are so dominated by this use as to suggest that their prime objective was the care and feeding of animals, rather than the storage and processing of crops. It is perhaps not surprising that all the known examples are situated on medium to large farms and most also possessed a conventional crop storage barn. Three examples of these 'specialized' buildings are illustrated in Figure 6.10 - *see* also Figure 6.11 for an interior view of one of the former lofted-over cattle shelters within the barn at Froghole, Mayfield.

Figure 6.11
One of the two adjacent formerly lofted-over cattle houses at Froghole, Mayfield (early 17th century) showing mortices (just visible) in crossbeam for former joists, feeding rack on right dividing the two bays, and the lean-to animal shelters to the rear and left. [383/12]

UNUSUAL LAYOUTS

A detailed study of any group of historic buildings will always bring to light the occasional atypical example, and barns are no exception. Most differences take the form of unusual flooring arrangements, presumably designed with specific purposes in mind, though these uses can today only be guessed. For example, a medieval barn at Chittinghurst, Wadhurst (Figure 6.12, A) was extended during the medieval period to give a large additional ground-floor room with a smaller first-floor chamber above. The design of the latter, fitted with shuttered windows and comb-decorated daub infill, is consistent with farm labourers' lodgings, an explanation in keeping with evidence from other barns. For instance, the barns at Mill Cottage, Salehurst (medieval) and Durrants, Warbleton (*c*1600) not only have upper chambers with shuttered windows, but also first-floor ceilings (Figure 6.12, B and C).

At Park Farm, Mountfield the end bay built in *c*1600 had both first-floor and attic rooms and was originally lit by no less than nine unglazed windows, all with shutters. In this instance the floored bay appears to represent an addition built onto the end of an earlier barn, rebuilt subsequently (*see* Figure 6.13). At Common Woods, Northiam (also *c*1600 and also shown in Figure 6.13) the room and chamber occupied one corner of the building only, divided off on one side of an open storage bay.

Finally in this group, is the barn at Hammerden, Ticehurst (mid 16th century) shown in Figures 6.14 and 6.15. This originally possessed an isolated floor across part of the midstrey at roof level: perhaps it served as a

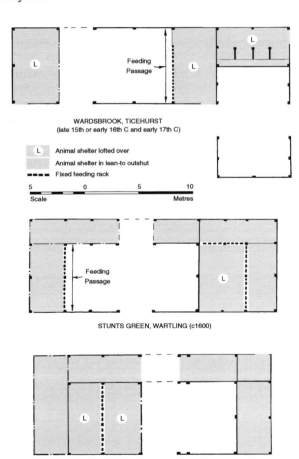

WARDSBROOK, TICEHURST
(late 15th or early 16th C and early 17th C)

L Animal shelter lofted over
Animal shelter in lean-to outshut
Fixed feeding rack

Scale Metres

STUNTS GREEN, WARTLING (c1600)

FROGHOLE, MAYFIELD (early 17th C)

Figure 6.10
Reconstructed ground-floor plans of three specialized 'cattle barns'.

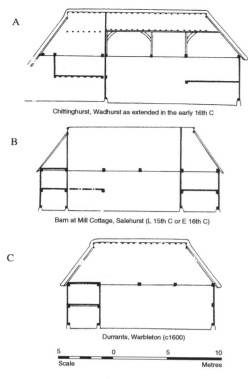

Figure A: Chittinghurst, Wadhurst as extended in the early 16th C

Figure B: Barn at Mill Cottage, Salehurst (L 15th C or E 16th C)

Figure C: Durrants, Warbleton (c1600)

Figure 6.12
Longitudinal sections through three barns
incorporating unusual internal layouts.

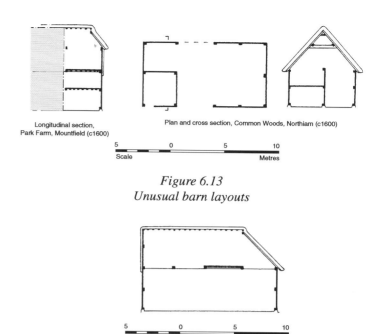

Longitudinal section, Park Farm, Mountfield (c1600)

Plan and cross section, Common Woods, Northiam (c1600)

Figure 6.13
Unusual barn layouts

Figure 6.14
Longitudinal section, Hammerden, Ticehurst (Mid 16th C)

store area, or even a granary. Certainly any grain stored at this level would have been inaccessible to rodents.

There are other atypical examples, though the above are sufficient to illustrate the type of variations found.

FITTINGS AND STALL ARRANGEMENTS IN ANIMAL SHELTERS

It is known from documentary evidence that agricultural buildings in the area were fitted with feeding racks, mangers and stall divisions from at least the 14th century. For example, on Icklesham Rectory Manor in 1349/50 12d per head was paid for ten animals pastured and 'in rack in winter', whilst on the same manor in 1353/4 the sum of 5 shillings was paid 'for five animals at rack in winter and not more as the cellarer had two oxen at rack and John de Saprerton [keeper of the rectory] had four cows which the abbot [of Battle] and seneschal conceded to him whilst he had cows in the winter, 20d from 5 calves at rack at that time . . . .'. There are similar references in later years.[8] In 1384-5 the cellarer of Battle Abbey made payments for the repair of mangers and racks on the abbey's home farm at Battle.[9]

It is of course possible that these fittings were

Figure 6.15
Evidence of floor over midstrey
at Hammerden, Ticehurst (mid 16th century).
Note the in-situ joist on the right. [241/18]

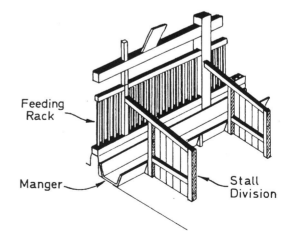

Feeding Rack

Manger

Stall Division

Figure 6.16
Typical fittings associated with animal shelters

Figure 6.17 (left)
Reconstruction of truss between crop storage area and former cattle shelter at Great Dixter, Northiam (15th C) showing fixed feeding rack

movable or only nailed into position, and would thus leaving no trace once relocated or destroyed. When the initial analysis of local barns was undertaken in 1982 no indisputable evidence of stalls and racks constructed as permanent features had been recognized within a medieval barn. Since then the evidence of an original fixed feeding rack has been recorded in the barn at Great Dixter (Figure 6.17 and *see* Case Study in Chapter 11) and there are strong indications of a second medieval example at Burgham in Etchingham (*see* Case Study in Chapter 11), and perhaps a third at Limden, Ticehurst. All were located in the downhill end wall, between the main body of the barn and a lean-to cattle shelter. In all three instances the outshuts have since been destroyed.

Feeding racks

Within the sample analysed in 1982 in about half of the barns which formerly incorporated secondary functions insufficient evidence survived to indicate whether or not feeding racks once existed, though in many it would appear that they probably did not. In only 17 cases was it possible to say with any certainty that such features did not exist as fixtures, whilst in 21

Figure 6.18
Fixed feeding rack between two open bays at Froghole, Mayfield (early 17th century).
The method of fixing the rack indicates that it was inserted after the frame had been erected, though whether at a fitting-out stage during construction or at some subsequent date in antiquity is unclear. [383/4]

Figure 6.19
Feeding rack between crop storage area and former lean-to cattle shelter at Swailes Green, Sedlescombe (early 18th century) [320/4]

Fig 6.20
Regularly spaced round-ended mortices for the removed slats of a feeding rack visible in the underside of a crossbeam at Thorneyfold, Dallington (early 18th century) [276/15]

instances positive evidence of their inclusion still survived. A further 16 racks were incorporated as part of historic alterations and extensions.

To those who have never seen a built-in feeding rack, at first sight they appear very unlikely-looking features, comprising as they do a series of vertically-set morticed-in slats spaced to give openings about 90-110 mm wide. Typical examples are shown in Figures 6.18 and 6.19. The slats are usually neat and always have rounded, smoothed edges so as not to cut or shed splinters into the animal's tongues. As in the example shown in Figure 6.20, in many instances the slats have been removed, but, if either the head beam or cill survive, their former existance is evidenced by the very distinctive closely-spaced round-ended mortices which accommodated them. Although the individual mortices are very similar to those used to fix staves supporting daub infill, the two cannot be confused, for those used within a feeding rack are very much more closely spaced.

The main difficulty with such a feature is in accepting that a vertical slatted wall could have been used to feed animals, for at first sight there is no obvious way of retaining the fodder in place against it. In ten

Figure 6.21
Loose sloping feeding rack in lean-to cattle
shelter at Goatley Manor, Northiam. The date
of the rack is unknown. [281/35]

Figure 6.22
Manger of unknown date within added lean-to
outshut at Boyces, Ewhurst. [240/27A]

recorded examples the answer is to be found in a row of large-diameter holes drilled diagonally into the main framework in order to accommodate slanting removable hurdles which held the fodder securely in place. The majority of racks, on the other hand, show no such fixings, and in these it would appear that a wide-meshed hemp net, known as a 'hay net', was utilized. Using this method the lower edge of the net was first tied to the lower end of the slats, held out horizontally to receive the fodder, and then tied back to the slatting in order to hold the feed in position. The location of the fixed racks, incorporated as they were into the side and cross-walls of the barns, is of particular interest, for in order to service them a clear feeding alley, together with access walk-ways, had to be left within the storage areas of the barn. This necessity would have considerably reduced the building's crop-storage capacity.

Feeding troughs or 'mangers'

The only other fixture encountered regarding the feeding of animals is a feeding trough or 'manger'. Few of these survive, and all belong to the second half of the 17th century or later. Typical arrangements are illustrated in Figures 6.22 and 6.23. As such fixtures are only nailed into position and leave no obvious evidence once removed, they were doubtless more common than now appears to have been the case, though it is equally possible that movable mangers were often used.

Stalls

In most buildings it is now impossible to tell whether the animal houses incorporated fitted stalls, or whether the beasts were either left un-tethered or restrained by some other means. In other parts of England it is known that cattle were usually tethered in pairs, their double stalls varying in width from *c*1.50 metres - 1.80 metres. Stalls for horses (?and draught oxen) were of similar width, though intended for one animal only, thus leaving sufficient room for grooming. Double stalls in stables were correspondingly wider.[10] The divisions between stalls intended for horses varied only in that they tended to be taller and longer in order to prevent the animals from biting and kicking each other.[11]

Where sufficient evidence survives within the sample of buildings here under discussion the stall divisions can be shown to have been 1.35 metres to 3.10 metres apart and appear to fall into two distinct groupings of 1.40 metres to 2.20 metres and 2.70 metres to 3.10 metres. Presumably the latter group (comprising six examples of which only two are confirmed) represent double stalls designed for horses (?or oxen).

The types of stall for which mortice evidence survives are illustrated in Figure 6.23, types A and B. Where the rails were nailed-on (as opposed to morticed-and-tenoned or halved to the main frame) stalls of this type would leave very little recognizable evidence once removed. Others, originally jointed into position, have probably been destroyed without trace by removal of the studs containing the evidence. Figure 6.24 shows the surviving stall division at Wardsbrook minor, Ticehurst - the only division within the sample to pre-date the agricultural revolution. It is of 'type C', with earth-fast posts at either end of the division. These continue upwards and are secured to the joists of the loft above.

Even though the stall division at Wardsbrook is

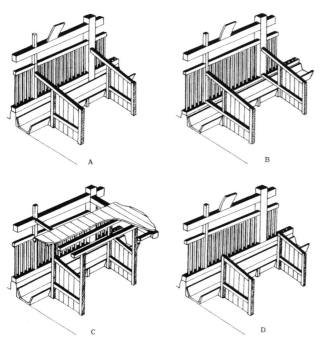

Figure 6.23
Details of stall divisions - methods of construction

likely to be contemporary with the 17th- or early-18th century re-framing of the loft floor, the posts are merely nailed to the joists and thus, if removed, would have left very little evidence. In other examples where the posts may have been jointed into position the loft floors have since been destroyed, obliterating all above-ground traces. Type D in Figure 6.23 is conjectural, for once removed it would leave no structural evidence whatsoever, comprising as it does isolated earth-fast partitions. Since it was the most basic of the four forms

Figure 6.24
Wardsbrook, Ticehurst. Surviving stall division and feeding trough. Note the fodder drop in the floor above. [285/3]

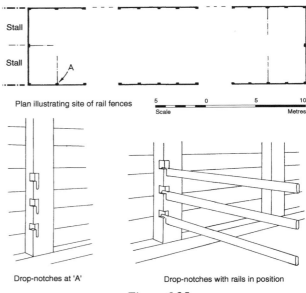

Figure 6.25
Great Dixter, Northiam. Details of pens.

of division, this type may have been common.

Stalled animals were tethered by a halter either tied around the head post, or, as at Wardsbrook minor, to a purpose-made iron ring secured to the side of the head post or manger supports. At Toll Farm, Warbleton, iron tethering rings survive fixed to the cillbeam. In this instance the animals were not confined by stall divisions (or at least not by any which have left recognizable evidence). This is an arrangement which may have existed elsewhere.

Rather than being tethered, cattle were in some instances housed loose either within all, or (more often) part of the shed. Whilst undertaking the survey many sheds were encountered divided up by modern fences. These were often makeshift affairs comprising one or two hurdles, or equally temporary arrangements consisting of nailed-on horizontal poles and rails. Such pens would rarely leave evidence. In some instances they were more permanently constructed. Two such examples once existed in the medieval major barn at Great Dixter, Northiam, where sets of mortices for fences, each incorporating three rails, were cut into the faces of the principal posts in order to divide off areas at both ends of the barn (Figure 6.25). The mortices in one principal post have notched heads allowing removal of the rails when necessary. These neatly-constructed works could be of any date, perhaps even medieval! Similar mortices exist for a rail fence between two lean-to cattle sheds in the *c*1600 extension at Stunts Green Farm, Wartling, as well as in several other barns within the rape. Others, no doubt, were not observed during recording works.

7 BARNS: DETAILS OF CONSTRUCTION WALLS AND CLADDING

A barn's constructional detail had little connection with its intended use, being influenced chiefly by the availability of materials, by regional styles, and by the preferences of the chosen craftsman. The client, it is true, did have a role to play, for it was he who controlled the finances and governed the general external appearance of the building, though his principal concern was with the building's layout and fitments.

The Weald, being an area lacking good building stone but abundant in timber and clay, is an area in which timber framing was adopted at all social levels. Of the 181 barns surveyed, only two (both brick-built structures of the early 18th century) were not of this material. It should be borne in mind that only good quality barns survive from before the late 16th and early 17th centuries. Although it is known that barns were common prior to this date, their method of construction is a matter of speculation.

The late 16th-/early 17th-century rebuild was, at least in part, spurred on by a need for larger barns capable of storing increased quantities of crops. Even accepting this, if the existing smaller structures which were being replaced had been well built in the manner of their successors, then surely many would merely have been extended, as indeed can be shown to have been the case with those barns which do survive. The complete lack of early barns on all but the larger and/or high-status holdings must make it likely that these earlier buildings were of an 'impermanent' nature, especially bearing in mind that the basic requirements of the barns remained unchanged at this time. Whether this impermanence was due to the method of framing, poor jointing, the use of small-scantling, immature or low-grade timber, or a combination of these factors will probably never be know. What it does seem safe to assume (bearing in mind the available building materials) is that some form of clay-infilled timber construction was used.

The successors to these assumed 'impermanent' barns make use of box-framed construction and are in all cases competently constructed, showing a high degree of skill in their neatly-formed joints and (in the majority of cases) neatly squared timbers. In some instances the timbers have chamfered leading edges. Except in late buildings, only rarely were large quantities of rough-edged, low-grade or reused timbers incorporated. Late 17th- and early 18th-century buildings show an increasing tendency towards more sloppily-designed work as regards infill framing and bracing.

In discussing the details of construction, it is intended to divide the structures into their component parts. This present chapter will discuss the main frame, wall design and wall coverings, whilst Chapter 8 deals with trusses, arcades and internal partitions. Chapter 9 addresses floor construction, and Chapter 10 will concentrate on roof design and roof coverings.

THE MAIN FRAME

The main frame is here taken to comprise the timbers shown in Figure 7.1: that is, the soleplates, principal posts, intermediate posts, side girts, end girts, wallplates and tiebeams. Those timbers below roof level which stiffen the main frame, help strengthen the wall infill, and (where relevant) form internal partitions, will be dealt with subsequently. The design of the main frame did not vary throughout the period here under discussion, and in many instances this continued to be

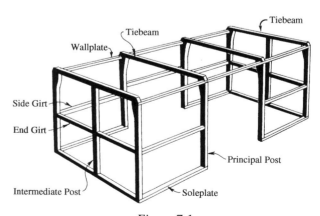

Figure 7.1
The components which make up the main frame of a timber-framed building

Figure 7.2
The frame at Iwood, Warbleton (early 17th century)
stripped for repair during conversion into a
dwelling in 1994. [590/18A]

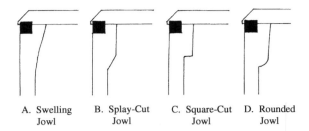

A. Swelling Jowl   B. Splay-Cut Jowl   C. Square-Cut Jowl   D. Rounded Jowl

Figure 7.5
The four basic shapes of jowl used in local barns.

the case until as late as the middle years of the 19th century.

The most important feature of any frame is the complex joint at the intersection of the principal post, wallplate and tiebeam, a joint upon which the building depended for its robustness. Its basic form, shown in Figure 7.3, remained unchanged from its introduction some time late in the 13th century. It is found in barns and dwellings alike. For its strength it relied upon a thickening or 'jowl' at the head of the principal post. This allowed the post to be jointed into both the wallplate and tiebeam, which were themselves dovetailed together. This arrangement is known as 'normal assembly'. In dwellings, where floors and chimneys helped strengthen the building, jowls were gradually abandoned locally during the early/mid 18th century, but in barn construction they were retained for their additional strength, being still commonly found in agricultural buildings constructed during the first half of the 19th

century. In such buildings they give a decidedly archaic impression.

In one or two early/mid 18th-century barns the end tiebeams are set level with the wallplates (*ie* in 'level' assembly) to which they are mortice-and-tenon jointed. The corners in those buildings which use level assembly are usually further strengthened by a diagonal dragon tie, as in the example at Cralle, Warbleton shown in Figure 7.4.

Several shapes of jowl have been used over the centuries: those found locally in barns are illustrated in Figure 7.5. By far the most common was the 'swelling' type, which was the predominant form until *c*1700. Its only rival prior to the mid 17th century was the relatively rare 'splay-cut' type. A cumbersome-looking 'square-cut' form is occasionally found in buildings dating from the late 17th century, and this, together with the earlier swelling and splay-cut styles continued to be used throughout the early/mid 18th century, combinations of the various types occasionally being found in a single building. However, by this date none of these forms were popular. Over half the surviving barns constructed during the early/mid 18th century have jowls with a rounded bowl (Figure 7.5, D), a type first recognized locally during the last quarter of the 17th century. It is this 'rounded' jowl which is found in the vast majority of late 18th- and early 19th-century barns.

The sturdiness of a frame is best reflected in the size of its principal posts. Most surviving barns which predate the late 16th-/early 17th-century great rebuild have principal posts of between 250 mm and 310 mm in width, though of lesser depth. The construction of 'permanent' barns on small and less prosperous farms for the first time during the late 16th and early 17th centuries is reflected by a dramatic increase in the number of surviving buildings with principal posts of between 200 mm and 240 mm, though (at least in those buildings which have survived) posts narrower than this were still rare. This was to change during the 18th century when, although if anything the surviving barns tend to be slightly taller, about half the examples surveyed had posts less than 200 mm wide. Their depth was not

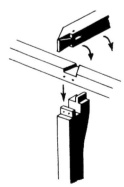

Figure 7.3
Typical joint at the head of a principal post

Figure 7.4
Corner joint incorporating a dragon tie, Cralle, Warbleton (early 18th century). [321/15]

Figure 7.6
Intermediate post in end wall of the medieval barn at Parkhill, Burwash. [192/4]

Figure 7.7
Intermediate post in a side wall of the medieval barn at Great Wigsell, Salehurst. The former weatherboard cladding (the presence of which is evidenced by fixing grooves in the posts) was probably removed when the lean-to outshuts were added. [316/23A]

affected. Thus, whereas most posts had previously been rectangular in section with their broad axis set along the building, they were now usually either set with their narrow face along the building, or were of square section. This narrowing-down of the posts in their strongest direction should be seen as nothing more than increased economy in the use of materials.

With the exception of four barns, the walls incorporate a single row of horizontal timbers or 'girding beams' mid-way up their height, these being known as 'side girts' if in a side wall or 'end girts' in an end wall. Their purpose was to divide the wall framing and infill into manageable heights, and thus add rigidity. The four barns which vary this arrangement each incorporate two lines of side girts and end girts, though at Wenbans, Wadhurst the second line is included to one side of the midstrey only, within the open storage bays (*see* Figure 6.6). During the late 18th and 19th centuries - beyond the period dealt with in this study - some timber-framed barns were built on relatively high brick ground walls, and in these the girding beams were on occasions omitted altogether.

The walls of many barns incorporate intermediate posts; that is, full-height posts set within the length or width of a bay. As Figures 7.6 and 7.7 illustrate, they are found in both side and end walls, and although their precise purpose is unclear, they were probably intended to give additional strength. Such posts were used in the end walls of about three-quarters of all surviving barns constructed during the study period, being most commonly omitted in narrow buildings, especially those having a span of less than 5.50 metres. In a few instances the design within the end walls was varied within a single building in that only one end incorporated an intermediate post. In some, but not all of the examples this was accompanied by the inclusion of a first floor at one end.

Bay lengths usually measure much less than the width of the building, and it is therefore not surprising

that intermediate posts in side walls are far less common than in end walls. They are found in only one in seven surviving barns, some of which show a combination of bays both with and without intermediates. Where such a combination exists, it is the shorter bays which lack intermediates. Indeed, no intermediate posts are known in a bay of less than 3.50 metres. Such posts are particularly common in medieval barns where they are found in almost two-thirds of all surviving examples. In this respect it is worth noting that medieval bay lengths tend to be longer than those in later buildings.

INFILL FRAMING

The main frames of local timber-framed buildings are infilled by studs. In barns intended to be weatherboarded the spacing of these studs was influenced by the need to support the boards, a point discussed more fully under claddings (*see* below). Where the frame was to be infilled with daub there was no such consideration. In these instances the number of studs was governed by fashion and bay length. Initially it was usual to divide the side walls of each bay into two panels by incorporating a single central stud above and below the side-girt, though occasionally additional studs were incorporated within the lower section. By the mid 17th century there was an increasing tendency to incorporate two studs per bay and, in some instances, even three. This was especially so if the bay length was excessive. The occasional differences found between the number of studs at upper and lower level is principally

Figure 7.8
Wall framing within side wall of the medieval
barn at Maplesden, Ticehurst. Some studs at
the lower level have been added, as have the
two short studs interrupted by the braces
at the upper level. [188/8]

Figure 7.10
Side wall within the formerly floored extension
of c1700 at Lattendens, Ashburnham. [385/7]

Figure 7.9
Side wall at Dewburys, Hooe (early 17th century).
At the lower level there was originally only one
stud, set immediately beneath that at the
upper level. [279/13A]

the result of the upper studs having been positioned so as to avoid the wall braces.

It is essential for all barns to incorporate at least some bracing in order to prevent the frame from racking (*ie* leaning over) and collapsing in high winds, though there was considerable room for variation in the number of braces included. Initially the upper level of the side walls was in most instances fully braced, regardless of the type of wall infill/covering used. From the time of the 'great rebuild' in the late 16th/early 17th century there was an increasing tendency at all social levels for some

of the bracing to be omitted. As the examples shown in Figure 7.11 demonstrate, this was particularly so with those braces flanking the wagon way in barns which incorporated only three bays, or adjacent to the intermediate trusses in larger barns. Even so, as late as the early 18th century a full complement of bracing was still being incorporated within almost half of the surviving barns then under construction.

To judge from the buildings which survive, the section of wall over a two-thirds-height wagon door was never braced. Even where a half-height door was included it was still usual in about two-thirds of the examples to omit the bracing, regardless of date or quality. The reason in the former group was probably the small depth of the wall panels, though in the latter group the governing factor appears to have been nothing more than carpenters' preference. This appears also to have been the case with the braces flanking intermediate posts in end walls. In these instances too only a third of the buildings incorporated bracing to the intermediate post. In contrast, corner braces in both side and end walls were never omitted, presumably being regarded as essential for the stability of the building.

Bracing was sometimes also incorporated into the lower section of a daub-infilled wall, and although only one example is known which post dates *c*1570, before that period bracing at this level is found in half the surviving examples. Typical is the arrangement at Kingsbank, Beckley, illustrated in Figure 7.12. With one

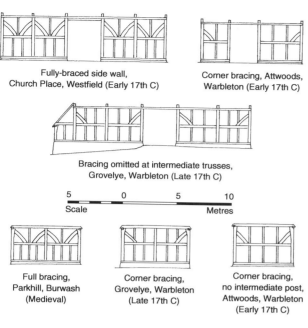

Fully-braced side wall, Church Place, Westfield (Early 17th C)

Corner bracing, Attwoods, Warbleton (Early 17th C)

Bracing omitted at intermediate trusses, Grovelye, Warbleton (Late 17th C)

Full bracing, Parkhill, Burwash (Medieval)

Corner bracing, Grovelye, Warbleton (Late 17th C)

Corner bracing, no intermediate post, Attwoods, Warbleton (Early 17th C)

Figure 7.11
Typical examples of wall bracing.
(Cladding omitted for the sake of clarity)

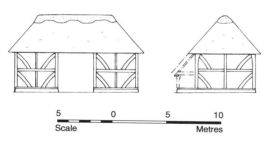

Figure 7.12
Bracing both above and below the side girts
at Kingsbank, Beckley (Medieval)

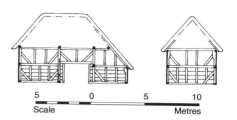

Figure 7.13
Bunces, Penhurst (1702)

Figure 7.14
End wall at Bunces, Penhurst (1702).
Note the rounded bowls to the jowls and the low-level
straight, almost square-section brace. The braces
at the upper level are reused from an earlier
building and at this level the frame was originally
daub infilled. [287/34]

exception (Pickdick, Brede) low-level bracing is unknown in weatherboarded walls predating *c*1700, though during the 18th century it was sometimes introduced in the form of straight raking struts. The earliest known example is Bunces, Penhurst, constructed in 1702 (Figures 7.13 and 7.14).[1] In most of these late examples the low-level bracing is intermittent and appears to have been intended as additional stiffening. It is probably no coincidence that by this period the main timbers used in the construction of the frames were becoming increasingly spindly. In contrast, the low-level bracing found in some early daub-infilled walls, such as Kingsbank, was probably incorporated either for aesthetic reasons or as the continuation of an earlier tradition. The frames of these buildings were certainly adequately braced without the need for extra rigidity.

The braces in all surviving barns which predate the mid 17th century comprise relatively thin plank-like lengths of timber, usually varying in depth from 180 mm to 270 mm and in width from 50 mm to 60 mm. Most are curved in their length. During the second half of the 17th century there was an increasing tendency for the braces to become thicker and, at the same time, less deep and usually straight. These late examples more closely resemble diagonally-set studs than braces. Such timbers are termed 'raking struts'. The precise point at which a brace becomes a strut is impossible to define accurately, though any brace of equal thickness to the studs in the same wall should certainly be classed as a raking strut. Once introduced early in the second half of the 17th century, they grew rapidly in popularity, having apparently entirely superseded the more archaic brace form by the mid 18th century. By this date many of the struts were long, spindly, and of square section.

All struts within the study area, at least as far as is known, stiffen the lower corner or 'foot' of the panel in which they occur, as is also the case with the majority of traditional bracing. This configuration is known as 'down bracing' or, alternatively, 'footbracing'. The

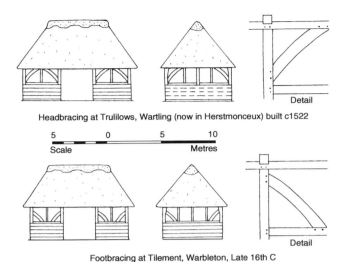

Headbracing at Trulilows, Wartling (now in Herstmonceux) built c1522

Footbracing at Tilement, Warbleton, Late 16th C

Figure 7.15
Examples of headbracing and footbracing

alternative form of traditional brace is that which triangulates the upper corner or 'head' of the panel in which it is located. This form is known as 'up bracing' or 'headbracing'. Examples of headbracing and footbracing are shown in Figure 7.15. In local housing it has been noted that although rare examples of headbracing occur throughout the period, braces of this form were only common for a relatively short time during the first third of the 16th century. Headbraces are, for instance, found in many houses incorporating medieval-style roof construction, but transitional plan types.[2] If, as seems likely, a similar date bias is true in barns, then several of the surviving 'medieval' barns probably belong to the early 16th century, for seven of the eighteen 'medieval' examples within the sample incorporate headbracing, as do two of the seventeen early/mid 16th-century barns. One of these is Trulilows, Wartling, which is shown in Figure 7.15. It was constructed within a year or two of 1522.[3]

As with the examples shown in Figure 7.15, most headbraces have a concave curvature, whilst curved footbraces are usually convex. Straight bracing was used, but was rare in barns constructed before the early 17th century and was usually avoided where the braces were intended to be visible externally. Once braces were designed to be hidden from public view (*see* below) straight braces became much more common, being found in approximately half the surviving barns built during the mid/late 17th century. Concave footbracing was also occasionally used during this latter period, whilst in some late barns a mixture of styles is to be found. In some instances this is due to the reuse of braces from earlier buildings. It is significant that the quality of finish in barns which incorporate mixed bracing tends to

be poor. After this period the use of straight raking struts rapidly took over from traditional bracing.

WALL CLADDINGS

Types of Cladding

The typical Sussex barn as it exists today is clad in black weatherboarding, though this has not always been the case. During the 15th, 16th and 17th centuries carpenters had the choice of two methods of cladding -

Figure 7.16
Barn at Norwoods, Ticehurst (early 17th century).
A rare survival of mixed weatherboarding
and daub infill. [382/36]

Figure 7.17
Interior view of Norwoods, Ticehurst. [382/32]

they could either infill the frame with lath and daub (similar to that used in dwellings) or clad it with boarding. Of the two materials, boarding was certainly the more suited, being better able to withstand the heavy-duty use to which the buildings would invariably be put. However, compared with daub, such claddings were very expensive, being costly in both materials and labour. It would appear that for many builders of barns, particularly the less prosperous, regular maintenance was regarded as preferable to excessive initial costs. As a compromise, a high proportion of builders chose to use a combination of the two materials (*see* Figures 7.15 to 7.17 and below).

Of those barns constructed on small farms of less than 50 acres during the late 16th and early 17th centuries over half of those which survive were initially fully daub infilled, whilst few were boarded throughout. In contrast, on farms in excess of 100 acres the reverse was true. A similar contrast between barns on small and large farms is recognizable throughout the study period, though there was an equally distinct progressive trend away from daub and towards the more general use of boarding. For example, although over half the surviving barns on small farms were fully daub infilled during the late 16th and early 17th centuries, no fully-daubed examples are known to have been constructed even by small farmers after the beginning of the 18th century. On farms of more than 100 acres few barns which survive from the mid 16th century were daub infilled throughout. A century later, by the mid 17th century, full daubing appears to have been abandoned in such buildings, whilst by that time fully weatherboarded examples account for six out of every seven surviving barns constructed on

farms of this size.

For many farmers and landlords of the 16th and 17th centuries the expense of cladding their barns throughout with boarding could not be justified. Yet, at the same time they recognized the need to reduce excessive maintenance costs. In particular it was the lower portion of the walls which suffered. Damage at this level was caused by a number of factors, but principally by farm animals and carts knocking and rubbing against the walls. Many therefore compromised by boarding their barns up to side-girt level, whilst infilling the upper section of the frame with daub. A rare survival of this configuration is to be seen at Norwoods in Ticehurst, illustrated in Figures 7.16 and 7.17. In virtually all instances the daub has since been replaced by weatherboarding. Such combinations formerly existed in about half the surviving barns constructed before *c*1570, many early examples being located on farms of no mean size and wealth. By the end of the 17th century such combinations were confined mostly to the smaller or relatively poor holdings.

As a further economy, in some barns only those walls most vulnerable to damage were partially boarded, the remaining walls being daub infilled down to ground level. Typical examples are to be found in the 16th-century barns at Church Farm and Little Harmers in Beckley. As Figure 7.18 illustrates, both had low-level boarding confined to one side wall only. In other instances, such as the late 16th-century barn at Bines, Ticehurst, shown in Figure 7.19, the end walls were fully daubed, whilst the side elevations were part boarded. The reasons for other combinations are less obvious, the most unusual of all being that in the medieval barn at the

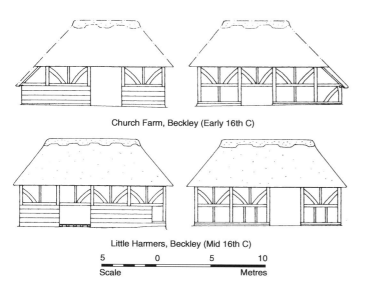

Church Farm, Beckley (Early 16th C)

Little Harmers, Beckley (Mid 16th C)

5   0   5   10
Scale   Metres

Figure 7.18
Combinations of infill and cladding

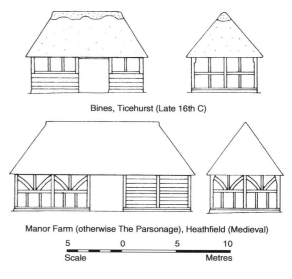

Bines, Ticehurst (Late 16th C)

Manor Farm (otherwise The Parsonage), Heathfield (Medieval)

5   0   5   10
Scale   Metres

Figure 7.19
Combinations of infill and cladding

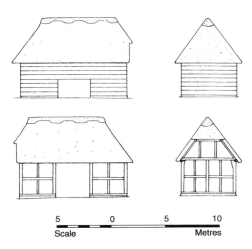

Figure 7.20
Stockherds, Beckley (late 17th century)

Parsonage, Heathfield (also shown in Figure 7.19) where the walls were originally daub infilled to one side of the midstrey, but fully boarded on the other. In another example dating from the late 17th century at Stockherds, Beckley (Figure 7.20) one side and one end wall were boarded throughout, whilst the other two walls were daub infilled. In this instance the principal weatherboarded wall faced the road, and thus the upper part may have been applied to add status. The same may be the case in the similarly-dated barn at Nortons, Battle, where all other walls were weatherboarded up to side-girt level only, though the lack of evidence for daub infill in this instance may equally be due to the former existence of a contemporary side lean-to, in which case the upper

portion of the main frame may have been left unclad. Similar low-level boarding may have been applied to the vulnerable walls of some farmhouses, though if so, it was applied over the daub infill and is today virtually impossible to detect.

To all intents and purposes by the early 18th century the use of daub in barns may be regarded as archaic. Its use is known in only three post-c1700 buildings, all relatively small and all incorporating combinations of weatherboarding and daub infill. They represent the last lingering examples of a bygone tradition. As the existing stock of barns fell due for repair these too, if daub infilled, were converted to weatherboard, though such alterations are by their very nature impossible to date accurately. Conversion often entailed the insertion of additional studs to give rigidity to the boarding, an early example of which is here illustrated in Figure 7.21 from Little Harmers, Beckley.

Daub Infilled Walls

In 1982 fragments of daub infill still survived in fifteen of the barns in the sample. All used the same methods of construction as found in housing. As depicted in Figure 7.22, the daub was applied to cleft oak laths (not hazel wattles) which were nailed (not woven) to one face of roughly-cleft staves. The heads of the staves were pushed up into small mortices in the soffit of the timbers, the bases then being knocked into a continuous 'v' notch cut into the upper surface of the frame. The mortices themselves are very distinctive, having been formed by drilling a pair of holes a short distance apart and then knocking out the intervening timber with a chisel, thus forming a narrow, round-ended

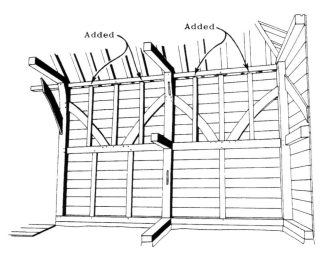

Figure 7.21
Little Harmers, Beckley. Wall framing designed
for daub infill, but adapted during the early 17th century
in order to support weatherboarding

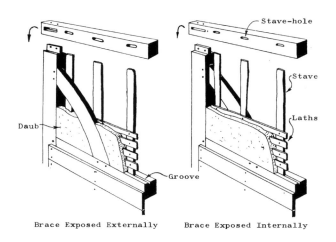

Figure 7.22
Details showing the methods used in
infilling the walls of local barns
with daub panels

Figure 7.23
Surviving daub infill with externally-exposed
brace within former external wall at
Tanhouse, Northiam (mid 16th century). *[214/16]*

Figure 7.24
Crockers, Northiam (late 17th century). *Braces*
concealed 'externally' (within open-fronted lean-to
outshut) by daub infill, but exposed internally. *[281/10]*

Figure 7.25
Externally-exposed brace in daub-infilled end wall
at Roadend, Beckley (early 18th century). *This is one*
of only two barns within the study area which
utilized long braces housed past the girding
beam, the other being the medieval barn at Burgham,
Etchingham. *This is a feature found quite commonly*
in Hampshire and West Sussex, but not in East
Sussex. *In this instance the lower part of the brace*
was sawn off when the section of wall below the
girding beam was removed. *[318/29A]*

mortice known as a 'stave hole'. Even when removed, former panels of daub infill are evidenced by these stave holes and 'v' grooves.

In agricultural buildings the only variation in design found throughout the study period is in the way the daub was treated at the braces of the main frame (*see*

Figures 7.22 to 7.25). In a very few instances (6 known examples) the braces are thick and the staves are nailed to their edges, thus leaving the side face of the brace visible in both the internal and external face of the wall. In the vast majority of examples, however, the staves were designed to pass to one side of the braces, leaving only one side exposed. In all medieval examples the braces were intended to be exposed externally, and, as in houses, this continued to be the case until the mid/late 16th century. In local houses during this period large-panel framing incorporating externally-exposed bracing was phased out in favour of small-panel framing, and eventually bracing was omitted.[4] With one exception, small-panel framing was not used locally in barns.[5] Thus the bracing was retained, though set to be visible from the interior only. The earliest local dated houses which

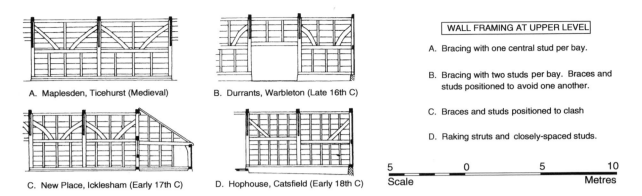

Figure 7.26
A selection of typical arrangements of wall framing designed to support weatherboarding.
The sample is arranged in chronological sequence.

lack externally-exposed braces are to be found in the mid 1560s, though it is likely that the design was already being adopted in a few high-status houses as early as the 1540s or 1550s. The new arrangement, however, quickly found favour at all social levels during the period 1570-1600. There is no reason to doubt a transitional period of similar date for barns. Indeed, this impression is supported by other architectural features, such as roof design. It should, however, be stressed that, as with the example shown in Figure 7.25, barns with externally-exposed bracing continued to be constructed after the period of transition. Todate, six such examples have been recognized, and these include Bunces, Penhurst, a small barn incorporating many up-to-date features and known to have been constructed in 1702. In two of the six buildings the bracing occurs in extensions, and here they may have been designed to be exposed in order to match the remainder of the building's existing appearance. In another the fragments of an earlier building may have been incorporated.

Weatherboarded Walls

Unlike daub infill, weatherboarding developed in its design during the period represented by the barns here under discussion, and this development has continued since with, for instance, the introduction of such features as softwood boarding. Modern boarding usually measures 160-200 mm in depth and has a tapered cross-section, narrowing from a little under 20 mm thick to virtually nothing. Each board is applied with its thick lower edge over-lapping the thin edge of the board beneath, thus giving a weatherproof joint. The supporting studwork for this modern-style boarding is normally set at centres of 600 mm or less, and it is this spacing which gives the first indications of a considerable variation in the past nature of boarding. In barns constructed prior to the early/mid 17th century

studs intended to support boarding are often positioned in excess of one metre apart and only very rarely below 750 mm. Indeed, especially in early barns, the walls commonly incorporate only one stud in addition to the bracing at their upper level, thus leaving long sections of unsupported boarding (Figure 7.26 A - for further examples *see* Figures 7.6 to 7.9). Additional studs were normally nailed in subsequently in order to help carry modern-style boarding.

In only a few instances, mostly where protected by an added lean-to outshut, does ancient boarding survive *in situ*. It is from these remains that the true extent of the changes can be fully appreciated. The early boards which survive are of a much heavier scantling than later boards, usually about 300 mm deep (and occasionally up to 450 mm) by 20-25 mm thick, hence the wider centres of the supporting studwork. They are not tapered, but are of rectangular section, and the surviving examples are mostly (but not exclusively) laid butt-edged with no attempt at excluding draughts. Indeed the flow of air would have been beneficial to the crops stored within.

At Great Lywood, Ardingly, in the Weald but outside the study area, two entire walls of original late 16th-century external boarding survived until 1996 where protected by a two-storeyed extension and a lean-to addition respectively.[6] In this instance the edges on the majority of the boards were splay cut to give a joint which allowed draughts to enter the barn, but prevented water penetration. What made the survival at Great Lywood particularly important was that one of the boarded walls was to a bay which not only incorporated a first floor, but also an attic floor. Whereas the boards serving the ground-floor and attic areas had splay-cut joints of the type used elsewhere within the building, those forming the wall of the first-floor area were rebated together. This refinement not only gave a waterproof joint, but also one which was draught proof. That this was an original feature rather than the result of selective

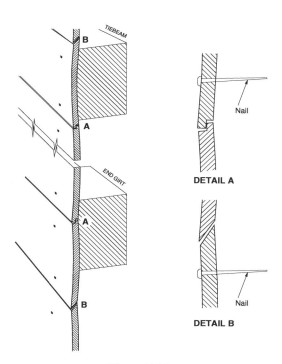

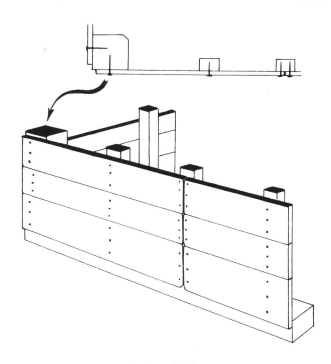

Figure 7.27
Details of late 16th-century weatherboarding
at Great Lywood, Ardingly.

Figure 7.29
Flush butt-edged boarding fixed across
the face of a timber frame.

Figure 7.28
Early butt-edged weatherboards surviving
near the eaves on the side wall of the early 17th-century
barn at Deudneys, Herstmonceux. [321/18]

21 mm thick, and were fixed at every stud by means of two hand-forged 75 mm long nails, set between 60 mm and 90 mm in from the edges of the boards. Additional nails were used where the boards crossed the braces. The board which coincided with the tiebeam was fixed with nails of rectangular cross section with chisel ends, but all other observed nails were pointed and had shanks which were approximately square in cross section. The boards were sawn and were, in the main, fixed 'dished' (*ie* so the edges of the boards warp outwards on the external face). The board at tiebeam level was the only example recognized which had been fixed 'domed' (*ie* the reverse of 'dishing'). Where the edges were splayed the splays had been achieved by hewing, whereas the rebates were neatly formed and were presumably planed.

Some of the Great Lywood boards were exceptionally long, but all surviving boards within the study area are fixed in relatively short lengths, as are the boards shown in Figure 7.28. As with those at Great Lywood, they are nailed across the face of the framing in similar fashion to modern boarding (*see* Figure 7.29). However, this has not always been the case. Of the eight surviving partially-boarded medieval barns within the sample only two had their boards fixed across the face of the principal posts. In four of the remaining cases the boards were accommodated in grooves cut into the sides of the main posts and in the other two examples rebates were used, a fixing method also recognized in one early 'post-medieval' barn. For further clarification of these

replacement of the boards was shown not only by the presence of a single set of fixing nails, but - more important - the survival of the transition boards between the two jointing types (*see* Figure 7.27). These transition boards had a splay cut down one edge and a rebate down the other. What the Great Lywood example demonstrates is that, at least in some instances, the design of the boarding was varied to suit the different uses of the spaces within the building.

The Great Lywood boards were of a relatively consistent cross section, averaging 320 mm deep by

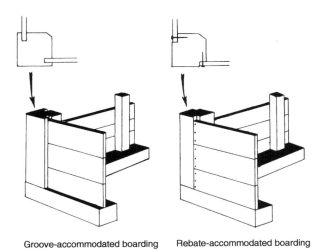

Groove-accommodated boarding   Rebate-accommodated boarding

Figure 7.30
Early methods of fixing weatherboarding

Figure 7.31
In-situ medieval groove-accommodated weatherboarding protected by an added lean-to outshut in the barn at Harts Farm, Hartfield. Note how the face of the side girt (at the base of the extant boarding) is inset from the face of the principal post so as to be flush with the exterior of the boarding. Beneath the side girt the groove in the face of the principal post is clearly visible where the boards have been removed. [815/8].

Figure 7.32
Interior view of the groove-accommodated medieval weatherboarding at Harts Farm, Hartfield. [815/12]

two earlier methods of fixing *see* Figure 7.30.

Although no examples of either groove-accommodated or rebate-accommodated boarding is known to survive within the study area, a medieval barn at Harts Farm, Hartfield, (outside the study area, but within the High Weald) retains one wall of 15th- or early 16th-century groove-accommodated weatherboarding protected by a lean-to outshut added in the 17th century.[7] Despite the grooves being 22 mm wide (which is about average) the boards are only 18 mm thick and thus could be sprung into position. All boards are 260 mm deep, are square edged and are butted against one another. As with the boarding at Great Lywood, Ardingly, they are nailed back to the footbraces and studs, towards the top and bottom of each board.

As can be seen from Figure 7.31, because both the upper and lower parts of the walls at Harts Farm were intended to be weatherboarded from the outset the external faces of the side girts and end girts are deliberately inset 25 mm from the external face of the principal posts and intermediate posts so as to be flush with the boarding. In this way a potential weathering problem along the top edge of the timbers was avoided. As a result of this the girding beams have the appearance of being part of the weatherboarding when the building is viewed from the exterior. Where boards are missing from the wall only one set of fixing nails/nail holes are visible on the frame, confirming that the surviving boards are primary to the building's construction.

Before the mid 16th century the use of weatherboarding appears to have been rare, known examples being limited to prosperous holdings. The use of such expensive methods of fixing can perhaps best be understood as a continuation of the tradition of boarded walling found in high-quality housing during the opening years of the 14th century and before.[8] The boards infilling the walls of these early houses were similarly accommodated in grooves. Not only were such methods of fixing unnecessarily expensive, but, if thick boards

Stud notched to allow
brace to pass

Brace set-in to avoid
line of stud

Figure 7.33
Methods of dealing with the intersection between a traditional-style plank-like brace and a stud

Figure 7.35
Late-style raking strut interrupting the line of a stud, which is angle-cut and nailed to the strut

Figure 7.34
Early-style bracing inset so as to pass against the inner face of the wall studs at New Place, Icklesham (early 17th century). [327/15]

Figure 7.36
Summertree, Warbleton (early/mid 18th century) Late-style wall framing incorporating closely-spaced studs to support flimsy weatherboarding. The studs at the ends are interrupted by straight raking struts which triangulate the frame. [288/25]

equal to the width of the grooves were used, they had one major drawback: the boards could be fixed into position only during fabrication, and could only be replaced using thinner boards or by modifying the grooves to rebates. It was perhaps for ease of maintenance that rebates were adopted in three of the surviving barns, and it must have been for this reason too - as well as for economy - that the boards were finally fixed across the face of the principal posts. As already noted, this more simple method was already in use by the close of the medieval era and is evidenced in some local barns built during that period. By the early/mid 16th century this alternative fixing method had become the norm, only one rebated example being known within a barn having a post-medieval form of roof construction.

Although the date can be ascertained for the adoption of more simple fixing methods, there are no clear indications as to when butt-edged, flush-faced boarding was superseded by the use of overlapping tapered boards. Indeed, it must be borne in mind that the transition to the new style of overlapping boards could have been slow, and was perhaps spread over a very long period. Certainly by the mid/late 17th century few low-level studs were set at over one metre centres. By the early/mid 18th century most studs were positioned less than 750 mm apart at both the upper and lower levels, a practice which suggests that by this date a change had occurred in the form of boarding being utilized. Indeed, early tapered boarding still survives on the early 18th-century barn at Thornden, Ashburnham. Although located on the east elevation (away from the prevailing winds) and from the 19th century onwards protected by an attached cowshed, the boards are heavily weathered and appear to be contemporary with the building.

Once the upper-level studs began to be set more closely together they increasingly clashed with the alignment of the wall braces, though during the early years it was still possible in many instances to avoid a clash by inserting the studs immediately adjacent to the feet of the braces, a method which continued to be normal until the early/mid 17th century (*see* Figure 7.26). Already during the late 16th century, however, studs were in some instances being notched around, interrupted by, or set to pass against the inner face of the braces, as shown in Figures 7.33 and 7.34. No one method became dominant until the early/mid 18th century, by which time the use of heavy, almost square-section raking struts (rather than traditional bracing) made it convenient to nail the studs onto the edge of the struts, as indicated in Figures 7.35 and 7.36.

8 BARNS: DETAILS OF CONSTRUCTION TRUSSES, ARCADES AND INTERNAL PARTITIONS

OPEN TRUSSES

Within barns open trusses are found in two locations - flanking the midstrey and separating adjacent open storage bays. Initially trusses in both locations were identical in their design, being arch braced from principal post to tiebeam in order to give lateral stability to the frame. Most arch-braced trusses have concave bracing, though (particularly from the late 16th century onwards) convex, straight, and even combinations of all three were also used. A selection of typical examples is shown in Figure 8.1. As in external walling, straight braces became particularly popular towards the end of

Figure 8.2
Longdown, Hooe (mid 16th century).
Typical trusses with curved braces. [323/10]

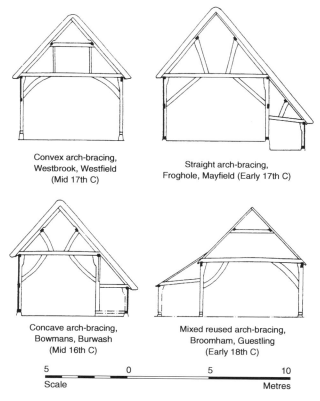

Convex arch-bracing,
Westbrook, Westfield
(Mid 17th C)

Straight arch-bracing,
Froghole, Mayfield (Early 17th C)

Concave arch-bracing,
Bowmans, Burwash
(Mid 16th C)

Mixed reused arch-bracing,
Broomham, Guestling
(Early 18th C)

5   0   5   10
Scale   Metres

Figure 8.1
A typical selection of arch-braced open trusses.

Figure 8.3
Randolphs, Iden (early 18th century).
A cumbersome-looking truss with chunky jowls and convex-curved braces. [318/3A]

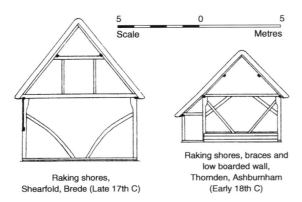

Figure 8.4
Trusses incorporating raking shores.

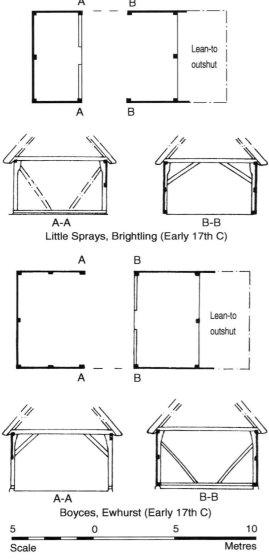

Figure 8.5
Barns with mixed forms of trusses

the study period, being present in two out of every five surviving barns built from the mid 17th century onwards. The majority of braces spring from between a third and half way down the principal posts, though both shorter and, more commonly, longer braces are found in barns of all periods.

During the early 17th century a new form of truss began to make its appearance flanking the midstrey. In this variation the principal posts were tied at their feet by means of a soleplate from which a pair of long, virtually square-section raking shores rise to brace the heads of the principal posts (Figure 8.4). In three early examples only one truss is thus shored, its opposite number being of typical arch-braced type. Two examples of this type are illustrated in Figure 8.5. Whilst still undertaking the arch brace's function of stiffening the frame, the new-style shores with their soleplate also prevented the walls from spreading at their base, until now a weak point. In addition to this they also helped in keeping both the loose crops and straw separated from the threshing floor. Although initially only occasionally used, shores became increasingly popular during the 17th century and are found in approximately half the surviving barns constructed during the first half of the 18th century. During the same period shores were being inserted into many existing buildings. A few trusses, such as that at Thornden shown in Figure 8.4, incorporate both arch bracing and raking shores as a contemporary feature, though these are rare. In some instances where shores have been added into an existing arch-braced truss the arch braces were removed: in others they were retained. In the barn at Farmhouse, Ninfield (Figure 8.6) the

Figure 8.6
Barn at Farmhouse, Ninfield (early 17th century)
showing shores added into the arch-braced trusses.
In one truss the original arch braces have been removed,
but they have been retained in the other. [322/22]

braces were removed from one truss, but not the other.

By the early 18th century a few of the new-style trusses also incorporated low cross walls, normally about a metre tall and of stud-and-board construction. An example, at Thornden in Ashburnham, is illustrated in Figure 8.4. Apparently, the purpose of these walls was to catch grain bouncing off the threshing floor, whilst keeping the threshed and unthreshed straw separated. As a secondary function, they were also useful in forming sheep pens for use during shearing.[1] Such walls were rare locally until after the mid 18th century.

ARCADES

In aisled barns the aisles are divided from the main body of the building by open arcades. The principal posts (in this context called 'arcade posts') are usually flanked by arch braces which rise to the wallplate or 'arcade plate' in order to strengthen the arcade and stiffen the main frame. Selected examples of arcade design are illustrated in Figures 8.7 and 8.8. As these show, full bracing was normal in the storage bays of the arcade, especially in the early buildings. From the late

16th century onwards some bracing was omitted in approximately a quarter of surviving examples, as is the case at Deudneys, Herstmonceux, shown in Figure 8.8. The same reduction in the quantity of bracing used is recognizable in external walls too. Presumably this was an economy measure aimed at reducing the over-designed nature of the earlier arcades and walls. As with open trusses, concave braces appear to have been usual in early barns, though other forms were later adopted in increasing numbers. Straight bracing was utilized in over half the surviving aisled barns constructed after the early 17th century.

Whether the arcade was braced or not within the area of the midstrey appears to have been a matter of carpenters' preference, and, as with the design of walling above the half-height wagon doors, the carpenters opted for its omission in over two-thirds of barns. In the remainder of examples the bracing is often noticeably short so as not to impede the movement of laden wagons.

A number of fully-aisled and single-aisled barns incorporate an end lean-to cattle house, and in these examples the arcade usually continues a short distance beyond the end arcade post so as to carry a flying

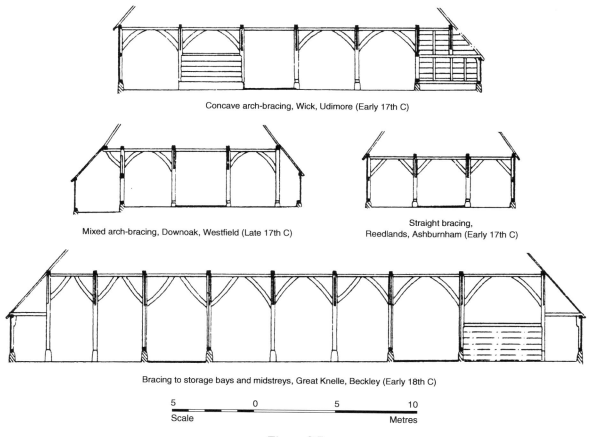

Concave arch-bracing, Wick, Udimore (Early 17th C)

Mixed arch-bracing, Downoak, Westfield (Late 17th C)

Straight bracing,
Reedlands, Ashburnham (Early 17th C)

Bracing to storage bays and midstreys, Great Knelle, Beckley (Early 18th C)

Figure 8.7
A selection of arcades used in aisled barns (see also Figure 8.8).

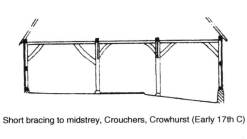

Short bracing to midstrey, Crouchers, Crowhurst (Early 17th C)

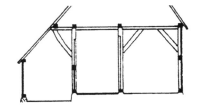

Mixed bracing, Old Farm Place, Catsfield (Early 18th C)

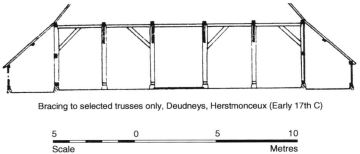

Bracing to selected trusses only, Deudneys, Herstmonceux (Early 17th C)

5	0	5	10
Scale			Metres

Figure 8.8
A selection of arcades used in aisled barns (see also Figure 8.7).

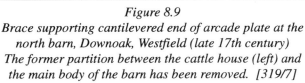

Figure 8.9
Brace supporting cantilevered end of arcade plate at the north barn, Downoak, Westfield (late 17th century)
The former partition between the cattle house (left) and the main body of the barn has been removed. [319/7]

Figure 8.10
The arcade at Cralle, Warbleton
(early 18th century). [274/31]

tiebeam supporting the jack rafters. In this way the partition between the cattle house and the barn's crop-storage area is in effect 'pushed back' into the main body of the barn, thereby considerably increasing the size of the cattle house. As the example from Downoak, Westfield shown in Figure 8.9 demonstrates, in order to give sufficient strength to the cantilevered end of the arcade plate an arch brace is incorporated beneath it.

TRUSSES BETWEEN CROP-STORAGE AREAS AND SPECIALIZED BAYS

Only nine examples of closed first-floor partitions between open crop-storage areas and specialized bays are known. These follow closely the design of the end walls (*qv*), except that intermediate posts tend to be more often omitted. As with the examples illustrated in Figure 8.11, most trusses between the main body of the barn and a specialized bay were left open at the upper level, whereas the surviving evidence suggests that the lower part of the truss was more usually infilled. However, it should be stressed that the majority of crossbeams within such trusses have been removed and thus details at this lower level are scarce. A selection of examples in which good details remain is shown in Figure 8.11. Where crossbeams survive, in two instances the trusses were originally closed by daub, in eight by boarded stud walls, and in at least four (perhaps as many as seven) by a feeding rack. Only in the medieval barn at Chittinghurst in Wadhurst is there known to have been no partition beneath the crossbeam.

Of the surviving barns which incorporate an open truss at the upper level, roughly three-quarters were merely braced to the principal posts using either arch bracing or footbracing, the latter arrangement being more common from the late 16th century onwards. With the exception of Bines in Ticehurst (which possessed no infill framing whatsoever) the remaining examples incorporated either an intermediate post or stud.

WALLS BETWEEN BARNS AND LEAN-TO OUTSHUTS

Prior to the mid 18th century most lean-to outshuts were intended as cattle sheds. It is therefore not surprising that about half the dividing walls between barn and lean-to incorporated feeding racks. With the

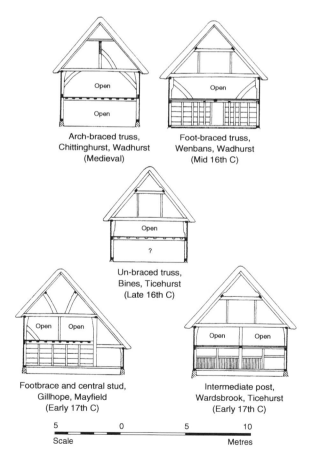

Figure 8.11
Trusses between crop storage areas
and floored bays

Figure 8.12
Bunces, Penhurst (1702) showing truss between midstrey (forground) and former end lean-to outshut (since rebuilt as a full bay - see Figure 8.13) [287/36]

Figure 8.13
Bunces, Penhurst (1702) showing relationship of truss illustrated in Figure 8.12 with former lean-to outshut, indicated by framing incorporated within side wall [287/37]

Figure 8.14
Two open 'partitions' at Gillhope, Mayfield (early 17th century). The open partition
in the foreground is illustated in Figure 8.11, where it is viewed from
the opposite direction. [185/18]

exception of three late examples (which were for some reason entirely open) the remainder of examples within the sample were closed at the lower level by a stud-and-board wall, or, in one instance, by a daub partition.

Some walls, irrespective of period, were infilled at their upper level using either daub or, less often, boarding, even though a closed partition was not necessary. Three-quarters of the surviving barns, however, incorporated an open partition, the studs either being omitted altogether or limited to one per bay. No such economies were made regarding the inclusion of bracing, which was maintained at the same quantity as elsewhere within the barn. In two instances headbracing was utilized in lieu of footbracing in order to give additional support to the wallplate and/or tiebeam.

9 BARNS: DETAILS OF CONSTRUCTION UPPER FLOORS

First floors were once relatively common within local barns, though today very few survive intact. The vast majority were removed either during the late 18th or 19th centuries when the floored bays were converted to open storage use. The floors are now mostly evidenced by mortices for removed crossbeams, the level of the crossbeam in relation to the girding beam in the end wall often giving an indication of the type of construction adopted. It should be stressed that not all crossbeams carried floors, though examples associated with open bays on both sides appear to have been rare.

To judge from the relative levels of the girding beams, the most popular method of flooring a bay within a barn was to use longitudinally-set joists as illustrated in Figure 9.1, though central-girder construction of the type shown in Figure 9.3 appears also to have been relatively common except in bays of less than 3.50 metres long. At Wardsbrook minor barn, Ticehurst, a medieval floor of longitudinally-set joists was re-framed - probably in the 17th century - using central-girder construction. In this

instance the girder is lodged over the crossbeam and end girt (*see* Figure 9.2). The surviving floors in the barn at Church House, Northiam also have lodged girders. Because of their wholly lodged methods of construction, if either of these floors had been removed they would

Figure 9.2
Floored bay at Wardsbrook Ticehurst.
Note the mortices in the crossbeam indicating the position of the original medieval floor and the replacement central-girder floor lodged over the crossbeam. [285/3]

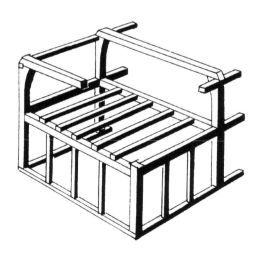

Figure 9.1
Typical arrangement of the joists within a barn in which the joists are aligned along the axis of the building, being morticed-and-tenoned into the crossbeam of the truss and lodged over the end girt.

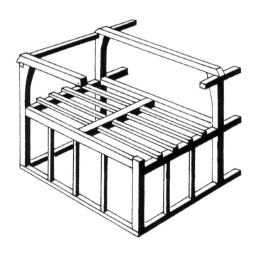

Figure 9.3
Alternative arrangement of joists within a barn in which the joists are aligned across the axis of the building, being morticed-and-tenoned into an axial girder and lodged over the side girts at the side walls.

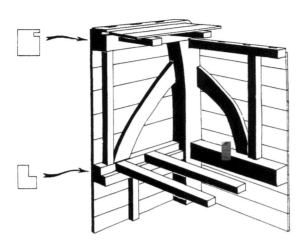

Figure 9.4
Durrants, Warbleton (late 16th century).
Reconstruction showing groove-accomodated
floorboards at attic-floor level and lodged
first-floor joists accommodated in a rebate.
For the evidence upon which this reconstruction
is based see Figure 9.5.

Figure 9.5
Durrants, Warbleton (late 16th century).
Evidence in the framing for the former first floor
and attic floor. [288/32]

Figure 9.6
Chittinghurst, Wadhurst (Medieval)
Crossbeam between midstrey and end bay
showing the large mortices for the joists of
the former floor. [284/6A]

have left no evidence of their former existence. Six other barns have their crossbeams and end girts set at a common level and in four of these the lack of mortices may indicate that the bays were never floored. Alternatively, they could have incorporated lodged joists, as was certainly the case at Durrant's, Warbleton. As Figures 9.4 and 9.5 demonstrate, in this instance the longitudinally-set first-floor joists were seated in purposely-cut rebates in the crossbeam and end girt in order to prevent movement. The joists in the sixth example, at Froghole, Mayfield (*see* Figure 6.11) were morticed into the crossbeams at both ends.

Only five examples of attic floors are known. Surprisingly, in two the joists were set longitudinally, being morticed into the tiebeams at both ends, a feature which must have made fabrication difficult. Central-girder construction was utilized in the remaining three examples.

In only seven buildings within the study area are the joist sizes known. Although relatively spindly joists were certainly sometimes used, heavy 130-160 mm joists more reminiscent of the medieval period are found in four mid 16th- and early 17th-century examples, their

size probably reflecting the heavy weights required to be carried. In two barns (one of medieval date, the other late 16th century) the sides of the tiebeam/crossbeam project above the floor level and are neatly grooved so as to accommodate the edge of the last floor board. One of these is Durrants illustrated in Figures 9.4 and 9.5. This feature illustrates well the high quality of construction found in some barns.

10 BARNS: DETAILS OF CONSTRUCTION
ROOFS

PITCHES AND COVERINGS

Much of the external character of a building is given to it by the steepness of its roof, and this in turn is to some extent influenced by the coverings it was designed to carry. For instance, in areas where heavy stone slabs were used the pitches are much shallower than in thatched areas where a certain steepness was essential to throw rainwater rapidly off the roof. Up to the mid 17th century the vast majority of barn roofs - and indeed house roofs - within the study area were constructed to a pitch of between 50 and 53 degrees, with only occasional examples falling either above or below this range. Although roofs within these parameters were still dominant after that date, there was an increasing trend towards less-steep pitches, up to a third of roofs over newly-built later barns being of less than 50 degrees, though very few were below 47 degrees and none fell below 45 degrees. The question which needs to be considered is whether this change reflects a variation in the types of covering being used - for example, a move away from thatch towards the more general use of plain tile - or was the change a mere whim of fashion?

Within the High Weald (excepting the area around

Figure 10.1
Interior of a thatched roof showing tar-impregnated rope ties around the rafters and the stain left on the rafters by the ties after they have either stretched and sagged or been removed.

Horsham, well to the west of the present study area) there was an absence of good stone roofing slabs. Given this fact, the cheapest and most easily accessible roofing material was thatch. According to L F Salzman, in medieval times thatch was held in place on the roof either by short straw ropes or, more often, by rods.[1] Hemp rope finally superseded these materials, although at what date this was first used is at present unclear. As yet no 16th, 17th or early 18th century documentary references are known to the purchase of hemp rope in connection with thatching, although there are constant references to the use of withies - that is, 'rope' made of twisted young twigs. What is certain is that by the 19th century the traditional fixings had given way locally to the use of tar-impregnated hemp rope. The use of this material has resulted in horizontal brown stains of the type shown in Figures 10.1 and 10.2 being visible on the rafters. The presence of these stains is clear and incontrovertible evidence of a former thatched covering.

Based upon rope-stain evidence of this kind 112 of the roofs within the sample can be shown to have once been thatched, whilst in comparison only 20 roofs show no rope stains on their rafters. Even with these 20 examples it should not automatically be assumed that other roof coverings were used, for it is quite possible that in these instances the thatch was superseded prior to the widespread local use of tar-impregnated hemp, or alternatively the ropes may not have been pulled tight or been sufficiently impregnated to leave a stain. Certainly the barn at Court Lodge, Wartling, which shows no signs of rope stains, had a thatched covering in 1830.[2]

Documentation suggests that thatch may not merely have been dominant, but virtually exclusive prior to the early/mid 18th century. For example, a survey of the buildings on the tenements held at the will of the lord of Etchingham Manor in 1597 lists four barns, three stables and four minor agricultural buildings: all were thatched.[3] The same was the case with the stable, two barns and a 'longhouse' at Robertsbridge Abbey in 1567 and with all but one of the six pre-1700 references to barn repair costs known to the authors.[4] The exception, the barns at Marley, Battle (which were tiled) were built by Battle Abbey in *c*1310 upon their home farm, and were thus buildings of considerable importance. As various abbey accounts indicate, their barns elsewhere were thatched.[5] In addition to this data, 17th- and 18th-century leases commonly note that the tenant was to supply the wheat-straw for re-thatching the barns when necessary.

There is no evidence locally for the use of reed thatch on farm buildings, though on occassions other thatching materials were used. For example, the decaying thatch removed from the roof of the barn at Iwood, Warbleton in 1994 was heather, as too was that covering the barn at Newhouse, Rotherfield, just outside the study area. According to the octogenarian thatcher responsible for the heather thatch covering at Rotherfield, this very woody material is not weather tight when first laid - for that to become so it required a covering of lichen to become established. Because of this, it was necessary to lay a thin undercloak of straw thatch over the rafters so as to serve as a temporary weathering. In this respect heather thatch was required to be laid in horizontal bands around the building, as shown in Figure 10.2.[6] This specification was not only used at Rotherfield, but was also recognized on the roof at Iwood when it was being stripped. Other thatching materials referred to in documents are broom and 'furze' (*ie* gorse).[7]

What is perhaps surprising to us is that persons of high status evidently had no qualms about using thatch upon their agricultural buildings, even when these stood close to their dwellings. For example, thatch was utilized on the 16th-century aisled barn adjacent to the house at Pebsham, Bexhill; on the prominently-sited early 17th-century barn opposite Thomas Stollion's mansion house at Iwood Place, Warbleton; and upon the medieval barn beside the entrance to Henry English's

Figure 10.2
Interior of the heather-thatched roof at
Newhouse, Rotherfield showing the horizontal
bands of straw undercloak.

great house at Wigsell, Salehurst. Likewise, from documentary evidence it is known that the barn of Nathaniel Powell, gent, adjacent to his mansion house at Court Lodge, Ewhurst had a thatched covering, as did the barns of John Everenden, gent. at Beech House, Sedlescombe.[8] On the other hand, some 16th- and 17th-century barns owned by status-conscious, newly-prosperous owner-occupiers may have been tiled from the outset. In this respect it may be no coincidence that the barns of John Cruttenden at Great Tott, Burwash, John Robinson at Tanhouse, Northiam, and the brothers, Thankful and John Frewen at Church House, Northiam, show no obvious evidence of having been thatched.

During the 18th century there are indications (both documentary and architectural) to suggest that the dominance of thatch was beginning to wane. A survey of Herrings Estate, Dallington, made in 1793/4 includes nine barns of which two were tiled.[9] Both are known to have been of mid/late 18th-century date. In addition, a third barn, although thatched, had tiled lean-to outshuts, probably representing extensions of the 18th century. Tiled 18th-century outshuts added to thatched barns are not uncommon, typical examples being those at Iwood Place and Batsford, both in Warbleton, and at Lea Bank, Whatlington. Apart from outshuts, architectural evidence for a more general use of tile during the late 17th and early 18th century is found in the increasing absence of rope stains: perhaps as many as a third of barns built during this period were intended to be tiled.

What does this data say about the tendancy to use less steep pitches during the latter part of the study period? Some argue that roofs pitched at less than 50 degrees were not suited to thatch. They suggest that the increasingly common use of relatively shallow roof pitches from the late 17th century onwards is strong evidence of the more general adoption of tile instead of thatch. In this respect it is worth bearing in mind that, although the architectural and documentary evidence supports a move away from thatch during the 18th and 19th centuries, only four of the seventeen low-pitched roofs within the sample of barns lack clear evidence of former thatched coverings, and the lowest pitches are not amongst them. This must suggest that, despite the more common use of tile, the adoption of lower roof pitches during this period has more to do with fashion than the intended type of roof covering. Unlike the case with heavy stone slabs, the pitches used for thatch and plain tile appear to have been interchangable.

ROOF TERMINALS

Of equal importance to roof pitch in setting the character of the local buildings is the choice of roof shape - the options available were sloping hipped ends,

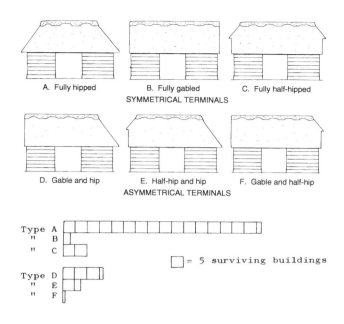

A. Fully hipped   B. Fully gabled   C. Fully half-hipped

SYMMETRICAL TERMINALS

D. Gable and hip   E. Half-hip and hip   F. Gable and half-hip

ASYMMETRICAL TERMINALS

Type A
" B
" C

☐ = 5 surviving buildings

Type D
" E
" F

Figure 10.3
Types of roof terminal and their popularity within
Hastings Rape prior to c1750

Figure 10.4
Bines, Ticehurst (late 16th century). A typical
fully-hipped roof. [JM168/2]

Figure 10.5
Wildings, Northiam (early 17th century). A rare example
of a barn with a fully-gabled roof. [211/11A]

vertical gables, half hips supported by stub gables, or a combination of these with one form at one end and an alternative form at the other. As Figure 10.3 demonstrates, during the period here under discussion the hip was by far the most common form of terminal used locally, the fully-hipped roof alone accounting for about two-thirds of all barns. It was consistent in its popularity throughout the 300 years covered by this study, and was used upon buildings of every size and quality. On the other hand, although the gable was the dominant roof terminal in many parts of England, fully-gabled buildings are rare in the south east. Within the sample there are only three fully-gabled barns of pre *c*1750. All three date from *c*1600 and two - those at Church House and Wildings, both in Northiam - are located upon the estate of the Worcestershire Frewen family.[10]

Introduced into houses with garrets during the mid/late 16th century, the half hip was common in such buildings throughout the 17th and 18th centuries. The earliest examples in a barn are those at Wenbans, Wadhurst, a pretentious late 16th-century building in which the half hips themselves incorporate an overhang (*see* Figure 6.6). In this instance the use of this form of terminal appears to have been for show, as was probably also the case in the prominently situated early 17th-century barn at Mount House in Burwash High Street. It should be stressed that in houses the half hip's main purpose was to gain sufficient headroom and light within a garret without completely abandoning the external hipped effect, and therefore it is not surprising

that such terminals were slow to be incorporated into barns. After Wenbans and Mount House it is virtually fifty years before the next examples are found, though from the late 17th century onwards half hips were utilized in about one in six newly constructed barn roofs. Whether this change was due to fashion (for the half hip had by this date become very popular in houses) or whether barns were by this time being more fully filled, is unknown. Certainly from the late 18th century, after the close of the study period, both half-hipped terminals and gables appear rapidly to have replaced the hip as the dominant forms of roof terminal.

Of the three possible combinations of asymmetrical terminals only two appear to have been utilized, there being but one known example of a gable and half-hipped combination. Initially, during the 15th and the majority of the 16th century, the hip and gable combination was the only alternative to the full-hipped roof: the type accounted for about a third of the barns built at this period. As is evident from Figure 10.6, barns of this type tend to give the impression that they have been shortened by the demolition of one end, but, except in very rare instances, this is not the case. For some

Figure 10.6
Combination of hip and gable at Clench Green,
Northiam (Late 16th century). [61/11]

Figure 10.7
Hip and half-hip combination at Manor Pound,
Wartling (early 18th century). [324/6]

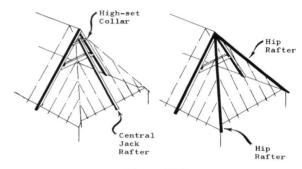

Figure 10.8
The two methods of framing a hip.
The timbers shown in solid outline are
the first components to be erected
in each case.

unclear reason the popularity of this combination waned during the late 16th and early 17th century, after which it disappeared from use. Its place was taken by roofs incorporating hip and half-hip combinations, though such configurations appear never to have become as popular as that of the hip and gable.

So much for the types and chronological distribution of asymmetrical terminals, but why were they employed? Was it to gain additional storage capacity at one end of the barn, or was perhaps appearance the main consideration? Of the 17 hipped-and-gabled examples, 11 possessed open crop storage bays throughout, whilst of the remaining six, half had the gable set at the floored end and the other half over the open crop storage area. Clearly, if additional storage was its aim, then different people had different priorities. Some of the hipped ends were continued down in the form of lean-to outshuts (as shown in Figures 10.6 and 10.7) but this was by no means always the case. Neither barn size nor location appears to have had any bearing on the use of such terminals either, the real swaying factor probably being nothing more than the preference of either the carpenter or his client.

The Use of High-Set Collars in association
with hipped and half-hipped terminals.

As illustrated by Figure 10.8, there were two methods of framing a hip or half-hip. In one, the pair of rafters supporting the head of the terminal incorporate a short collar set just below the apex in order to support the central jack rafter during pitching. Using this method the end pair of rafters, together with the central jack were the first to be erected. With the second method there is neither a high-set collar nor central jack rafter, the end pair of rafters and the two hip rafters being raised first, the jacks being fitted later. When viewed externally the first method results in a small gablet at the head of the

hip or half-hip, whereas the second (with a very few exceptions) does not. The two variations relate to the method of pitching, and therefore result from the preference of the carpenter, not the client.

In houses the use of high-set collars disappeared very rapidly once the new method had been introduced during the middle years of the 17th century, but in barns they were still occasionally used as late as 1750. Even so, terminals lacking high-set collars had become the norm by the early 18th century.[11] The more rapid adoption of the new technique in housing was probably due to the existence in such buildings of attic floors which allowed easy access to ridge level for fixing the timbers during erection of the frame.

During the transition period a few barns are found which utilize a high-set collar in one terminal only. All three recorded instances involve barns with a hip and half-hip combination, and in all cases it is the half-hip that lacks the collar. At Stockherds in Beckley, however, there is a small gablet at the head of the half-hip (as is also the case at Wardsbrook major) whilst in addition the pair of rafters carrying the head of the half-hip are prevented from over-turning by a peg fixed through the side purlin, a feature noticed in some other roofs.

MEDIEVAL ROOFS

Two types of roof were used within the Rape of Hastings during the medieval period: those incorporating crownposts and those comprising merely paired rafters and collars. As will be obvious from Figure 10.9, both types are closely related - the only difference is that one of the two forms incorporates a collar purlin running beneath its collars, supported off the tiebeams by crownposts. In Kent and East Sussex roofs of both types were progressively superseded by clasped-side-purlin construction during the period *c*1490-1540. It should, however, be stressed that rare examples of paired-rafter-and-collar construction are found in houses dating from as late as *c*1570. Furthermore, although no barn within the study area has been tree-ring dated, two examples in Sussex with crownpost roofs have been dated. One of these is the huge aisled barn at Falmer Court near Brighton, the other is an un-aisled barn from Cowfold, now re-erected at the Weald and Downland Open Air Museum. Both were constructed during the first half of the 16th century. That at Falmer Court was built between 1505 and 1525, whilst the timbers used to build the example from Cowfold were felled in 1536 - a surprisingly late date for such a roof.[12]

Only 20 barns within the sample show evidence of medieval roofs, 13 being of crownpost construction and five of paired-rafter-and-collar type. In two other instances the exact form is unclear. The method of jointing collar to rafter is common to both forms. Details are known in 14 of the 20 roofs - all but one make use of dovetailed halvings rather than more expensive mortice-and-tenon joints. The exception is a barn on the manorial demesne farm of Great Wigsell, Salehurst.

Of the 13 crownpost roofs within the sample, no fewer than nine have been rebuilt, leaving only mortice evidence of the crownposts and their associated bracing, although in three instances the original rafters were reused. Eleven, or possibly twelve, of the thirteen examples incorporated open crownposts with footbracing to the tiebeam, and this design can be assumed to have been the norm in local medieval barns. In only three buildings, however, did the crownposts each possess a pair of footbraces, whilst in at least seven of the remaining eight or nine examples the single footbrace was set on alternate sides in each truss. Examples are shown in Figures 10.10, 10.11 and 10.12. This alternating design must indicate economy, for although adequate in keeping the crownpost vertical, a single brace would not normally have been regarded as aesthetically acceptable. Admittedly, by excluding one of the braces it would have made handling the crops over

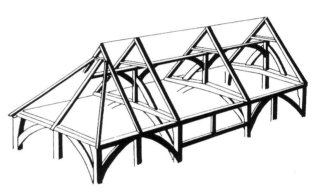

Figure 10.10
Medieval roof at Limden, Ticehurst.

Figure 10.11
Crownpost roof at Chittinghurst, Wadhurst,
showing the alternating footbraces.
The side purlins and associated struts are
later additions. [283/34]

A. Crownpost Construction at Chittinghurst, Wadhurst.

B. Paired-rafter-and-collar construction at Yewtree, Northiam.

C. Methods used in jointing collars to rafters.

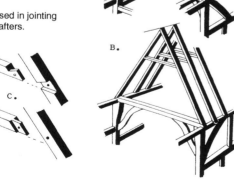

Figure 10.9
Medieval roof construction.

Figure 10.12
Manor Farm, Heathfield showing alternating
one-way 'residual' footbraces to the crownposts.
The roof pitch has been lowered by removing
the collars and re-setting the rafters over
the collar purlin. [153/22]

Figure 10.13 (left)
Manor Farm,
Heathfield showing
the full height of one
of the crownposts,
indicating the small
size of the 'residual'
footbraces.
[153/24]

Figure 10.14
Early clasped-side-purlin roof at
Trulilows, Wartling (c1522). [275/30]

the tiebeams much easier, though it is unlikely that at this period the unthreshed crops stored within the barns were stacked sufficiently high for this to be an issue. Certainly in the case of the crownposts at Manor Farm, Heathfield (Figures 10.12 and 10.13) the braces are so small as to be hardly worth including and would not have caused an obstruction when handling crops! Utilitarian straight bracing is used in lieu of more normal curved bracing in two of the three sets of crownposts which retain their footbraces, economy again being the reason. In contrast, those crownposts incorporated into a gable had a full complement of braces and, being visible from the exterior, were probably curved.

Economies of the type mentioned above may have been less common with regards the headbraces rising from crownpost to collar purlin, though as only four roofs survive complete with their crownposts, the sample is too limited to allow positive conclusions to be drawn. However, in those examples which survive, two possess a full complement, even though, significantly, all four

barns incorporate only one footbrace per crownpost. In one instance the headbraces are curved even though the footbraces are straight. These apparent inconsistencies between the treatment of the head and footbracing are perhaps explained by the more important functions of the longitudinal headbraces: they provided additional support to the collar purlin and helped in preventing the roof from overturning in high wind.

CLASPED-SIDE-PURLIN ROOFS

Although clasped-side-purlin construction was common during the medieval period further west in the country and was the normal form of roof used in Hampshire from the early 15th century, and despite its occasional use locally by the closing years of the 15th century, it was only during the second quarter of the 16th century that it finally superseded the medieval form as the normal type of roof built in East Sussex.[13] The earliest confirmed example within the sample is that at Trulilows, Wartling, constructed a few years after 1522.[14] As indicated by Figure 10.14, it incorporates rafters of heavy, wide, 'medieval' section.

Accounting for 114 of the 146 roofs found on new works and 28 of those on the 36 alterations and extensions within the sample, clasped-side-purlin

Collar only   Collar and Queen-Studs   Raking Struts

Figure 10.15
Types of truss used in clasped-side-purlin roofs.

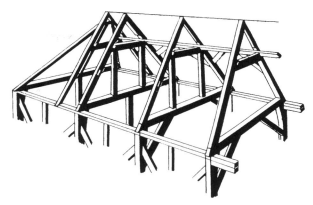

Figure 10.17
Roof at Walters Farm, Salehurst
(probably late 16th century).

Figure 10.16
Over-designed roof at Longdown, Hooe
(mid 16th century). In the foreground is a queen-stud
truss and in the background a truss with raking
struts (one strut removed and refixed as a collar).
A hip to the rear of this truss was removed when the
barn was extended. The collar in the extreme
foreground is located beneath the head of the hip.
Note also the intermediate collar located part way
along the central bay. [323/11]

construction is by far the most common roof type to have survived. Throughout its long period of use several design variations have occurred, and it is with these that the following section is concerned.

Roof Trusses

Three methods were used to support the side purlins - simple collars without any timberwork beneath

them, collars strengthened from beneath by queen-studs rising from the tiebeams, and a third method which omitted the collars and instead supported the purlins by means of raking timbers or 'raking struts' rising from the tiebeams (*see* Figure 10.15). In early side-purlin roofs predating *c*1570 it was the queen-stud truss which was most favoured, accounting for about three-quarters of the total examples, whilst the remainder made use of raking-struts or, in the over-designed early roof at Longdown, Hooe shown in Figure 10.16, a combination of types. By the mid 17th century, however, fewer than one surviving newly-built roof in six made use of queen studs, raking struts by this time accounting for about half the side-purlin roofs. The remainder made use of collars only. Raking struts were particularly popular in houses which incorporated open attic areas where they allowed free passage through the trusses without collars to impede headroom. If barns were more fully filled by this date, the more widespread adoption of this form of truss may have been for similar reasons - it would have allowed unthreshed crops to be handled more easily over the tiebeams.

Raking-struts give direct support from the tiebeam to the side purlins, whereas queen-studs support the purlins indirectly via a collar. This collar was in itself capable of carrying the purlins by keeping them a set distance apart, and by *c*1600 collar trusses were occasionally used. Perhaps the earliest known local example is that at Walters Farm, Salehurst shown in Figure 10.17 where such a truss is used in conjunction with two of normal queen-stud type. However, at least four of the six collar-truss roofs typologically dated to the early 1600s may in truth belong to the last two decades of the 16th century.

As the collar truss used less timber and required fewer joints than its rivals, it is perhaps not surprising that once introduced it found rapid favour. To judge from the sample analysed, by the late 17th century a third

Figure 10.18
Double tier of clasped side purlins at Pebsham,
Bexhill (mid 16th century). This is the only example
of its type known within the Rape of Hastings.

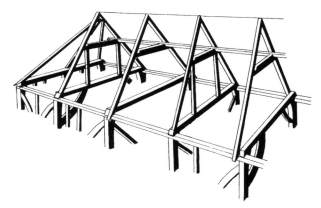

Figure 10.19
Alternating collar and queen-stud trusses at
Marley, Battle, rebuilt c1729.

Figure 10.20
A typical collar-truss roof with its trusses
set between the tiebeams of the main frame.

of all surviving roofs then being constructed were of this type, a proportion which appears to have remained relatively constant throughout the early/mid 18th century. This, however, is not the full story, for by this date the collar truss was also commonly being alternated with queen-studs and raking-struts, especially in the larger barns where, because of the length, carpenters were reluctant to remove all support up from the tiebeam in case the roof spread. Thus, when the nine-bay barn at Marley Farm, Battle shown in Figure 10.19 was rebuilt after being blown down by a tornado in 1729, queen-studs were alternated with collar trusses.[15] Likewise, the central truss in the four-bay barn at Lower Snailham, Guestling incorporates queen-studs, although all others trusses are of collar type.

Collars have always been used to give additional support to the side purlins where thought necessary. For instance, intermediate collars are found set midway between the roof trusses in the late 17th-century barn at Shearfold Farm, Brede, and in the mid 18th-century barn at Little Worge, Brightling. In both instances the bay lengths are excessive. The same feature is found in the over-designed roof of c1540 at Longdown, Hooe shown in Figure 10.16. The most common position for such collars, however, is beneath the head of a hip where they give support to the ends of the side purlins, especially where the hip is located some distance away from the adjacent truss.

In three-bay fully-hipped roofs the number of collars was sometimes reduced by omitting those over the trusses, and replacing them by a single collar set midway along the length of the barn. A typical example of this arrangement is illustrated in Figure 10.20. Similar adjustments are sometimes found in larger barns. Roofs of this general type tend to post-date the middle years of the 17th century.

Principal Rafters

One of the problems posed by the use of clasped-side-purlin construction was the collar/rafter joint. Rafters of deeper section were used at the trusses in order

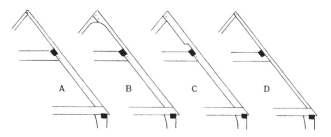

Figure 10.21
Types of principal rafter.
A = Diminished,   B = Diminished with jowl at head,
C = Notched.   D = Common rafters and
principal rafters of equal scantling.

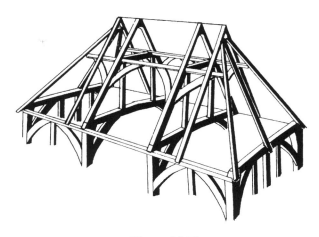

Figure 10.22
A fully-windbraced, fully-hipped roof at
Trulilows, Wartling (c1525)

Figure 10.23
A fully-windbraced, fully-hipped roof at
Parsonage Farm, Hooe (mid 16th century) [279/19A]

to give additional strength, though this resulted in their soffits being set lower than those of the common rafters, thus fouling the line of the purlin. Two alternative methods of overcoming this problem were adopted. In the first (Figure 10.21, A) the principal rafters were reduced or 'diminished' to common-rafter depth above collar level, whilst in the second (Figure 10.21, C) a notch was cut into the rafter in order to accommodate the purlin, the notch being longer than the depth of the purlin in order that the latter could be easily slotted into position during construction. Which method was chosen depended solely upon the carpenter's preference, there apparently being no geographical trends within the study area.

Initially it was the diminished rafter which was most common, and in six early examples a jowl was incorporated at the apex (as illustrated in Figure 10.21, B). This latter feature has also been noted in a few dwellings. By the late 16th/early 17th centuries the number of barns being constructed with either diminished or notched principal rafters were about equal, though during the early 17th century the need for heavy scantling principal rafters was increasingly doubted and roofs with their common rafters and principal rafters of equal depth were developed (Figure 10.21, D). This system was very quickly adopted as the normal method of construction. The new style did not entirely replace the old, but does appear to have been used in about two-thirds of all barn roofs of clasped-side-purlin type constructed from the mid 17th century onwards. A few carpenters struck a compromise, using principal rafters of slightly greater depth than the commons, accommodating the purlins in a shallow, accurately-cut notch.

The Use of Windbracing

The purpose of windbracing is to prevent the roof from overturning or 'racking', either partially or completely, in high wind. The same is achieved by the triangulating effect of a hip or, to a lesser degree, a half-hip, and thus in theory windbracing is unnecessary in a fully-hipped roof. It is therefore at first sight surprising that six of the fully-hipped roofs of pre c1570 are fully windbraced (*see* Figures 10.22 and 10.23) whilst the remainder only omit one or two braces. It seems probable that this was the result of the transplantation of a roof type from an area where gables predominate, introducing hipped terminals, but otherwise retaining all constructional details. Bearing the above in mind, it is clear that in discussing the use of windbracing it is necessary to consider not only date, but also the type of terminal adopted.

That the use of windbracing within the study area declined over time is beyond doubt. Roofs which lack any form of bracing are present by the late 16th century and had become the norm by the mid 17th century. It is likely that traditional windbracing had been entirely abandoned in side-purlin construction by c1700, though the surviving sample is too small to prove this point.

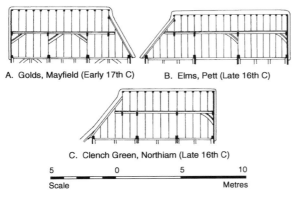

A. Golds, Mayfield (Early 17th C)   B. Elms, Pett (Late 16th C)

C. Clench Green, Northiam (Late 16th C)

Scale   Metres

Figure 10.24
Partial windbracing in barns having a
combination of hipped and gabled terminals.

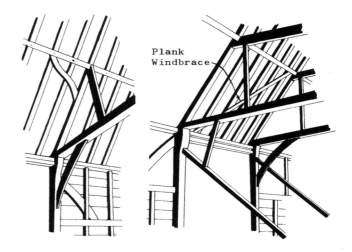

Plank Windbrace

Figure 10.25 (above left)
Ogee windbrace at Wick Farm, Udimore
(early 17th century)

Figure 10.26 (above right)
Plank windbracing, Merriments, Salehurst
(early 18th century, but before 1728)

As would be expected, there was a greater readiness to omit first some, and then all windbracing from fully-hipped roofs than from those incorporating other types of terminals. It was in roofs without any hipped ends that the braces lingered longest, being retained in varying degrees in the majority of such roofs dating from the mid 17th century.

Of the thirteen 16th- and early 17th-century barns with roofs which incorporate a hip opposed by a gable, only one, a 17th-century building, lacks windbracing, whilst five are fully braced and two virtually so. The remaining five show very clearly that the carpenters were aware that, if the roof did move, it would be away from the hip. In three cases the arrangement of the braces is identical, with full bracing to the central bay and gable (Figure 10.24, A), thus giving one pair of braces triangulating in the already strong direction and two in the direction in which the roof was most likely to move. Windbraces are strong in compression, but, being merely notched over the back of the purlins, have no tensile strength. At Elms Farm, Pett, the pair of braces triangulating in the 'strong' direction (in which the roof is unlikely to move) are omitted altogether, thus leaving two pairs strengthening the weak direction (*see* Figure 10.24, B), whilst at Clench Green, Northiam one pair only, against the gable, is present (*see* Figure 10.24, C). Likewise, in those barns which incorporate a hip and half hip and possess intermittent windbracing, all the braces in the 'weak' direction are present.

In preventing the overturning of a roof the windbrace undertook the same task as the headbrace of a crownpost. In crownpost construction, although straight footbraces seem to have been relatively common, this appears to be less true with headbracing (*see* above) and the same is the case with early windbracing. For example, in only six of the 25 barns typologically dated to the 16th century is the windbracing straight. This was not to be the case for very long, however. Straight bracing became increasingly popular during the early 17th century, whilst no examples are known of curved windbracing after *c*1630. Of the curved braces, those at Wick Farm, Udimore, are of ogee type (*see* Figure 10.25), whilst convex curves are also occasionally encountered. Most, however, are concave.

Mention should be made of a crude alternative form of windbracing which was occasionally used during the closing years of the 17th century and first half of the 18th century. It comprised long planks nailed to the underside of the rafters and running across the roof at approximately 45 degrees. The earliest dated example is found in a house built in 1673. In all, only three examples are known in barn roofs. Those at Merriments, Salehurst (built prior to 1728) are neatly jointed into the wallplate and reach up to side-purlin level (Figure 10.26).

INTERRUPTED-SIDE-PURLIN ROOFS

The essential feature of this type of roof is that the side purlins of each bay are jointed into the principal rafters, instead of extending the length of the roof in one uninterrupted line, as is the case in clasped-side-purlin construction. There are two basic divisions of the family: those in which the common rafters are laid over the purlin as in continuous-side-purlin roofs (butted-side-purlin construction) and those in which the rafters are interrupted by and jointed into the purlin (butt-purlin construction). The two types are shown in Figure 10.27. The former style is the earlier, being found occasionally

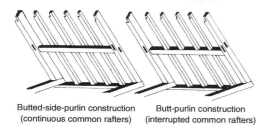

Butted-side-purlin construction
(continuous common rafters)

Butt-purlin construction
(interrupted common rafters)

Figure 10.27
The two types of interrupted-side-purlin roof

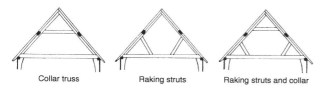

Collar truss

Raking struts

Raking struts and collar

Figure 10.28
Types of truss used in association with roofs
of interrupted-side-purlin type.

Figure 10.29
Butt-purlins
incorporated
into hipped
terminal at
Cralle,
Warbleton,
c1720.

Figure 10.30
Quedley, Ticehurst (mid 18th century)
Staggered butt-purlin roof incorporating windbraces
which interrupt the common rafters. [317/5]

in local houses dating from the closing years of the 15th century, whilst the butt-purlin appears not to make its debut locally until the closing years of the 16th century. In the barns surveyed, butted-side-purlin construction was used in only four instances. All are composite roofs, of which at least three were built by a single carpenter working during the opening years of the 17th century. These four roofs are described under composite construction (*see* below). The earliest examples of barns with butt-purlin roofs belong to the late 17th century, though they never became common during the study period. Only 15 examples are currently known, two of which are over minor extensions. One composite roof incorporates a single bay of butt-purlin construction.

Butt-purlins can either be set in line or staggered, the early examples invariably being set in line. As has already been stated, no early examples survive over barns. Of the 13 roofs possessing more than one bay, all but one late 17th-century example are of staggered type.

Trusses either incorporate small raking struts, collars, or, in two instances, a combination of both (*see* Figure 10.28). Of those surveyed, collar trusses outnumber those incorporating raking struts by almost four to one, no roof with raking struts being known after the early 18th century. The barn of *c*1725 at Hill House, Crowhurst, incorporates a double row of staggered purlins, and possesses very short bay lengths with two roof bays to every bay in the main frame (*see* Figure 12.28). Much of the material is reused and it is likely that in this instance the double sets of purlins and the length of the bays are so constructed in order to allow short lengths of second-hand material to be used. However, short roof bays are a feature which has been noted in 18th-century roofs over local houses. The Hill House roof incorporates return butt purlins to its hips, a feature also found at Cralle Place, Warbleton (*c*1720) and at Hophouse Farm, Catsfield (early 18th century). As shown in Figure 10.29, the hips at Cralle Place incorporate a central principal rafter which interrupts the purlins, which are in turn staggered. Heavy straight strut-like windbraces are found in two of the late roofs. In both instances the windbraces interrupt the common rafters, which are morticed into them (*see* Figure 10.30). One of these, the mid/late 18th-century example rebuilt over the barn at Redpale Farm, Warbleton, also incorporates an interrupted ridgeboard, and is therefore almost certain to have been built quite late in the 18th century.

Figure 10.31
Staggered-butt-purlin roof at Manor Pound,
Wartling (early 18th century). [324/3]

COMPOSITE ROOFS

There are five hybrid roofs within the sample and these are best described in a section of their own. An unusual example of clasped-side-purlin construction has also been included.

Three of the composite examples can be dealt with together: they are all in Warbleton, date from the early 17th century, and are the work of a single carpenter. Two of the barns are twins and are located on farms which from 1598 were in single ownership. In all three examples the main body of the roof construction is of butted-side-purlin type with twin purlins and raking struts to the principal rafters. In contrast, the hipped ends make use of normal side-purlin construction, the single row of purlins being jointed into the last pair of principal rafters and carried beneath the head of the hip by means of a collar (Figure 10.32). At Woodlands Barn one terminal was initially gabled, though for some reason it was converted to a hip sometime during the 17th century. It may be that this adjustment was made before erection, during fabrication of the frame, for the walls of the building were initially intended to be partially daub infilled, though this was varied to full weatherboarding before all the stave holes were fully cut.

A fourth roof, over an extension at Holmshurst, Burwash, is so similar to the Warbleton examples as to suggest that it too was constructed by the same carpenter. The extension is probably contemporary with the house, which is dated 1610. It may be significant that both the owner of Holmshurst and that of the Warbleton Estate

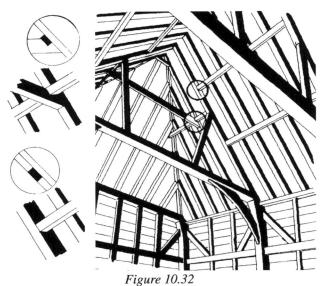

Figure 10.32
Composite roof, Iwood, Warbleton (early 17th century)

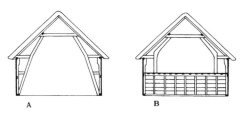

A   B

Figure 10.33
Little Worge, Brightling (mid 18th century).

were heavily involved in the local iron industry.

At Grovelye, also in Warbleton Parish the late 17th-century barn employs a mixture of clasped-side-purlin and butt-purlin construction. In this instance only the central bay of the five-bay roof is of butt-purlin type, the two bays at each end being of clasped-side-purlin construction with reduced principal rafters to the side-purlin trusses. The trusses incorporate raking-struts. It is possible that the design of this roof was in some way influenced by the other three, earlier composite examples within the same parish.

The sixth hybrid is that over the mid 18th-century barn at Little Worge, Brightling. This building, which may post-date 1750, has a standard clasped-side-purlin roof, though it incorporates four trusses which lack tiebeams as such, stub tiebeams being jointed instead into long, almost base-cruck-like 'sling braces' rising from ground level (*see* Figure 10.33, A). The two end bays of the building are floored, the trusses between the open and floored sections being fitted with a crossbeam. In these trusses too the tiebeams are trimmed by cranked timbers, in this instance rising from the crossbeam (*see* Figure 10.33, B). The building is a late hybrid and should be treated as an isolated example.

11 BARNS: SELECTED EXAMPLES. THE MEDIEVAL PERIOD

BATSFORD, WARBLETON. (NGR TQ 6305 1609)
[ESRO HBR 1/415]

Prior to *c*1670 Batsford was alternatively known as 'Reades'. The first reference to it so far identified was in 1640 when it formed part of the demesne lands of the manor of Warbleton. It then had 70 acres of land associated with it.[1] The barn is a four-bay 15th-century structure measuring 12.80 metres x 6.85 metres (41'11" x 22'5"). Originally it lacked outshuts and was fully open internally, having two crop storage bays on the west side of the midstrey and one on the east. Because of the excessive height of the frame the tall doors do not reach to wallplate level. Instead there is a dropped head, the soffit of which incorporates a pendant which may have acted as a door stop. The barn is heavily framed and very well finished. Its walls were originally daub infilled throughout with footbracing at the upper level and

headbracing below. All braces were exposed to view externally. Intermediate posts are incorporated within the side walls of the eastern bay, as well as in the end walls. All open trusses have short arch braces. Although the roof has been rebuilt to a more shallow pitch, the rafters have been reused and there is sufficient surviving detail to make an accurate reconstruction, including an assessment of the original pitch. All three crownposts incorporated two-way footbracing to the tiebeam. Both

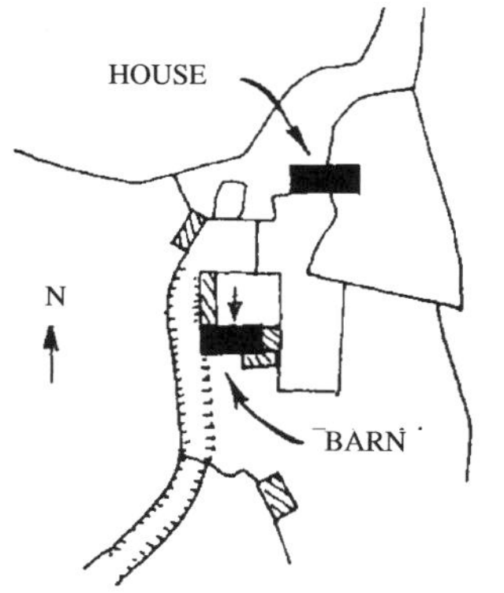

Figure 11.1
Plan of the farmstead as in 1838.

Figure 11.2
Exterior of Batsford from the south. [275/15]

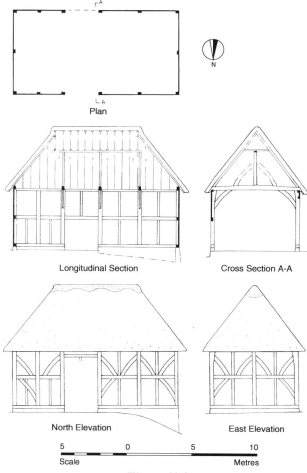

Plan

Longitudinal Section

Cross Section A-A

North Elevation

East Elevation

Scale — Metres

Figure 11.3
Reconstruction drawings of Batsford as built.

93

Figure 11.4
Detail of wall framing in north wall of
western bay. [466/27]

terminals were hipped.

It was probably in *c*1700 that an end and side lean-to cattle shelter was added. A fixed feeding rack was fitted between the side lean-to and the main body of the barn, and stall divisions were built within the end lean-to. The threshing floor was also rebuilt at about the same period. It reuses an earlier central-girder floor raised off the ground on brick-and-stone piers. Measuring 190 mm x 125 mm, the joists are heavy, as are the 225 mm x 38 mm boards which make up the threshing floor. The boards are individually pegged to the joists using dowels of 35 mm diameter. It may have been at this period too that the daub infill was replaced by weatherboarding. The roof was rebuilt in the 19th century, at which date a single-storeyed open-fronted shelter shed was added at right angles, projecting north-westwards from the building. The complex was converted into a dwelling in 1991.

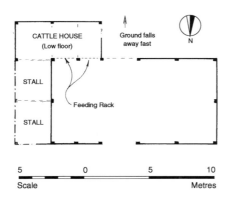

Figure 11.5
Ground plan of Batsford as altered in c1700.

BURGHAM, ETCHINGHAM. NGR TQ 7022 2791
[ESRO HBR 1/1047]

In 1421 Burgham was a farm of 65 acres, and the acreage is consistently described in the documents as either 65 or 70 acres until after 1742. By 1837 a holding called Newick had been merged, increasing the size to 128 acres.[2] The barn consists of three bays, fully open, with clear evidence of an original lean-to cattle shed at the down-hill end. The arrangement of the rails within the end wall suggests that there was originally a feeding rack dividing the outshut from the main body of the barn - certainly the frame between the two lacked infill at its upper level. A full-height doorway (with double plates above) gives access to the barn from the present farm track, whilst the half-height doorway within the rear wall leads into a field. A particular feature of this barn is its

Figure 11.6
Exterior of Burgham viewed from the east.
[487/4]

Figure 11.7
(Right)
Burgham. Detail
of crownpost roof.
The footbraces
shown in
Figure 11.8 have
been removed
[487/8]

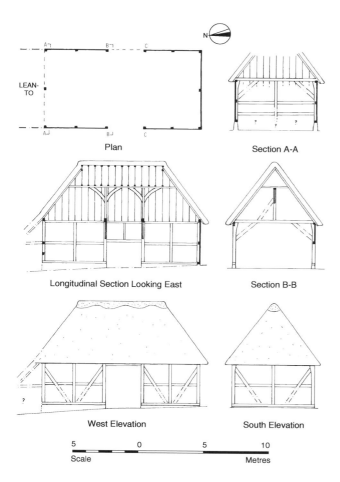

Plan

Section A-A

Longitudinal Section Looking East

Section B-B

West Elevation

South Elevation

Scale
5   0   5   10
Metres

Figure 11.8
Reconstruction drawings of Burgham as built.

long externally-exposed straight braces, which are housed past the side girts. Braces of this type have been recorded in only one other local barn, - Roadend, Beckley - which example appears to be of much later date. The arrangement of single alternating footbraces to the crownposts is typical of the region.

At some subsequent, but uncertain date a southern end lean-to outshut was added and a slatted feeding rack (now partially removed) was inserted into the original southern wall of the barn. The present southern lean-to is a rebuild dating from the late 18th or 19th century: its tiebeams are set higher than those of its predecessor. Other alterations include replacement of the daub infill within the external walls by weatherboarding supported by inserted studs and struts, and the conversion of the rear doorway from half-height to full-height type. Planning permission for conversion into a dwelling was granted in the late 1980s, but it is not known whether this has been implemented.

GREAT BUCKHURST, WESTFIELD
NGR TQ 7940 1590 *[ESRO HBR 1/1421]*

Nothing is currently known about the early history of the farm upon which this very idiosyncratic non-standard five-bay medieval barn is located. At 15.60 metres (51'3") long, it is a good size building, but at only 4.90 metres (16'1") wide overall its main posts it

Figure 11.10
Front (south) elevation of Great Buckhurst. [816/22]

Figure 11.11
Interior of Great Buckhurst looking east. [816/14]

95

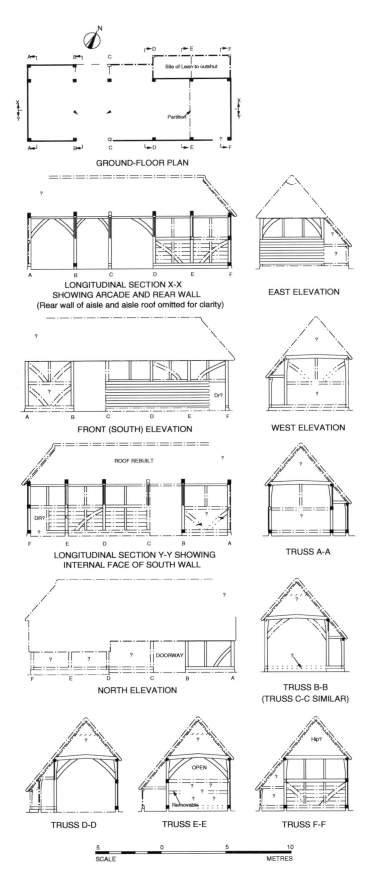

GROUND-FLOOR PLAN

LONGITUDINAL SECTION X-X
SHOWING ARCADE AND REAR WALL
(Rear wall of aisle and aisle roof omitted for clarity)

EAST ELEVATION

FRONT (SOUTH) ELEVATION

WEST ELEVATION

LONGITUDINAL SECTION Y-Y SHOWING
INTERNAL FACE OF SOUTH WALL

TRUSS A-A

NORTH ELEVATION

TRUSS B-B
(TRUSS C-C SIMILAR)

TRUSS D-D   TRUSS E-E   TRUSS F-F

SCALE   METRES

Figure 11.12 (Left)
Reconstruction drawings of Great Buckhurst
as first built.

Figure 11.13
Great Buckhurst showing surviving part
of rear aisle. [816/16]

is surprisingly narrow, especially bearing in mind its height – 3.95 metres (12'11") from underside of soleplate to top of wallplate. Admittedly within the three western bays the width was increased by the inclusion of a narrow 1.15 metre (3'10") rear aisle.

What is surprising is that the aisle was restricted in its length to the three western bays of the building only, even though the crop-storage area originally extended a full bay further eastwards. This is despite the fact that the bay sizes suggest that – like the aisle – the crop storage area should have terminated at truss D-D, for although bay C-D is similar in length to bay A-B, bay D-E to its east is half a metre shorter and is equal in length to the formerly partitioned-off easternmost bay. Usually adjacent crop storage bays are of identical length. Yet the structural evidence clearly indicates that truss D-D was of fully-open type, and that it was the truss to the east (*ie* E-E) which was originally closed by some form of ground-floor partition. Thus, in its original form the barn comprised an aisled single-bay crop storage area to the west of the midstrey and a pair of unequal crop storage bays to the east – one aisled and the other not.

The easternmost bay (E-F) was divided from the remainder of the building on the ground floor, but not above. There is some evidence to suggest two means of access to this area, one from the main body of the barn and a second opening in the front wall. Whereas the three western bays were aisled along their rear, the two eastern bays had a rear lean-to outshut. The peg holes for this outshut's tiebeams are set at a considerably lower level than those in the rear aisle, indicating that the outshut was wider than the aisle. Even so, it was not large: from the location of the peg holes its width can be estimated at *c*1.80 metres (*c*5'11"). The original use of the outshut is uncertain, though either during the 17th or 18th century a feeding rack was inserted into the wall between it and the main body of the barn, indicating that by then it was in use as a cattle house. This could have been its original function.

Generally the timbers of the main frame are neatly finished and are of average scantling for the period. Although the main frame is of standard construction for the area, as with the layout the pattern of bracing chosen to triangulate the walls is idiosyncratic. Usually the pattern adopted is very predictable, but not so here. For instance, the upper level of the eastern end wall uses headbracing with two studs, whereas the western end wall was footbraced at this level and incorporated only one stud (or perhaps an intermediate post). Furthermore, at its lower level the eastern end wall is footbraced, with the long braces housed past the wall studs, but there are no mortices in the principal posts for any form of low-level bracing within the western end wall, unless braces flanked the central stud/intermediate post. Although the western wall does not appear to incorporate low-level bracing, there is ample evidence in the form of mortices for low-level footbracing elsewhere within the building.

Stave holes in the undersides of the wallplates and tiebeams indicate that all walls above side-girt and end-girt level were originally daub infilled, with the braces exposed externally and masked by daub internally. In contrast, the rear wall of the two eastern bays, the eastern end wall, and the eastern three bays of the south elevation (beyond the wagon way) were always intended to be weatherboarded below side-girt and end-girt level. This combination of walls weatherboarded at their vulnerable low level and daub infilled above is not unusual. However, in this instance stave holes indicate that the rear and eastern end wall of the surviving section of rear aisle was also daub infilled, rather than weatherboarded. Annoyingly, the side girt and end girt within the main walls of this bay have been replaced, removing any evidence of stave holes. Therefore, it is not known how the lower parts of the south wall and the western end wall of this western bay were clad.

The use of daub infill within the rear aisle makes it likely that these lower levels were likewise daub infilled, and some evidence in support of this is to be found in the fact that the side girt within the south wall of this bay is set higher than in the eastern bays.

The roof has been entirely reconstructed reusing some material from the original. These rafters are from a medieval-style roof of paired-rafter-and-collar type, with the collars halved onto the rafters. One rafter has a second halving for the high-set collar of a former hipped end. Some of the rafters show rope-stain evidence for a former thatched covering. There are no indications of peg holes in the side faces of the cambered tiebeams for crownposts.

At the time of writing Great Buckhurst was in the process of being converted into a dwelling.

GREAT DIXTER, NORTHIAM. NGR TQ 8196 2516
[ESRO HBR 1/440]

This is the largest known surviving medieval barn within the study area. It is built upon the demesne lands of the manor, just beyond the high-end crosswing of the impressive mansion built, almost certainly, by Sir Thomas de Etchingham during the 1460s or 1470s. Sir Thomas was at that time the most extensive land owner within the study area and he used Great Dixter as an occasional home, his principal houses being at nearby Etchingham and Udimore. After his death in 1479 the estates were split between his two daughters, Dixter being one of the properties left to his daughter Margaret, wife of Sir John Elrington.[3]

The barn is of seven bays and measures 26.85 metres x 7.80 metres (88'1" x 25'7") excluding a now destroyed down-hill end lean-to cattle outshut. The eastern bay may once have incorporated a first floor. The

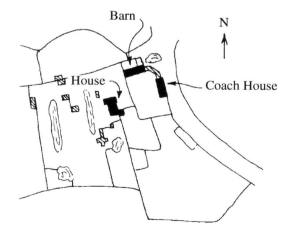

Figure 11.14
Plan showing the house and farmstead in the 1870s.

Figure 11.15
North elevation of Great Dixter in 1979. [281/11]

Figure 11.16
Great Dixter. Round-ended mortices in the soffit of the girding beam in the western end wall indicating the position of a former fixed feeding rack. [508/16]

Figure 11.17
Great Dixter. Notches cut into the northern principal post of truss G-G for removable rail fencing. [281/21]

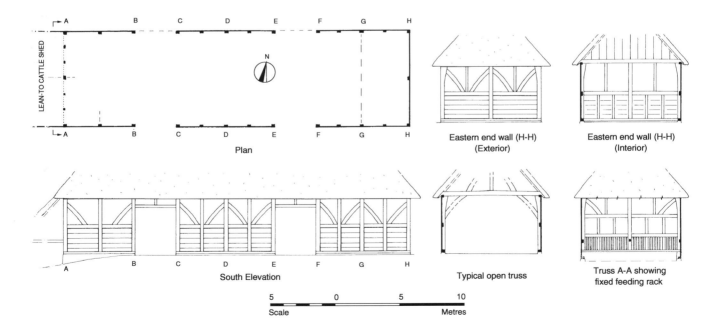

Figure 11.18
Reconstruction drawings of Great Dixter as first built.

Figure 11.19
Great Dixter. Northern wall of bays F-G and G-H.
Some of the studs at both levels have been
added in. Note the two mortices in the central
principal post for a crossbeam with arch-bracing
above. The notches shown in Figure 11.17
are just visible lower down in this post. [281/13]

Figure 11.20
Great Dixter. Eastern end wall. By comparing
this view with the same wall as shown in
Figure 11.18 it will be obvious which studs were
added in when the building had its original
low-level boarding and high-level daub replaced
by weatherboarding. [281/12]

barn has two midstreys, each served by a tall doorway facing south (towards the front yard of the mansion) with half-height doors within the opposite elevation. Mortices are cut into some of the main posts, indicating that areas within the barn were once divided off with rails to form pens, though the date of these is not known (for details *see* Figures 6.25 and 11.17). The evidence for the former end cattle outshut was only recognized in 1990, despite the inclusion of mortices for a contemporary slatted feeding rack incorporated into the western end wall of the main frame. The distinctive closely spaced round-ended mortices which supported the slats are shown in Figure 11.16. This evidence represents the earliest confirmed use of a fitted feeding rack locally.

All wall framing is typical of the period, with intermediate posts to each bay. At the lower level the walls were originally infilled with boards fitted into neatly-formed grooves cut into the principal posts and intermediate posts and supported by intermediate studs. Daub formerly infilled the upper part of the frame and a few areas of this still survive *in situ*. Externally-exposed footbraces stiffen the frame at this level. The easternmost truss appears to have incorporated a crossbeam with footbracing above (*see* Figure 11.19). Otherwise all internal trusses were arch braced. The roof has been entirely rebuilt, though mortices indicate crownpost construction with two-way footbraces to each crownpost. The terminals were hipped.

The building is now fully weatherboarded and has been for some considerable time. Some areas of the wall framing have had new studs and struts inserted. The wagon doors have been adjusted so that the full-height doors now face away from the house. At the western end (on the site of the medieval cattle outshut) has been

added a mid 19th-century brick-built oasthouse, the cooling floor of which is located within the western bays of the barn. At the opposite end a cart shed links the building to a coach house of *c*1700. The present roof incorporates late kingpost trusses. The building currently remains in agricultural use.

KINGSBANK BECKLEY. NGR TQ 8543 2345
[ESRO HBR 1/536]

The name 'Kingsbank' is derived from the King family who were the owner occupiers in the 19th century. Prior to then it was called Great Harmers, and in the early 16th century it was known as Bixley. It appears

Figure 11.21
Kingsbank, Beckley. House and barn viewed
from north in 1979. Note the oasthouse in the
background, to the left of the barn. [293/14]

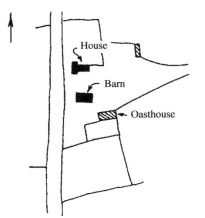

Figure 11.22

Kingsbank. Plan showing the house and farmstead in c1840.

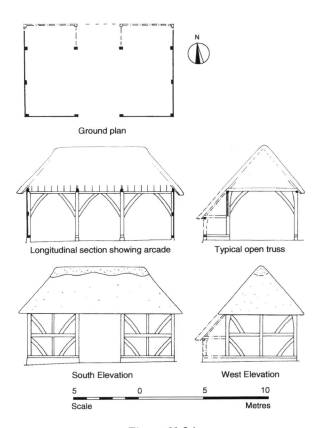

Ground plan

Longitudinal section showing arcade

Typical open truss

South Elevation

West Elevation

Figure 11.24
Kingsbank. Reconstruction drawings of the building as first built.

Figure 11.23
Kingsbank. Two-tier footbracing within formerly daub-infilled external walls. [318/10A]

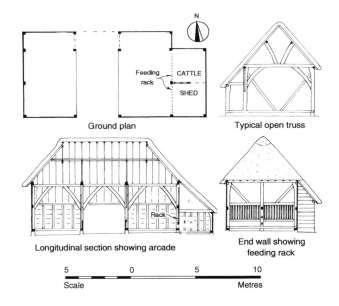

Ground plan

Typical open truss

Longitudinal section showing arcade

End wall showing feeding rack

Figure 11.25
Kingsbank. Reconstruction drawings showing the building's appearance after alterations of c1700.

never to have been a large farm - in 1538 it was described as 32 acres of land and wood: this was subsequently increased to 36 acres. In 1839 25¾ acres of that total was plainland: the remainder was woodland.[4]

Given the historical background, it is perhaps not surprising that this is a relatively small three-bay barn. It incorporates a rear aisle and has overall dimensions of 11.55 metres x c6.85 metres (37'10" x c22'6"). Single-bay crop storage areas flank the midstrey. Originally the walls were daub infilled throughout, with externally

Figure 11.26
Kingsbank. Interior looking east showing the
alterations carried out in c1700. [318/11A]

BARN AT MILL COTTAGE FARM, SALEHURST.
NGR TQ 7421 2570 *[ESRO HBR 1/82 - Revised]*

The present name of the farm relates to a windmill which used to stand on the property. Its earlier name is recorded in 1543 as 'Springets, Garswynes and Conyngarde' suggesting that it represented an engrossment of three manorial holdings. It then amounted to 80 acres - a not inconsiderable farm at that date. By 1570 a further holding had been merged, giving 98 acres in total. The cottage, immediately to the east of the barn, represents the attached kitchen of a once much larger medieval house.[5]

By Wealden standards this is a relatively large barn of five bays. Although the partitions have been removed, originally the bays at either end of the building were fully divided off from the central area by daub partitions and were fully floored. In addition to its first floor, the eastern bay also had an attic floor and may have served as domestic accommodation. It was entered by a doorway in the end wall, facing towards the house.

Figure 11.27
Barn at Mill Cottage Farm, Salehurst.
Exterior from south during conversion
into a dwelling in 1991. [529/11A]

Figure 11.28
Barn at Mill Cottage Farm, Salehurst.
General view of interior looking north west. [57/22A]

exposed footbracing at both the lower and upper levels. The arcade and open trusses are fully arch braced, the braces being long and relatively steeply set.

Around 1700 the roof was totally rebuilt reusing some of the rafters from the original paired-rafter-and-collar roof. At the same period the aisle was totally reconstructed and a lean-to cattle shed (with stall division) was added onto the eastern end. The medieval eastern wall was modified to incorporate a fixed feeding rack nailed into position. All daub infill within the medieval part was removed and replaced by weatherboarding supported by added-in studs. Raking shores were inserted into the open trusses. The new roof is of clasped-side-purlin design with curved struts supporting the purlins off the tiebeams All rafters are of equal scantling. There are high-set collars at the apex of the hips.

Kingsbank was one of the barns severely damaged during the October 1987 storm. It has since been repaired and is in use as a general purpose store.

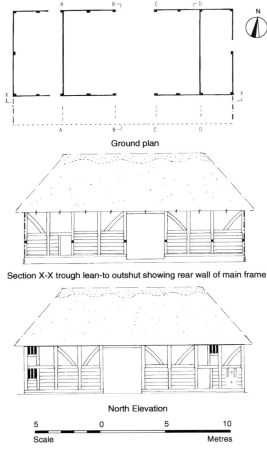

Figure 11.29
Barn at Mill Cottage Farm, Salehurst.
Reconstruction drawings of the barn as
first built. (See also Figures 11.30 and 11.31)

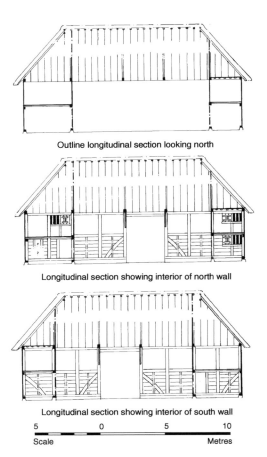

Figure 11.30
Barn at Mill Cottage Farm, Salehurst.
Reconstruction drawings of the barn as
first built. (See also Figures 11.29 and 11.31)

In contrast, the western end bay was served by two opposed doors, that in the north elevation being wide. Both end bays had windows fitted with sliding shutters. Along the southern wall, on the downhill side of the barn, extended a lean-to cattle outshut, but whether this was enclosed or open to a yard is not known. What is certain is that the lean-to was fully partitioned from the main body of the barn. Both openings leading to the midstrey are of full height, though the height of the southern opening may have been restricted further south, depending upon whether the former southern lean-to extended across the midstrey.

The building contains many interesting constructional details. The intermediate posts dividing each bay should be noted, as should the neatly formed rebates cut into the external leading edges of the principal posts and intermediate posts for half-height weatherboarding. The boards were strengthened by widely spaced, relatively slender studs fitted into long, round-ended mortices somewhat similar to the mortices

used locally for staves. The mortices are most easily recognized within the eastern wall, where during the initial survey carried out in 1972 they were erroneously assumed to indicate daub infill. This is now known not to have been the case. In total the positions of five unglazed windows can be recognized. Four have grooves for sliding shutters, whereas that in the east wall at first-floor level does not. Perhaps here the shutter groove was omitted in error, for a row of five nail holes in the soffit of the tiebeam shows where an applied runner was fitted, whilst a stain on the jamb and extra peg holes in the cill and jamb mark where the lower runner supporting the shutter was fixed. The barn's roof was entirely rebuilt in the mid 20th century.

Several alterations made prior to *c*1750 are recognizable, though these have proved impossible to either sequence or closely date. The most significant was the addition of a lean-to cattle house against the western two bays of the northern wall, and the insertion of an associated feeding rack into the old external wall. In addition, the eastern open storage bay had an upper floor inserted into it. The floor was located relatively low in the frame and was of central-girder construction. Its relatively early date of insertion is indicated by the fact that the eastern end bay was still separately divided off and floored at this date. A further historical alteration involved converting the southern wagon door to half-height type by the insertion of a new rail with notched-in studs above. This insertion was later removed. It is possible that the medieval southern lean-to was destroyed when the half-height door was formed, for although not heavily weathered, there is, none-the-less, some weathering on the southern face of the frame. Having been redundant and semi-derelict for a number of years, the building was converted into a dwelling in 1991.

YEWTREE, NORTHIAM. NGR TQ 8296 2267
[ESRO HBR 1/684]

Nothing is known about the early history of this property. By 1641 it was a farm of 61¾ acres.[6]

Yewtree is a three-bay barn measuring 10.55 metres x 6.05 metres (34'8" x 19'10"), fully open internally. The full-height doorway faces north towards the highway. There is a gentle cross fall to the site, with

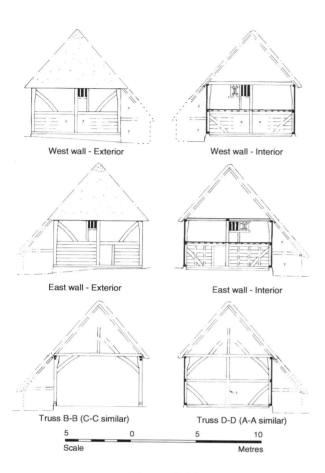

West wall - Exterior

West wall - Interior

East wall - Exterior

East wall - Interior

Truss B-B (C-C similar)

Truss D-D (A-A similar)

Figure 11.31
Barn at Mill Cottage Farm, Salehurst.
Reconstruction drawings of the barn as
first built. (See also Figures 11.29 and 11.30)

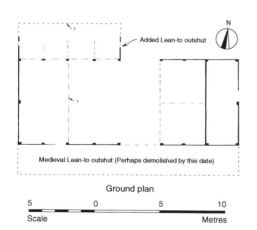

Added Lean-to outshut

Medieval Lean-to outshut (Perhaps demolished by this date)

Ground plan

Figure 11.32
Barn at Mill Cottage Farm, Salehurst.
Reconstruction plan of the building as
it existed in the mid 18th century.

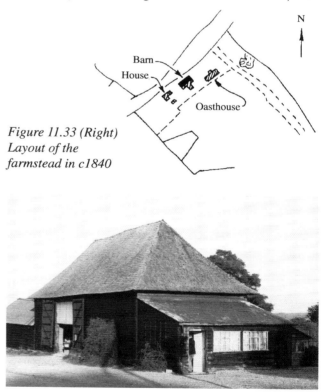

Barn
House
Oasthouse

Figure 11.33 (Right)
Layout of the
farmstead in c1840

Figure 11.34
Exterior of Yewtree, Northiam in 1977. [210/9]

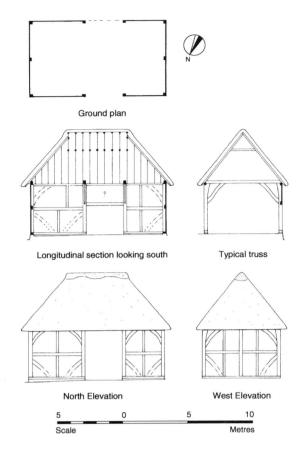

Ground plan

Longitudinal section looking south

Typical truss

North Elevation

West Elevation

5   0   5   10
Scale   Metres

Figure 11.35
Yewtree, Northiam. Reconstruction drawings
of the barn as first built.

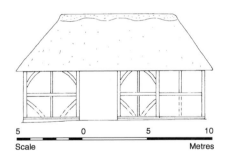

5   0   5   10
Scale   Metres

Figure 11.36
Yewtree, Northiam. North elevation as
extended in the 16th century.

a slight drop outside the rear doorway. There are no indications to suggest original lean-to outshuts. All walls were originally daub infilled (evidenced by stave holes) with headbracing at the upper level and footbracing below. All braces were exposed externally. Note from the reconstruction drawings the variation in the amount

of bracing between the front (north) elevation and the rear (south) elevation - the latter are shown in dotted outline in the long section. The arch braces in the two open trusses have a noticeable uneven curvature. Fully hipped, the roof is of paired-rafter-and-collar construction absent of crownposts (*see* Figure 11.37). Rope stains indicate a former thatched covering: it is now shingled.

In the mid 16th century a bay was added in order to increase the storage capacity, giving a revised overall length of 14.20 metres (46'8"). The extension was achieved by moving the western wall *in-toto* to its new location and inserting a completely new truss on the line of the old western wall. The truss lacks braces. Although daub infilled, the walls of the new bay likewise lack bracing. The northern wallplate of the extension has been reused from elsewhere. The roof construction over the extension is identical to that of the original section, though this may not reflect an early date. The high-set collar which carried the head of the original western hip was retained *in situ*, but the hip and jack rafters from this were reused within the extension.

Although now replaced by later extensions, evidently a southern lean-to outshut was added to the building. From the style of the studs and struts inserted into the original frame, it would appear that the early daub infill was retained until the 19th century, when it was replaced by weatherboarding.

The building served for a number of years as an annex to a tearooms, but is now converted into a dwelling.

12 BARNS: SELECTED EXAMPLES. THE POST-MEDIEVAL PERIOD

BINES, TICEHURST. NGR TQ 6713 2793.
[ESRO HBR 1/50]

In 1618 Bines was described as a house, barn, close, orchard, garden and 33¾ acres (*see* page 27). The boundaries of the farm remained the same until after 1840.[1] Subsequent to 1840 the house was demolished, leaving the barn isolated, and in the 1970s the same fate befell the barn. This was a three-bay late 16th-century barn which measured 10.25 metres x 5.90 metres (33'8" x 19'4"). The bay on the west of the midstrey was the longer of the two end bays and was of open crop storage type, whereas the smaller eastern bay was originally floored.

Although the lower half of the northern (rear) wall was boarded from the outset, all other walls were initially daub infilled, with the wall bracing inset so as to be masked from view externally. In this instance the section

Figure 12.2
Interior of Bines looking southeast towards former floored bay. The shores in the open truss are added. [49/14]

Figure 12.3
Wall framing in southeast corner of Bines showing intact daub at upper level, together with inset braces. [49/12]

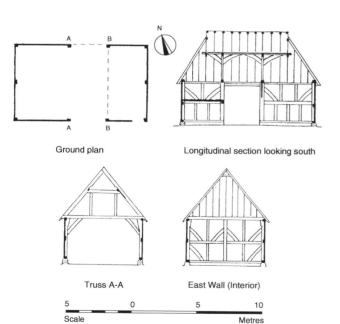

Ground plan   Longitudinal section looking south

Truss A-A   East Wall (Interior)

Scale   5   0   5   10   Metres

Figure 12.1
Reconstruction drawings of Bines.

of walling above the half-height northern doorway was also braced. Truss A-A, dividing the midstrey from the crop storage area, incorporated straight arch braces, whereas the upper part of truss B-B, between the midstrey and lofted area, lacked braces. As the crossbeam was removed in antiquity, it is not known

Figure 12.4
Bines, Ticehurst. Detail of fully windbraced
and fully hipped clasped-side-purlin roof. [49/13]

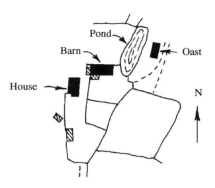

Figure 12.5
Bowmans, Burwash. Plan of the
farmstead as in 1839.

whether the area beneath it was open to the midstrey or partitioned off from it.

Despite being fully hipped, the clasped-side-purlin roof incorporated a full complement of curved windbraces. The trusses had collars, queen studs, and notched principal rafters. Rope stains on the rafters indicated a former thatched covering.

It was probably in the 17th century that the daub panels within the lower parts of the south, east and west walls were removed and replaced by weatherboarding supported upon new, added-in studs. In addition, a doorway was cut through the eastern end of the south wall so as to give independent access to the floored end. At a subsequent date the upper floor was removed, shores were added into truss B-B, and the daub panels within the upper parts of the walls were clad with weatherboarding to match that at the lower levels. However, unlike at the lower levels, the daub was not removed and at the time of survey in 1971 much of it still survived behind the weatherboarding. For an external photograph of the building *see* Figure 10.4.

BOWMANS, BURWASH. (NGR TQ 6810 2291)
[ESRO HBR1/768]

The 1839 tithe map and award give the size of this farm as 160½ acres, of which 26¼ acres was woodland.[2] However, this acreage is known to include what had been a house and 35 acres of land called Kymland (merged into Bowmans in 1680) and another part of Kymland amounting to 30 acres, the acquisition date of which is unknown. John Cony was in possession in 1711, in which year Bowmans was rated at £20 and Kymland at £9.[3] Bowmans was held of the manor of Burwash, but the manorial records are of little help in reconstructing the original acreage - in 1673 the tenement was described

Figure 12.6
Bowmans, Burwash. Exterior from south
showing the front of the building. [384/6A]

as a messuage and lands (fields named) being 11 acres, part of a tenement called Bowmans held at a quitrent of 6/-; in 1726 it was referred to as a messuage and 30 acres, quitrent 6/-, whilst in 1840 it was a messuage and 50 acres held at the same quitrent.[4] All these totals appear to fall short of the true size, though they may exclude woodland.

As the tithe map shows, the house, barn, oasthouse and two other buildings formed a loose cluster with the house and barn built at right angles to one another. Both date from the middle years of the 16th century. The barn is of four bays and measures 12.55 metres x 6.35 metres (41'2" x 20'10"). Originally the layout comprised an open storage bay on either side of the midstrey with a floored bay to the west, fully partitioned from the remainder of the building. The two storage bays are of noticeably unequal size. The full-height doors face south, towards the house. It is a neatly framed building using heavy timbers. As the reconstruction drawings show, the walls of the floored bay incorporated unglazed

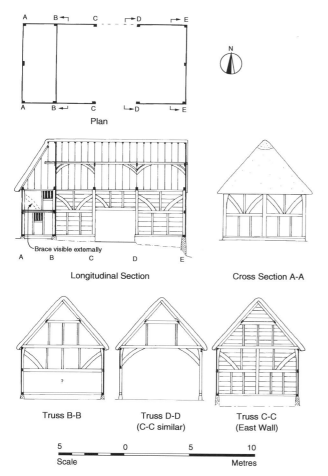

Figure 12.7
Reconstruction drawings of Bowmans,
Burwash, as built.

Figure 12.8
Bowmans, Burwash. Interior looking southwest showing
former floored bay in distance and half-height
wagon doorway on right. [384/4A]

windows and were daub infilled. In contrast, those within the storage areas were originally weatherboarded. Both open trusses have short arch braces: the closed truss was footbraced and stave holes indicate that it was daub infilled. The roof is of clasped-side-purlin construction with notched principal rafters and an almost full complement of relatively short, curved windbraces. All trusses have a collar with queen studs beneath.

It was probably in the 18th century that a lean-to cattle house was constructed to the south of the two western bays. The existing walls were at that date modified to incorporate a fixed slatted feeding rack with angle-bored holes to accommodate removable slanting hurdles. As part of these alterations both the upper floor and the internal partition within the main body of the barn were removed to increase the storage capacity of the building. The eastern gable has been converted into a half hip. As part of a programme of 20th-century repair, all walls are now infilled with plaster with the framing exposed externally.

The barn still survives in an unconverted state, but in 1982 was no longer in agricultural use.

BUSH BARN (FORMERLY NETHER OCKHAM), SALEHURST. NGR TQ 7350 2514.
[ESRO HBR1/479]

Although now isolated, this barn formerly served a farm called Nether Ockham, the house and detached kitchen of which stood close to the northwest of the barn.[5] This was a substantial farm comprising a freehold of the manor of Etchingham called Nether Ockham held at the substantial quitrent of 20/-, and a further freehold called Bugsell otherwise Ponts held of Bodiam Manor, quitrent 12/-. It is shown as amounting to 181¾ acres in an estate map of the 1640s. The property had already been bought into the Iridge Estate by 1597 and continued to form part of that estate in 1654. Therefore the barn, which dates from the early 17th century, was almost certainly built by the estate.[6]

Figure 12.9
Bush Barn, Salehurst. Exterior from southeast.
The second barn formerly stood at right angles
against the end wall in the foreground. [290/31]

Figure 12.10
Bush Barn, Salehurst. Looking towards former floored
bay with restricted-width wagon doorway
on right. The infill framing in the end wall has
been replaced. [290/34]

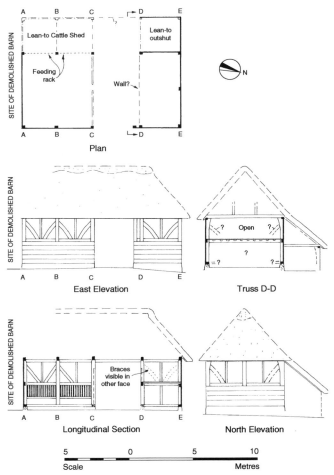

Figure 12.11
Reconstruction drawings of Bush Barn,
Salehurst, as built.

As confirmed by the tithe map, the surviving structure was formerly attached at its southern end to another now destroyed barn set at right angles to it. The surviving building is of four bays and measures 12.40 metres x 6.10 metres (40'8" x 20'1") and always had a 2.80 metre (9'2") lean-to outshut running along its western side. The full-height wagon door leading into the midstrey faces east. When first built, the area to the north incorporated a first floor, whilst that to the south served as a pair of open storage bays. The southern two bays of the lean-to outshut were designed as a cattle house served by a fixed slatted feeding rack between it and the storage area. Therefore, the storage area was probably intended principally to store the fodder crops. Quite probably the main crops were stored and processed within the now lost barn which adjoined the southern wall of the building.

As was once common practice, the external walls were originally weatherboarded at their lower level and daub infilled above. This upper level incorporated a full set of externally exposed curved footbraces, though some have now been replaced. As shown in Figures 12.10 and 12.11, the full-height wagon doorway is restricted in width on its northern side.

Internally the truss to the north of the midstrey originally incorporated a crossbeam (mortice visible in Figure 12.10) and was either footbraced or unbraced above this level: the truss immediately to the south of the midstrey has never incorporated arch bracing, but instead has long down-going shores. The truss crossing the crop storage area was never braced. Later rough studwork now infills the southern end wall but, although apparently footbraced, originally this truss was left open, the wall of the adjacent building having been utilized at this point. This must indicate that the destroyed barn to the south was either of the same date or, more likely, earlier. The wall between the floored bay and the rear

Figure 12.12
Bush Barn, Salehurst. Interior of open crop storage
area showing bracing and intact staves for former
daub infill in upper part of east wall. [290/32]

Figure 12.13
Common Woods, Northiam.
Exterior from southwest. [210/25]

lean-to outshut was daub infilled, but the southern end of this wall was left open at the upper level and incorporated straight, rather than curved footbraces. Below this open section of wall was a fixed slatted feeding rack (removed, but evidenced by the mortices for the slats). The main roof has been entirely rebuilt to a shallow pitch, whilst the rear outshut has been widened and its roof rebuilt flat.

At the time of survey in 1979 the building was redundant and semi-derelict. It was still standing in 1991.

COMMON WOODS, NORTHIAM.
NGR TQ 8210 2284. *[ESRO HBR1/443]*

By 1567 this and other adjacent land formed part of the estate attached to Tufton Place in Northiam, but without knowing the tenancy of the individual blocks of land it would be dangerous to attribute an acreage to this particular farm. At that date four adjacent tenements were held of Robertsbridge Manor and comprised a copyhold house, kitchen, barn, 14 acres of pasture and 7¼ acres of woodland called Nytingales held at a quitrent of 15d; another copyhold house, barn and kitchen with 28 acres of pasture called Gullaches otherwise Motyns held at a quitrent of 5/1d; 3¾ acres of copyhold pasture with 8½ acres of woodland called Munkynland held at 8d; and 17½ acres of copyhold pasture with 42½ acres of woodland called Kinges held at a quitrent of 8d.[7] In the mid/late 17th century the pasture (but not the woodland) upon Munkynland was sold, and by 1700 all the other lands mentioned above had been conveyed to William Duncombe, who was occupying all of them as a single farm. Its size was then about 120 acres, of which approximately half was woodland. Subsequently a further 23 acres were added, bringing the total size by

Figure 12.14
Common Woods, Northiam.
Interior looking south. Note the stave holes
extending part way across the soffit of the
tiebeam in the foreground. [282/5A]

1840 to 142½ acres, of which 60 acres was woodland.[8]

The barn upon the holding dated from the early 17th century and was of four bays. It measured 11.50 metres x 6.25 metres (37'8" x 20'7") and had its full-height entry facing west, away from the farm track. There were two short open storage bays on the up-hill side of the barn, whilst the down hill bay was originally divided axially, the rear half being open to the rest of the building. However, the front half was originally partitioned off to form a ground-floor room and a first-floor chamber, the latter with open eaves and an unglazed window.

All walls were originally infilled with daub throughout (evidenced by stave holes). Footbraces within the side and end walls stiffened the frame, but these braces were inset so as not to be visible from the

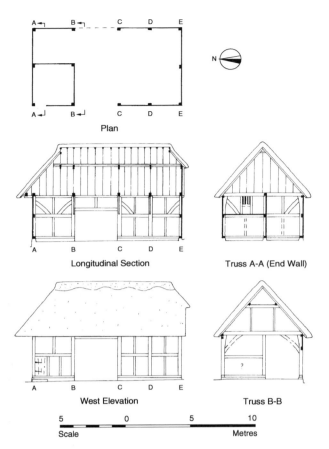

Plan

Longitudinal Section

Truss A-A (End Wall)

West Elevation

Truss B-B

Figure 12.15
Reconstruction drawings of Common Woods,
Northiam, as built.

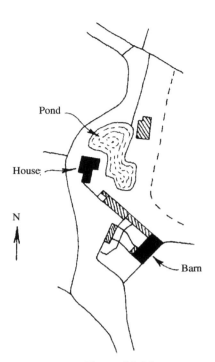

Figure 12.16
Great Bigknowle, Heathfield. Plan of the
farmstead as in c1840.

Figure 12.17
Great Bigknowle, Heathfield. Exterior from
southeast. [382/25]

exterior. All three internal trusses were arch braced, without shores. The side-purlin roof had equal-scantling rafters throughout, and there was no windbracing. All roof trusses had queen studs beneath the collars. The roof terminals were asymmetrical in their design in that the terminal over the partially floored bay was a hip, whilst that over the crop storage area was a half hip: both were supported at the apex by high-set collars. Rope stains indicate a former thatched covering.

Lean-to outshuts were added at both ends of the building during the 18th century. These always had weatherboarded walls. The original daub infill was replaced by weatherboarding at this time and the former thatched roof was tiled. The building was totally destroyed by high winds in the 1980s.

GREAT BIGKNOWLE, HEATHFIELD
NGR TQ 6228 2443. *[ESRO HBR 1/760]*

Great Bigknowle occupies a north facing slope below formerly open land known as Heathfield Down. The history is complex and has yet to be researched in

full. Its lands were held of at least two manors - Burwash (upon which the house and buildings were situated) and Burghurst. In 1673 that part held of Burwash amounted to 26 acres, whilst in 1706 the lands held of Burghurst were described as being 50 acres in extent. The Heathfield tithe award gives the acreage in 1840 as 102a.1r.7p, but whether extra land had been added or whether the balance was held of another manor is unclear.[9]

The late 16th century barn is of four bays, with side and end aisles and a down-hill end lean-to cattle shed. Overall it measures 17.10 metres x 9.60 metres

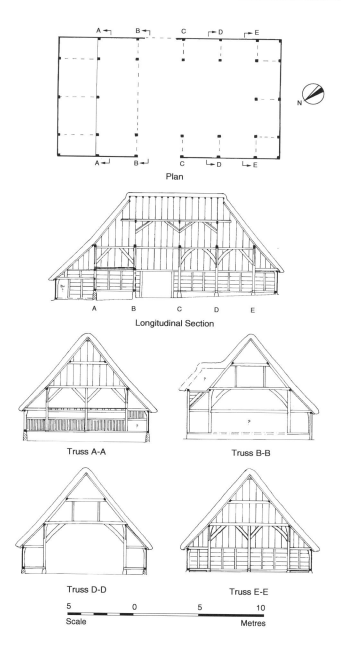

Plan

Longitudinal Section

Truss A-A

Truss B-B

Truss D-D

Truss E-E

Figure 12.18
Reconstruction drawings of Great Bigknowle,
Heathfield, as built.

Figure 12.19
Great Bigknowle, Heathfield.
Interior looking southwest towards return
end aisle. [382/22]

(56'1" x 31'6"). Its midstrey is located off-centre and is entered by a wagon porch in the northwestern wall, facing towards the road. There is a low rear door of restricted width. On the up-hill side of the midstrey are two crop storage bays with an end aisle beyond: on the opposite side is just one bay which was originally floored and may have been divided off from the remainder of the barn on the ground floor. Beyond this is a lean-to cattle house with a fixed feeding rack between it and the floored end (*see Figure 12.18,* A-A). Note the curious high-level section of feeding rack - perhaps designed for a horse - at one end of the wall.

This is an exceptionally well proportioned building with a mixture of curved and straight arch braces to its arcades and braced intermediate posts in the end arcades. The side walls were always weatherboarded. Straight windbraced clasped-side-purlin construction is used for the fully-hipped roof, which was originally thatched. The trusses incorporate queen studs and have principal rafters which are reduced in depth above collar level. Note the low eaves level of the downhill lean-to cattle shed.

The date at which the upper floor was removed is uncertain. Apart from this alteration, the replacement of the thatch by a mixture of corrugated iron and tile, and the destruction of the roof over the wagon porch, in 1982 the barn remained very much as first built. It is now converted into a dwelling.

Figure 12.20
Great Bigknowle, Heathfield. Detail
of arcade. [382/18]

Figure 12.21
Hammerden, Ticehurst. Exterior
from south. [49/20]

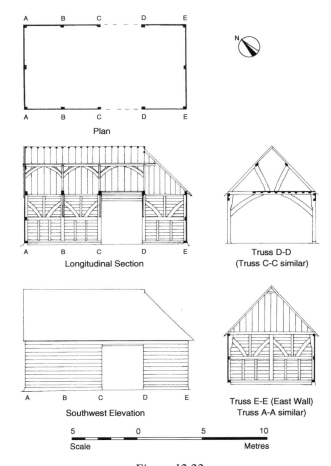

Figure 12.22
Reconstruction drawings of Hammerden,
Ticehurst, as built.

HAMMERDEN, TICEHURST. NGR TQ 6623 2713
[ESRO HBR1/349]

Hammerden formed the demesne lands of the extensive Ticehurst manor of the same name. It was acquired in 1558 by Bernard Randolph, a lawyer who, in 1563, was admitted to the office of Common Sergeant of the City of London. From at least this date until his death in 1583 he must have spent most of his time resident within the city, though he also had a country residence at Wardsbrook, just two miles to the northeast of Hammerden. The Randolphs and their relations, the Apsleys, continued as owners until 1833 when it was purchased into the estate of the Courthopes of Whiligh in Ticehurst.[10] The farm was large, amounting in both 1614 and 1775 to approximate 274 acres, mostly plainland.[11]

A map of 1614 shows a house, the barn, and three other small outbuildings.[12] Already by that date the barn (demolished in the 1980s) had been built. Dating from the middle years of the 16th century, this substantially built four-bay structure measured *c*12.50 metres x *c*6.80 metres (*c*41'0" x *c*22'4"). Internally it was open throughout, having two crop storage bays to the northwest of the midstrey and one to the southeast. Unusually, both wagon doors were of identical height,

Figure 12.23
Hammerden, Ticehurst. Interior looking across midstrey showing mortices for removed high-level floor. Note the retained joist on the right. The rear wagon door on the left has at some date been reduced to half height. In addition, the southeast end wall has been re-infilled using late studwork, the hipped end has been re-framed and the common rafters have been reset, framed against a ridge board. All these alterations appear to be associated with repairs made in the 19th century. [241/16]

Figure 12.24
Hammerden, Ticehurst. Interior looking across early 18th-century cattle house showing the first floor. Note the doorway in the far wall. [241/19]

being nearly the same height as the walls. A lofted area extended across two-thirds the width of the barn above the midstrey. There was no evidence to suggest the former existence of outshuts, and at this period there were no floored ends.

This was an exceptionally well finished building. Its walls were always fully weatherboarded and incorporated a full complement of footbraces within the upper level. All trusses were arch braced, the braces being set high and at a shallow angle. There was a good, fully windbraced clasped-side-purlin roof with curved struts supporting the purlins at the trusses. The principal rafters were of reduced type. There were no obvious indications of the roof having been thatched.

The most curious feature of the barn was its partial floor at tiebeam level above the threshing floor. Most of the joists had been removed, but one still survived next to the wagon door in the southwest wall (*see* Figure 12.23). This proved that the mortices did not relate to a former use of the timbers.

In the early 18th century the building was extended northwest by one bay so as to give a lofted-over cattle house. The extension was timber framed, but used regularly-spaced stud infill, a feature which was also at this date added into the walls of the original part of the building. Central-girder construction was used to support the joists of the first floor, which incorporated a trap door in the southeast corner. A feeding trough

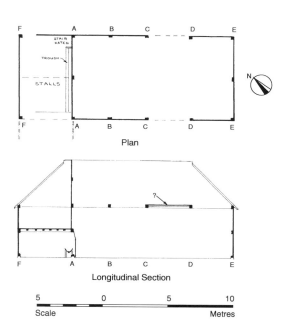

Plan

Longitudinal Section

5	0	5	10
Scale | | | Metres

Figure 12.25
Reconstruction drawings of Hammerden, Ticehurst, as extended in the early 18th century.

survived at the time of survey, but the stall divisions (if they were originally fitted) had been rebuilt. The southwest wall of the extension showed no signs of infill framing at ground-floor level, indicating that the later single-storeyed southwestern range replaced one of earlier date upon the same site. The matching northeastern range was entirely modern.

HILL HOUSE, CROWHURST. NGR TQ 7513 1198
[ESRO HBR1/557]

Originally a copyhold tenement of Crowhurst Manor called Beards, at some as yet uncertain date between 1580 and 1670 this 30 acre farm was increased to 124 acres by the engrossment of other copyhold and freehold farms and lands called Nashes, Bennets, Flecham and Greenstreet. By 1670 the combined holding was in the owner occupation of Richard Alchorne, gentleman. Between 1714 and 1725 his widow conveyed it to Ralph Norton, gentleman, who was already in occupation by 1702.[13] A datestone (with the initials ${}_R{}^N{}_A$) indicates that he made considerable improvements to the house in 1725, including brick encasing the earlier parts.

The five-bay barn at Hill House was probably rebuilt at the same date as the alterations were made to the house - certainly it belongs to the first half of the 18th century. It is one of only two early (*ie* pre 1750) brick-built barns within the study area, the other being Pelsham in Peasmarsh. Designed as a rear-aisled structure measuring 15.30 metres x 8.70 metres (50'3" x 28'7") overall, internally it is of open crop-storage type throughout with two bays on either side of the midstrey. The full-height doors face west, towards the house.

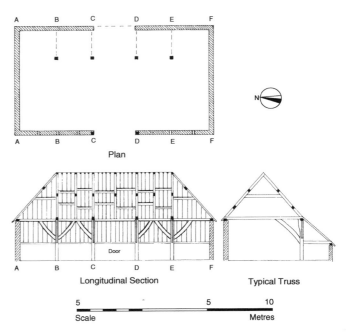

Figure 12.28
Reconstruction drawings of barn at Hill House, Crowhurst, as built.

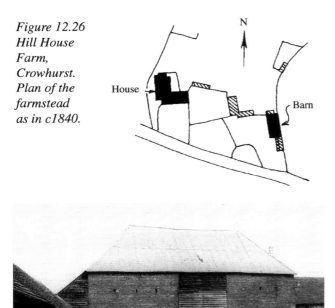

Figure 12.26
Hill House Farm, Crowhurst. Plan of the farmstead as in c1840.

Figure 12.27
Hill House Farm, Crowhurst. Exterior from west. [352/1]

Figure 12.29
Hill House Farm, Crowhurst. Rear arcade viewed from south. [323/22]

Figure 12.30
Hill House, Crowhurst.
Roof viewed from south. [323/21]

All external walls are one-and-a-half bricks thick, laid in English bond. Within the front wall are incorporated narrow ventilation slits. Principal posts are included flanking the wagon doors within this wall. Traditional timber-framing is used for the arcade, and this has long, convex arch braces rising from the arcade posts to the arcade plate and tiebeams. As the reconstruction drawings show, there is a complete lack of bracing to the front section of the trusses, against the brick wall. The roof is of staggered-butt-purlin construction with two tiers of purlins within very short bays - two to each bay of the arcade. Much of the material is reused. The end tiebeams and wallplates are set in level assembly and are linked by dragon ties.

At the time of survey in 1980 much of the rear aisle had been demolished, thereby converting the building into an open-fronted structure. It is now converted into a dwelling.

LEA BANK, WHATLINGTON. NGR TQ 7578 2161
[ESRO HBR1/542]

This was a small copyhold farm called Highpopinghothe, held of Robertsbridge Manor at the high quitrent of 12/-. In 1567 it was described as

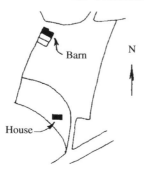

Figure 12.31
Lea Bank,
Whatlington. Plan of
the farmstead
as in c1840.

consisting of 23 acres, being 17 acres of pasture and 6 acres of wood, held by the heirs of Thomas Kempe. No buildings are mentioned at that date. Although the boundaries of the property appear not to have altered, the farm was measured in 1840 as comprising 32¼ acres.[14] Both the house and barn appear to have been built in the late 16th or early 17th century, but whether they were in owner occupation or tenanted at this period is unknown. The barn is of four bays, measures 12.85 metres x 6.30 metres (42'2" x 20'8"), and has two open storage bays to the east of the midstrey and a lofted-over cattle house to the west. The loft above the cattle house was always open to the main body of the barn (*see* Figure 6.7). Full-height doors facing north (away from the house) give access to the barn, with half-height doors to the south.

Despite the small size of the farm, the walls of the barn were designed to be weatherboarded from the outset. They are fitted with a full complement of footbraces at the higher level. The braces are inset so as to pass the internal face of the studs (*see* Plate 12.34). Short arch braces triangulate the trusses of the open storage bays. Curiously, stave holes are cut into the

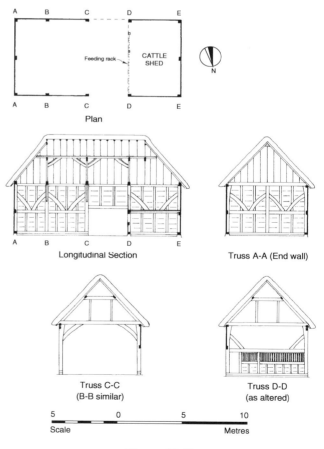

Figure 12.32
Reconstruction drawing of Lea Bank, Whatlington
as altered soon after construction.

*Figure 12.33
Lea Bank, Whatlington.
Exterior from southwest. [320/5]*

*Figure 12.34
Lea Bank, Whatlington.
Detail of wall framing within eastern
bay of north wall showing braces inset so as
to pass against the internal face of the studs
(two studs original, three added later). [320/6]*

soffit of the tiebeam (between the braces) within truss C-C adjacent to the midstrey: their purpose is unknown. Truss D-D retains its crossbeam, beneath which at an early date was inserted an added-in feeding rack. This allowed the animals to be fed from the midstrey. The area above was left open and is footbraced.

Despite both ends being hipped, the clasped-side-purlin roof is windbraced. It has reduced principal

rafters and queen studs to the trusses.

Lean-to outshuts have been added to the south and east of the barn and the thatched roof covering has been replaced by tile. The building was redundant at the time of survey in 1980: it is now converted into a dwelling.

LITTLE HARMERS, BECKLEY.
NGR TQ 8529 2280 *[ESRO HBR1/537]*

Little Harmers, formerly called Harmers, was a copyhold tenement held of the prebendal manor of Brightling at an annual quitrent of 3/-. In the manorial records it is variously described as a messuage and 80 acres, or alternatively a messuage and 40 acres. Significantly, despite the 80 acre description, upon the admission of William Piper, youngest son and heir of George Piper in 1535 the homage presented that there was only 40 acres of land and wood attached to the tenement. The 40 acre description equates relatively well with the entry in the Beckley tithe award of 1842 which describes the farm as comprising a farmhouse, cottage, barn, oasthouse, lodge and 46½ acres, being 26¾ acres of plainland and 19¾ acres of woodland. Likewise, the £8 ratable value given for the property in the land tax in 1711 suggests a holding of about 40 acres, though it should be stressed that the then owner, Mary White, was also assessed £8 for other lands and £5 for woodlands.[15]

It is significant for the context of the barn that during the middle years of the 16th century - around the time when the barn was built - the owner, William Piper, was renting extra lands in order to augment his holding. For instance, in 1542 the homage of the manor presented that another tenant of the manor, Lord Windsor and his son, 'have leased to William Piper for a term of 12 years without licence' a barn and lands (60 acres) called Betts, lands (38 acres) called Goseleys, lands (20 acres) called Sweets, and lands (15 acres) called Fermys.[16] Thus, Piper was leasing at least 133 acres in addition to that which he owned. The entry illustrates well the danger of assessing the size of an agricultural unit based solely upon details of ownership.

Built during the middle years of the 16th century, the four-bay barn at Little Harmers was semi-derelict when surveyed

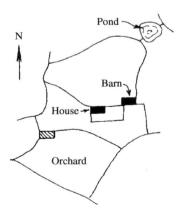

*Figure 12.35
Little Harmers, Beckley.
Plan of the farmstead
as in c1840.*

Figure 12.36
Little Harmers, Beckley.
Exterior from south. [318/16A]

Figure 12.37
Little Harmers, Beckley.
Detail of north wall, eastern bays. [318/18A]

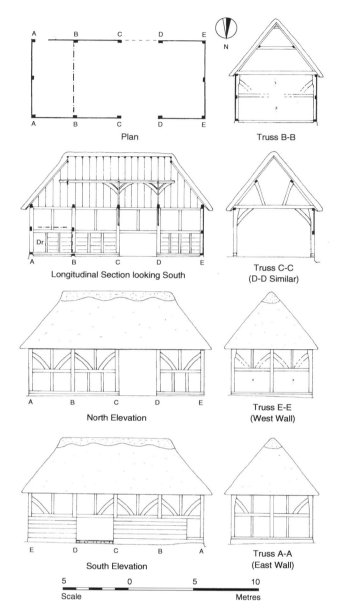

Figure 12.38
Reconstruction drawing of Little Harmers, Beckley,
as built.

in 1980 and fell down soon afterwards. It measured 13.30 metres x 6.25 metres (43'8" x 20'6") and incorporated equal-sized storage bays flanking the midstrey, with either a partially or wholly partitioned-off bay at the eastern end. This area was separately accessed and was originally floored. The full-height wagon doors giving access to the midstrey faced north.

As Figures 12.36 to 12.39 show, this was a well built and neatly framed structure. At its lower level the south wall (facing into the cattle yard) was always intended to be weatherboarded, whereas all other walls were originally daub infilled. Because of this variation, the studs within the lower section of the south wall were set at closer centres than elsewhere so as to support the boarding. The frame was stiffened at the upper level by externally-exposed curved footbraces. Note in Figure 12.38 the variation in the framing between the east and west elevations, and the use of a single brace over the half-height doorway in the south wall.

Little is known regarding the design of the internal partition between the storage area and the floored end bay, the crossbeam having been removed and the tiebeam replaced. However, mortices in the principal posts showed that it was footbraced at the upper level, whilst a long slip mortice lower down the northern post suggests that a feeding rack may have been inserted at some date. Both open trusses incorporated standard curved arch bracing. Above was a well proportioned roof of clasped-side-purlin type with reduced principal rafters. The trusses flanking the midstrey were fitted with well proportioned curved windbraces, and here the purlins were carried off the tiebeams by raking struts. There was never a roof truss above truss B-B: presumably this was

117

Figure 12.39
Little Harmers, Beckley.
Detail of roof showing windbraces. [318/20A]

Figure 12.40
Lower Float, Udimore.
Exterior from west. [169/33A]

Figure 12.41
Lower Float, Udimore.
Exterior from south showing added lean-to
outshuts. [169/34A]

because of its closeness to the apex of the hip.

In the early 17th century the daub infill was removed and the walls were weatherboarded, additional studs being added into the upper levels in order to give extra support to the boarding. The nailed-in studs were neatly notched so as to pass the existing wall braces. Subsequently, a lean-to outshut (with feeding rack and opposed entrance doors in the north and south walls) was added onto the western end. Shores were inserted into the trusses flanking the midstrey.

LOWER FLOAT, UDIMORE. NGR TQ 8817 1809
[ESRO HBR1/480]

Historically Lower Float Farm was known as Sparrows (after a former owner) and was a freehold tenement of Udimore Manor called Wellers and Lower Disnex, held at a quitrent of 3/4d + 1 hen, later commuted to 4/4d total. In 1597 the owner was Thomas Burdett, and in 1716 Edward Neeve esq. of London, at

which date it was tenanted by John Card. Although abutments are given in the 1597 manorial survey, the manorial documents do not quote acreages. However, from the boundaries the area of the farm can be reconstructed as 49½ acres.[17]

It was a three-bay late 16th-century barn which measured 12.70 metres x 6.20 metres (41'8" X 20'5") with an open storage bay on either side of the centrally placed midstrey. There were no indications of original outshuts. The full-height doors faced towards the highway.

All walls were originally daub infilled. As usual, footbraces at the upper level stiffened the frame - they were visible externally. The two internal trusses were arch braced, though down-going shores were added later. Fully hipped, the roof was of clasped-side-purlin design with collar-and-queen-stud trusses, slender straight windbraces, and diminished principal rafters.

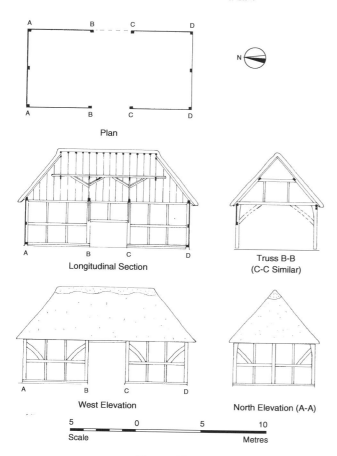

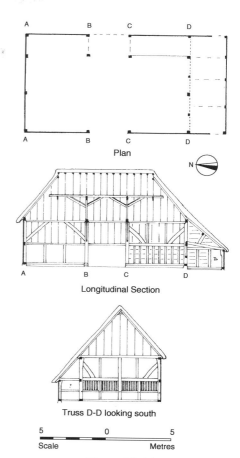

Figure 12.42
*Reconstruction drawing of Lower Float, Udimore,
as built.*

Figure 12.44
*Reconstruction drawing of Lower Float, Udimore,
as extended in the late 17th century.*

Figure 12.43
Lower Float, Udimore. Detail of roof.
[289/3]

Figure 12.45
*Lower Float, Udimore. Detail of feeding rack
added into truss D-D. [289/4]*

In the late 17th century, or perhaps the early 18th century, lean-to outshuts were added to the south and east to give an overall ground-floor area of 15.40 metres x 7.80 metres (50'6" x 25'7"). The wider end lean-to served as a cattle house and was fitted with

an added-in feeding rack located between it and the main body of the barn. Angle-bored holes were used to secure slanting hurdles against the rack. There were no indications of former stall divisions within the outshut. The side outshut served as an aisle at its northern end and a boarded-out 'cornhole' at its southern end.

The additions were traditionally framed with weatherboarded walls to the cattle outshut, but daub infill to the eastern wall of the side outshut. Arcade braces were inserted to replace the original eastern wall of the northern bay. At the time of survey in 1979 the roof was still thatched, but the building was then in a poor state of repair. It was demolished in1980.

Figure 12.46
Lower Float, Udimore. Dereliction and demolition, 1980. [331/20A]

PEBSHAM, BEXHILL. NGR TQ 7649 0892
[ESRO HBR 1/112]

Pebsham, a sub-manor of Robertsbridge, was held in the mid 16th century first by Anthony Pelham esq., and then by his son, Herbert Pelham esq. Both were absentee owners who lived elsewhere in East Sussex, and thus the demesne lands were tenanted when the barn was built. Neither the acreage nor the name of the tenant at that time are known. A 20-year lease of part of the demesne made by Pelham to William Smith, yeoman, in 1586 included the mansion house (described as 'where John Martin lived), a 'harbour', the east end of the great barn with the stable, and named fields amounting to over

Figure 12.47
Pebsham, Bexhill. Exterior from the south. [88/26A]

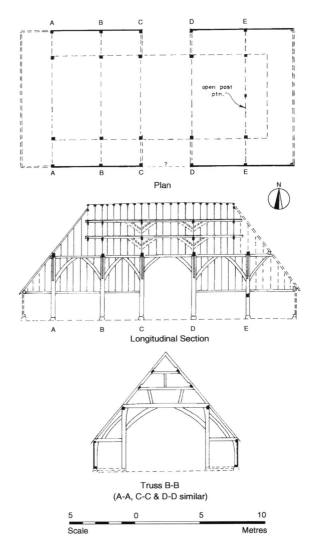

Figure 12.48
Reconstruction drawing of Pebsham, Bexhill, as built.

102 acres.[18] Evidently the western end of the barn and the other demesne lands were let separately, unless, that is, Pelham kept some lands in hand.

The barn was destroyed by fire in the 1980s. When built, it measured *c*21.25 metres x 10.90 metres (*c*69'8" x 35'9") overall the aisles and outshut and was a four-and-a-half bay fully aisled structure with a return aisle to west and an end lean-to outshut with cantilevered tiebeam to east (*see* Figure 6.5). The outshut served as the stable mentioned in the 1586 lease. The midstrey was placed almost central, with a two-bay open storage area to the west and a single-bay open storage area to the east, the latter divided from the end outshut by an open partition. There were no wagon porches, the full-height doors (on the north) being inset, on the line of the arcade.

The low walls of the aisle were weatherboarded,

*Figure 12.49 (Above)
Pebsham, Bexhill. Interior of
mid 16th-century section of barn
showing typical open truss and
roof. [88/21A]*

*Figure 12.50 (Right)
Reconstruction drawing of
Pebsham, Bexhill, as extended.*

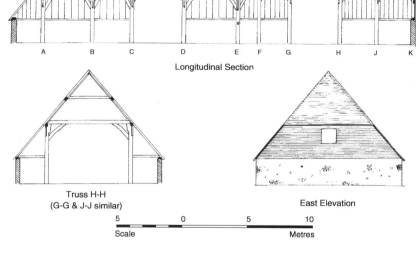

Plan

Longitudinal Section

Truss H-H
(G-G & J-J similar)

East Elevation

5   0   5   10
Scale   Metres

but, as they were constructed of reused material, they could have represented a later rebuild. This would be consistent with the redundant mortices in the arcade posts which suggest former tiebeams set lower than those present at the time of survey. However, it is possible that the arcade posts were reused from an earlier structure. All trusses were arch braced, the braces being set high and at a relatively shallow angle. Note in the reconstruction drawing the high shores in the aisle, set above the tiebeams. The arcade was fully braced, though the braces to the midstrey were shorter so as to improve headroom. The roof was a good example of clasped-side-purlin construction with two tiers of purlins, both tiers originally windbraced. Beneath the lower tier of collars were queen studs set to a slight rake, whilst above was a crown stud rising to the upper collar. All principal rafters were notched to take the purlins. Both terminals were originally of hipped type.

A neatly inscribed date, 1743, on an arcade post commemorated the date when the eastern outshut was destroyed and the barn extended by four bays, giving an

overall length of 31.10 metres. At this date the entire space was utilized for crop storage, loading being improved by the provision of a second midstrey. Wagon porches were constructed to protect the tall northern

*Figure 12.51
Pebsham, Bexhill. Roof over 1743 extension.
[88/23A]*

doorways. Some of the single-storeyed ranges around the yards may also have been of this date, but these were not inspected at the time of survey. Although the 1743 extension was fully framed, its construction was typical of the period with rounded bowls to the jowls on the arcade posts and short straight bracing to the arcades. Except at the upper level within the end wall (where weatherboarded stud infill was used) all of the external walls were of flint cobbles dressed in brick. Note from the illustrations the hatch within the end wall at first-floor level. Also typical of the period was the staggered-butt-purlin construction used for the roof, framed in five short bays which do not coincide with the tiebeams beneath. There was no ridge board at the apex.

REEDLANDS, ASHBURNHAM.
NGR TQ 6777 1572 *[ESRO HBR 1/564]*

When the majority of Ashburnham Estate was sold to William Relf by John Ashburnham in 1611 Reedlands was described as 23 acres of land: there was no reference to buildings upon the property. Both the house and barn were probably constructed soon afterwards, for when it was sold by Relf to George Thatcher in 1634 it was a

23 acre working farm.[19]   Certainly the barn (now demolished) was dated on typological evidence to the early 17th century. It was a small three-bay structure which measured 9.25 metres x 6.86 metres (30'4" x 22'6") overall its contemporary rear aisle. The open storage areas on either side of the midstrey were quite short in relation to the width of the wagon doors. The walls were initially daub infilled throughout and incorporated straight footbracing to stiffen the frame. The braces were not exposed externally. Straight, relatively spindly braces strengthened the trusses and arcade. Although the roof had been largely rebuilt, sufficient remained to indicate that it was originally fully hipped and was of clasped-side-purlin construction. The purlins were supported off the tiebeam by means of raking struts. All framing within the barn was of relatively slight scantling.

Reedlands continued to function as a 23 acre tenanted holding until 1724 when lands called Potkins

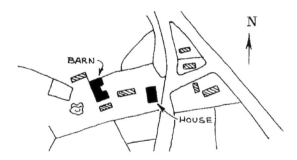

Figure 12.52
Reedlands, Ashburnham. Plan of farmstead as in c.1840

Figure 12.53
Reedlands, Ashburnham. Exterior from southwest.
[322/26]

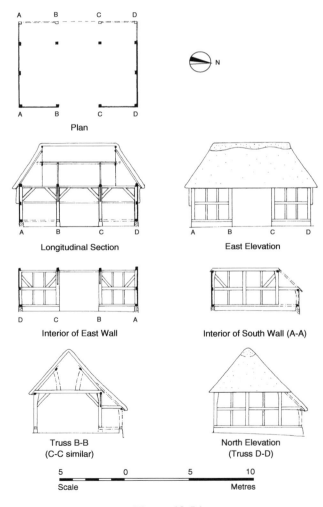

Figure 12.54
Reconstruction drawing of Reedlands, Ashburnham, as built.

Figure 12.55
Reedlands, Ashburnham. Wall framing showing
southern end of east wall (left) and southern end
wall (right). Note mortice in principal post
for missing footbrace. [322/27]

Figure 12.56
Reedlands, Ashburnham. Interior showing
area to north of midstrey, with the eastern wall of the
initial building on the right and the single-bay
extension on the left. The infill framing to the original
end wall has been removed, thereby converting the
truss to open type. [322/29]

and Kemps were merged into it, increasing the holding to 73 acres. It continued to be tenanted.[20] Presumably in response to the added acreage, in the mid 18th century the building was extended by the addition of a 3.05 metre (10'0") northern storage bay, complete with rear aisle. The principal posts of this bay had late style jowls with rounded bowls, whilst the walls were infilled with closely-spaced studs and raking struts, all intended to carry weatherboarding. It must have been at this period that the daub infill of the earlier section was replaced by boarding. The roof of the extension was of butt-purlin construction with a half-hipped terminal, absent of high-set collar at its apex. At this date the roof was still thatched, though it was later tiled. By 1840 lean-to outshuts had been added along the eastern side of the building.

SWAILES GREEN, SEDLESCOMBE.
NGR TQ 7714 2101 *[ESRO HBR 1/541 (Revised)]*

In the mid 16th century this was a small 12-acre copyhold farm called Vyles and Upathomes, held of the manor of Robertsbridge at a quitrent of 6/-. As is still the case, the barn stood on the opposite side of the public highway to the house. In 1567 the owner held no other adjoining land. By 1638 it had been acquired by Henry Barnes of Ewhurst, who was the owner of a small local estate.[21]

The western end of the barn at Swailes Green dates from the mid/late 17th century and represents a very typical small three-bay structure. Measuring 9.45 metres x 5.80 metres (31'0" x 19'0") it incorporated an

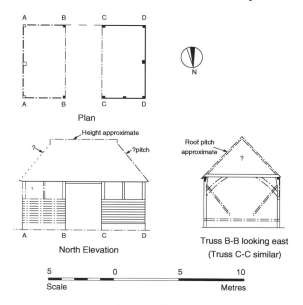

Figure 12.57
Reconstruction drawing of
Swailes Green, Sedlescombe, as built.

123

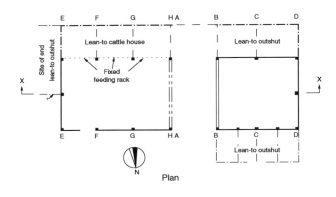

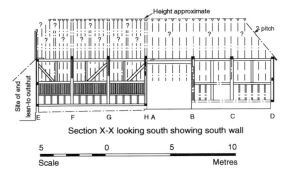

Section X-X looking south showing south wall

5   0   5   10

Scale   Metres

Figure 12.58
Reconstruction drawing of
Swailes Green, Sedlescombe, as extended.

Figure 12.59
North-eastern corner of frame as extended, showing
jowled post, level assembly and dragon tie.

open crop storage area on either side of the midstrey, the full-height doorway leading into which faced north towards the highway. In this initial phase the upper parts of its walls were daub infilled with the braces inset so as to be masked from view externally. The roof was hipped, but has been rebuilt subsequently.

This is a rare example of a small barn which was adapted to suit changed circumstances by adding a major extension as an alternative to demolition and total reconstruction. This phase of adaptation occurred in the early/mid 18th century, presumably in response to the increased size of the farm, for by 1753 other lands had been merged to give a holding of 65½ acres. It was at that date owned by John Holman of neighbouring Bodiam.[22] The original barn was more than doubled in size by the construction of three eastern bays and by the addition of a rear lean-to cattle house. The rear cattle house has been demolished, but the fixed feeding rack

between it and the main body of the barn remains in place (*see* Figure 6.19). As is to be expected of work carried out *c*1740, the extension has jowled principal posts, but its fully weatherboarded walls are infilled with closely-spaced studwork interrupted by raking struts. Despite the main trusses being in normal assembly, the eastern end wall is in level assembly and incorporates dragon ties at the corners (Figure 12.59). At this date the eastern roof terminal was of half-hipped type, though this was converted into a gable when the roof was subsequently rebuilt to a lower pitch.

Further lean-to outshuts were incorporated. That at the eastern end (now demolished) was certainly contemporary with the other mid 18th-century alterations, but the date of the lean-to at the western end of the northern wall is more uncertain. Some features suggest that it too was added during this period, but the details within its external walls suggest that it is later. One possibility is that the 18th-century lean-to was itself reconstructed at a later date. This lean-to, which is the only part to incorporate a first floor, cannot be earlier than the main 18th-century addition: it is built over the original wagon entrance, which was closed-down when the main extension was built. At this date the midstrey was moved into the original eastern bay of the barn, making it more central to the enlarged structure.

13   MALTHOUSES AND OASTHOUSES

Next to barns, the most common group of historical agricultural buildings to survive within the High Weald are oasthouses. With their very distinctive cowl-topped conical roofs, oast kilns remain a very distinctive feature of the local landscape. Most date from the 19th century and therefore fall outside the scope of this present study. However, early examples survive in sufficient numbers to give a reasonable indication of their size and form. They were very different from their successors.

When hops were first introduced into eastern Sussex during the middle years of the 16th century both hop processing and malt manufacture (from barley and, perhaps more usually in the Sussex Weald, from oats) shared the same facilities. Despite the advise of Reynold Scot in his treatise 'a Perfitte Platforme of a Hoppe Garden' first published in 1574 that what he called 'a common oste' (*ie.* a malt or corn drying kiln) was not good enough and that only a purpose-built structure would do, dual-purpose oasts were commonly used until at least the mid/late 18th century, after which the domestic production of malt ceased locally.[1]

In the early years the processing appears sometimes to have been carried out either within the service area of the farmhouse, or within a detached multi-purpose service building located close to the house (*see* Chapter 15). But, as the acreage dedicated to hops increased, specialist buildings (either of the type described by Scot as early as 1574 or of modified form) began to be built. Indeed, during the 17th century some service blocks (identified as '*coquina*' or 'kitchen' in the 16th-century documents) were converted solely to hop drying and malt manufacture. Examples are Wardsbrook, Ticehurst, and Beestons, Warbleton.[2]

Oasthouses were often referred to in 16th-, 17th- and early 18th-century documentary sources as malthouses, suggesting that malt manufacture was initially their most important function, and this use of the term 'malthouse' remained for some time after the drying of hops had become their primary purpose. The term 'hop house' is occasionally encountered, but the modern term 'oasthouse' is only rarely found at this period,

despite common references to 'oast kilns' and 'oast hairs' (a form of horse-hair sacking placed over the slatted drying floor of the kiln).

Even during the medieval period a few documentary references are known to specialized malthouses on major properties within the study area. For example, one such building is recorded at Robertsbridge Abbey, and this remained in use under secular control after the dissolution.[3] The earliest known local references to structures intended specifically for the processing of hops are a 'hoppehouse' used by a Rye brewer in 1585 and another mentioned at Northbridge Street, Salehurst, in 1597.[4] The latter example - a former medieval hall house - had then only recently been converted into a 'hop house'. It survives today as 21 Northbridge Street, though the layout during its hop-house phase has been obliterated by later alterations.

Initially very rare, by the mid 17th century purpose-designed specialist oasthouses were beginning to be built more commonly, and with an ever increasing acreage devoted to the growing of hops the number of such buildings continued to rise. Already by 1672 one farm in four within Mountfield Manor possessed such a building.[5] An analysis of early 18th-century inventories (spread throughout the rape) suggests that by the early 1700s a third of all farms had some involvement in the cultivation of hops and most of these possessed an oasthouse. By the late 17th and early 18th centuries oasthouses had become the second most common farm buildings in the area, exceeded in numbers only by barns. A phenomenal increase in hop production during the 19th century, coupled with improved drying techniques, resulted in most of the old-style oasthouses being swept away in favour of new improved designs incorporating the now characteristic clusters of cowl-capped brick roundels.[6]

Within the study area only 23 oasthouses are currently known which can be shown to have been built during the period here under discussion. Others no doubt await discovery, incorporated into the stowage bays of their successors. The 23 examples which have been studied range in date from *c*1600 (a building which appears to have been called a stable in 1682 and was first called a malthouse in 1697) through to the mid 18th century.[7] Before discussing them it is advisable to describe, albeit briefly, the processes for which they were built.

The Manufacture of Malt

Perhaps the best local description of an early malthouse with no hop-drying interests is that which existed at Abbey Farm, Salehurst in 1567.[8] The building is described as containing a stone cistern (for steeping the barley or oats), two malting rooms (upon the floors of which the steeped barley/oats were laid out to germinate) and an oast which comprised a furnace or hearth area with slatted floor above, upon which the crop was spread and kiln-dried in order to arrest further germination. Adjacent to the malthouse at Abbey Farm was a brewhouse, together with three watermills under a single roof, one of which was a maltmill for mashing the malt before it was used in brewing.

The Robertsbridge Abbey maltings were intended to produce malt on an industrial scale. Even so, all malthouses, including those which catered for purely domestic needs, would have required some form of steeping cistern or vat, a germination floor, and some form of oast kiln. A few early 18th-century inventories mention oasthouses which contained within them either a hand-driven 'steel mill' or a malt quern for mashing the malt (*see* Figure 13.20). Other inventories make clear that most people both stored and mashed their malt within the attic areas of their houses. The mashed malt was then carried down for use within the brewhouse.

Hop Drying

Ignoring the steeping vats and malt mills, the main elements of a malthouse were also essential for the drying of hops, though the process was different. To summarize, the picked hops were brought in from the gardens, hoisted to the first floor and laid out evenly upon the slatted floor of the oast. Here they were dried by passing hot air through them, rising from the kiln(s) or hearth(s) beneath. The crop was then allowed to cool, either by leaving them where they had been dried or by moving them into a separate area, depending upon the quantity of crop to be dried. Finally, they were compressed by treading them into hop pockets (long sacks) hung from a purpose-cut circular hole in the upper floor. When full, the pockets were sewn up for storage.[9]

DESIGN TYPES

Although only a small number of early oasthouses have been studied, it is possible to recognize four distinct design variations. These are here described as types A-D. Two of the buildings within the sample have been altered to such an extent that classification is no longer possible. The four types can be summarized as follows:-
A. Central drying kiln flanked by un-floored areas.
B. End drying kiln with an un-floored area to one side.
C. End drying kiln with a floored area to one side.
D. 'T' plan with the drying floor in the head of the 'T'.

Type A - The 'Scot' Pattern
Central drying kiln flanked by un-floored areas

In 1574 Reynold Scot, in his book on the cultivation of hops, gave an illustration and description of his design for an ideal hop-oast (Figure 13.1).[10] He suggested that the building should measure from 18 to 19 foot (5.50-5.80 metres) long by 8 foot (2.45 metres) wide and should be divided in its length into three compartments. The central section, 8 foot (2.45 metres) square, was to incorporate a hearth with a slatted drying floor above, whilst the rooms on either side were, apparently, to be left open from floor to roof. The room from which the hearth was stoked was presumably also intended to house the fuel, whilst that on the opposite side received the hops.

Hoppers Croft, Burwash (17th century) and Langham Cottage, Robertsbridge (*c*1700) are the only oasthouses of 'Scot design' at present known to survive within the study area (Figure 13.2).[11] Both have long been converted into dwellings, and thus much of the detail within both structures has been obliterated. Measuring 12.80 metres x 4.00 metres (42'1" x 13'2") and 8.76 metres x 3.40 metres (28'9" x 11'2") respectively, both are much larger than described by Scot. The drying chamber at Hoppers Croft was spacious, measuring 4.60 metres x 4.00 metres (15'1" x 13'2"), whereas that at Langham Cottage measured only 1.85 metres x 3.40 metres (6'0" x 11'2").

At Langham Cottage the section of roof over the drying chamber has been severely charred by fire, a

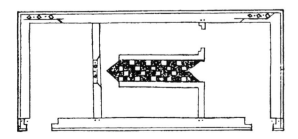

Figure 13.1
Scot's plan for an ideal oasthouse.

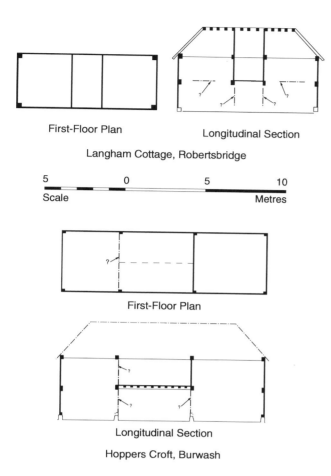

First-Floor Plan   Longitudinal Section

Langham Cottage, Robertsbridge

First-Floor Plan

Longitudinal Section

Hoppers Croft, Burwash

Figure 13.2
Reconstruction details of Type-A oasthouses.

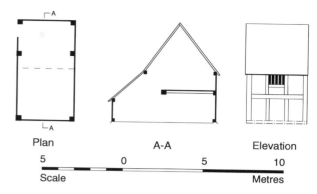

Plan   A-A   Elevation

Figure 13.3
Reconstruction drawings of Cross Cottage,
Warbleton, as first built.

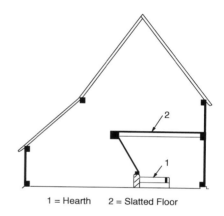

1 = Hearth   2 = Slatted Floor

Figure 13.4
Conjectural reconstruction through Cross Cottage.

reminder of the wisdom in Scot's advice that oasthouses should be placed 'somewhat distant from your house to avoid the danger of fire'. True to Scot's design, the end bays at Hoppers Croft were open to the roof, and this is likely to have been the case at Langham Cottage too, though in this instance the point cannot now be proven.

Type B
End drying kiln with an un-floored area to one side

As in the Scot pattern, the three buildings which make up this group possessed only a drying-floor at first-floor level during the earliest stages of their development, though, unlike Scot's design, they incorporated but one ground-floor area in addition to the hearth-space beneath the drying floor.

The smallest of the three is that which now forms the period-A portion of Cross Cottage, Rushlake Green, Warbleton (Figure 13.3). Of 17th-century date, the building initially comprised a single bay with a lean-to outshut on one side. It measured only 3.75 metres x

6.55 metres (12'4" x 21'5"). On the first floor the drying area was limited to a space 3.75 metres x 3.30 metres (12'4" x 10'10"): the remainder of the bay, together with the lean-to outshut, was open from ground floor to roof. The roof itself is soot-blackened, indicating that wood, not charcoal, was used to fire the hearths during the building's early years. Scot confirms that wood was utilized in oasthouses as fuel. An idea of how the building functioned (based on a similar example at Cranbrook) is shown in the conjectural reconstruction given in Figure 13.4.[12] The example from Cranbrook incorporated a partition dividing the drying chamber from the adjacent open area, though the extent of smoke-blackening shows clearly that no such partition existed at Cross Cottage. Instead the drying chamber was entirely open to the adjacent non-floored area.

Another small 17th-century oasthouse existed until the 1970s at Copens Farm, Ticehurst. As Figure 13.5 shows, in its initial form its layout closely resembled that of Cross Cottage, except that the 7.35 metre x 4.70 metre (24'0" x 15'5") building consisted of two unequal bays and did not possess a lean-to outshut. As at Cross Cottage, however, the drying floor was limited to only part of the structure, the drying chamber itself being open to the adjacent non-floored bay.

A modification of the Cross Cottage/Copens design is to be found at Rafters, Iden (also illustrated in Figure 13.5). In this instance the oasthouse was inserted into the end of a mid/late 17th-century barn, probably during the middle years of the 18th century. The drying chamber is partitioned off from the adjacent midstrey of the barn, though the partition incorporates a wide central opening so as to allow easy access for loading.

Already by the early 18th century the oasthouses at both Copens and Cross Cottage were regarded as too small in size and basic in design. Both were extended and improved. Three bays were added to Cross Cottage during the opening years of the 18th century, whilst Copens was modified and extended by one bay soon afterwards.

Type C
End drying kiln with a floored area to one side
(Figures 13.6 - 13.8)

To judge from the surviving buildings, this was the most commonly adopted design during the 17th and

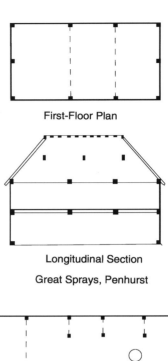

First-Floor Plan

Longitudinal Section

Great Sprays, Penhurst

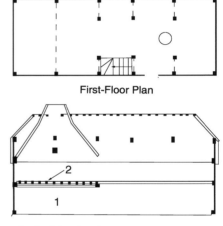

First-Floor Plan

Longitudinal Section [1 = Hearth. 2 = Slatted Floor]

Hampden Lodge, Mayfield

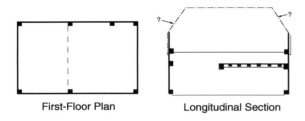

First-Floor Plan

Longitudinal Section

Copens, Ticehurst

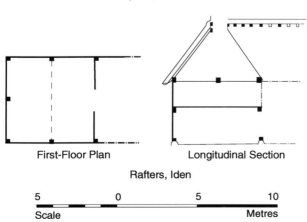

First-Floor Plan

Longitudinal Section

Rafters, Iden

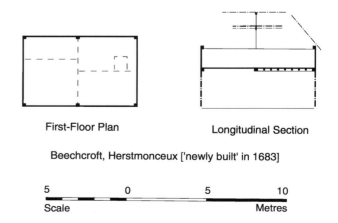

First-Floor Plan

Longitudinal Section

Beechcroft, Herstmonceux ['newly built' in 1683]

Figure 13.5
Details of two Type-B oasthouses

Figure 13.6
Three examples of Type-C1 oasthouses

early/mid 18th centuries. The sample available for analysis includes four modifications to earlier buildings, not all of which were initially built as oasthouses. In size they range from two to five bays of construction and vary from 5.70 metres x 3.70 metres (18'8" x 12'0") to 13.55 metres x 5.35 metres (44'6" x 17'7"), but most are 9.50 metres (31'0") or less in length and 5.00 metres (16'3") or less in width. All are similar in that their first-floor layouts comprise either two or, occasionally, three activity areas set in sequence within a single range. The drying floor is located at one end of the building in all cases. Three distinct variations of plan type are recognizable:-

C1   Drying floor and adjacent area with no physical barriers between them (five examples). Three examples of this type are illustrated in Figure 13.6.

C2   As C1, but the two areas separated by a partition (nine examples). Two examples are illustrated in Figure 13.7.

C3   A combination of types C1 and C2, the drying floor having an undivided adjacent area (as in C1) beyond which is an additional partitioned-off chamber. Only two examples are known, of which one - Great Sprays, Penhurst, as extended - is shown in Figure 13.8.

In most instances, especially in those buildings which predate the middle years of the 18th century, the area adjacent to the kiln is equal to or smaller than the space taken up by the drying floor itself. The area

beneath the drying floor originally housed the hearths (all now removed), whilst the space adjacent to the hearth presumably acted as a fuel store and pocketing area. In their period-B forms at least two of the buildings (Hayes, Northiam and Great Sprays, Penhurst) incorporated separate ground-floor rooms utilized for ancillary functions (*see* below).

At least one of the three oasthouses built by Walter Roberts during the 1660s and 1670s upon farms on his Boarzell Estate, Ticehurst, was of this type. Erected in 1667 on his farm at Flimwell in the extreme northeast of the parish, the agreement made between him, his tenant, and two carpenters indicates that the building was to measure 30 foot by 15 foot (4.55 metres by 9.15 metres) in plan, was to have a partition between the chamber and the oast (that is, the drying floor was to be divided off from the adjacent area) and it was to have three doors and a stairs. An indication of the building's height is the length of its main posts - they were to measure 10 foot (3.05 metres) between the soleplate and the wallplate. This measurement is very similar to those in the surviving buildings. The timber frame was to be infilled with 'loam' (*ie* daub).[13] A second oasthouse built upon the same estate in 1671 was slightly larger. Its wall posts were to be the same height, but in plan it was to measure 32 foot by either 16 or 17 foot (9.75 metres by either 4.90 or 5.20 metres) and was to include an 'outlet' - almost certainly a lean-to outshut.[14] The agreement specifically states that the building was to incorporate two kilns, but the size of the structure suggests that this

1 Hearth   2 Slatted Floor

First-Floor Plan   Longitudinal Section

Little Bucksteep, Warbleton

First-Floor Plan   Longitudinal Section

Wedds, Ticehurst

5   0   5   10

Scale   Metres

Figure 13.7
Two examples of Type-C2 oasthouses

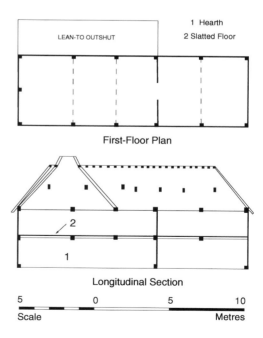

1 Hearth   2 Slatted Floor

LEAN-TO OUTSHUT

First-Floor Plan

Longitudinal Section

5   0   5   10

Scale   Metres

Figure 13.8
Great Sprays, Penhurst, as extended.
An example of a Type-C3 oasthouse

Figure 13.9
Type-D oasthouse at Homestead, Brightling
[250/29A]

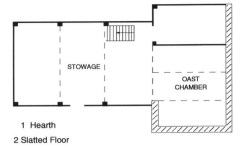

STOWAGE

OAST
CHAMBER

1 Hearth
2 Slatted Floor

First-Floor Plan

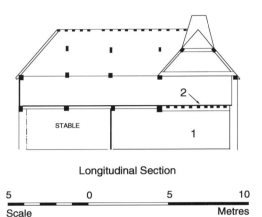

STABLE

2

1

Longitudinal Section

5   0   5   10
Scale   Metres

Figure 13.10
Type-D oasthouse at Homestead, Brightling.
reconstruction drawing prior to extension.

indicated that the drying floor was to be served by two hearths (*see* ' The Plenum Chamber ' below), rather than suggesting that the building was intended to incorporate two separate drying areas. The oasthouse covered by the third agreement was larger still, measuring 36 foot by 16 foot (10.95 metres x 4.85 metres) but the details give no indications as to its internal layout.[15]

Type D.
'T' plan oasthouse

The most elaborate of the surviving early-style oasthouses is the 'T' plan in which the drying floor is located within a crosswing set at one end of an extensive stowage range. These are essentially a mid/late 18th-century form. Indeed, only two known examples fall within the period covered by this study, and these only just. Homestead Farm, Brightling (Figures 13.9 and 13.10) was built in this form by Ashburnham Estate, whilst at Silverden, Northiam, the crosswing housing the kilns was added to an existing 16th-century structure of uncertain use (Figure 13.11). The first-floor plan of Homestead is shown in Figure 13.10. As will be noticed, there was never a partition between the drying chamber and the main body of the building. Much of the ground floor of the stowage range was devoted to ancillary functions (*see* below).

This general design appears to have been popular on the Ashburnham Estate, for other similar examples can be seen at Haselden Farm, Dallington, and Church Farm, Penhurst, the latter being inscribed with the initials J A (for John Ashburnham) and the date 1776.

THE PLENUM CHAMBER (Figure 13.12)

The Plenum chamber is the name generally given to that part of the ground floor which accommodated the

Figure 13.11
Silverden Oasthouse, Northiam, c.1900
The main range on the left is the original 16th-century building, into which an oast kiln had evidently been inserted, as indicated by the small cowl rising above its roof. The added range on the right was built to house an additional oast kiln, and cut rafters in the roof indicate the location of its cowl. This latter cowl was removed when the brick roundel was added at its far end in the mid/late 19th century. [300/25]

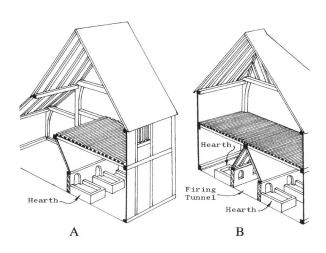

Figure 13.12
Details of hearth arrangements.

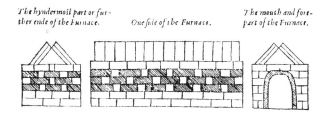

Figure 13.13
Scot's design for a kiln as shown in his
publication of 1574 (modified in 1576 reprint).

hearths. Within all the early buildings so far identified the hearths and other fittings have been stripped out, and thus for information regarding the internal arrangements it is necessary to rely upon later examples. In so doing there is always the danger that the methods described are more sophisticated than those utilized during the study period. For this reason, only the basics are given here and the reader is directed to the more details study of oasthouse in Sussex and Kent carried out by Gwen Jones and John Bell.[16]

The simplest arrangement is that shown by Scot in 1574 (modified in his 1576 reprint) where he illustrates a rectangular brick hearth or 'furnace' positioned centrally beneath the drying floor (Figures 13.1 and 13.13). That which survived until recently at Little Golford, Cranbrook, Kent was in essence similar, but comprised a pair of small brick hearths set centrally beneath the drying floor. This is most likely the arrangement referred to in Walter Roberts' agreement to build an oasthouse with two kilns in 1671 (*see* above). The hearths at Little Golford were located against a low brick wall, the fires being tended through arched openings built into the wall.[17] A slanting timber-and-daub partition rose from the wall to the edge of the drying floor, thus preventing the heat from the hearths from escaping into the adjacent area, whilst channelling it up to the entire area of the slatted drying floor above. This represented an improvement over Scot's design. Local surviving late 18th- and early 19th-century examples closely follow this 'improved' pattern, except that usually two rows of hearths are arranged in parallel, separated by a firing passage (Figure 13.12, B). In these instances the sloping partitions supported by the side walls of the passage meet in a point, thereby effectively forming a firing tunnel between the banks of hearths.

Considering that the two hearths at Little Golford served a drying floor of only 10 square metres and that most of the surviving early oasthouses possess drying floors of 20-30 square metres, it seems likely that these more complex arrangements incorporating firing tunnels would have been relatively common. Indeed, a survey of Ashburnham Estate made in 1830 describes the type-D oasthouse at Homestead Farm, Brightling (with its 26 square metre drying floor) as containing four 'fireplaces' (*ie.* hearths), whilst the 30 square metre period-B drying floor at Great Sprays was served by six. The type-D oasthouse at Church Farm, Penhurst (dated 1776) incorporated no less than eight 'fireplaces', whilst others possessed as many as fourteen .[18]

THE DRYING CHAMBER

Initially, except for its slatted floor and perhaps some form of low-level internal boarding against the face of the walls, the drying chamber differed in no appreciable way from any other first-floor chamber, the hot air (having passed through the bed of hops or barley/oats lying on the floor) being allowed to disperse throughout the building and out through the windows. Anthony Cronk has implied that it was not until the 18th century that interest was shown in improving the rate of air flow through the drying chamber so that it passed through the drying floor more rapidly, thereby allowing a thicker bed of hops to be processed.[19] However, Gwen Jones suggests that improvements were perhaps in some instances already being made in this respect during the 17th century.[20]

Regardless of when they were first introduced, these improvements were achieved by framing an inverted funnel of timber and plaster within the roof space above the drying floor, the upper end of the funnel terminating above the roof-line either in a tile-hung or boarded conical-shaped vent somewhat like a tapering, cylindrical chimney cap (*see* Figures 13.9, 13.11 (left), 13.15 and 13.17). Arrangements of this type which predate the late 18th century (or at least the remains and/or evidence of them) survive at Stunts Green, Wartling;

Great Sprays, Penhurst; Hampden Lodge, Mayfield; Homestead Farm, Brightling; Rafters, Iden; Wardsbrook, Ticehurst; and Woodlands, Warbleton. Only that in the mid 18th-century oasthouse at Homestead Farm can be proved to be contemporary with the building. The evidence within the early 17th-century example at Stunts Green is quite compelling and could represent the earliest example yet known (Figure 13.16). Despite this, it must be stressed that the earliest reference to the building at Stunts Green as an oasthouse is in 1697: it appears to have been in use as a stables in 1682.[21] Those arrangements at Great Sprays and Wardsbrook show clear evidence of representing later modifications.

Some indications as to the date at which these improved techniques began to be commonly employed is to be found in the work of the cartographers of the time. In early maps buildings were sketched in elevation, and although these sketches are probably rarely accurate representations of the buildings themselves, they do give an indication of the surveyor's impression of what a house, cottage, barn or oasthouse looked like.

Six plans drawn before 1730 are known to the authors which depict oasthouses, though none show any features projecting through the roof, even though some of the sketches, such as that of Great Sprays, Penhurst in 1717 (where the oasthouse still survives) and the late 17th century plan of Silverhill Farm, Salehurst, show the buildings in clear detail.[22] It should, however, be stressed that a number of plans, such as that dated 1641 showing Stonehouse, Warbleton, that of the 1640s showing Nether Ockham, Salehurst, and a plan of Brightling Place made in 1717 do depict a small building with a 'chimney' close to the house.[23] The problem is that at least some of these buildings - and perhaps all - represent detached kitchens. However, the building shown on a 1748 plan of Southings Farm, Westfield, is certainly an oasthouse and it is illustrated with a

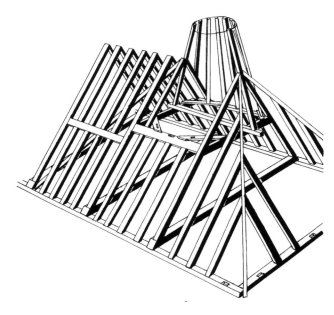

*Figure 13.15
Details of conical vent at Homestead, Brightling.
The timbers were originally masked internally
by lath and daub.*

Longitudinal Section

5   0   5
Scale   Metres

*Figure 13.16 (left)
Stunts Green, Wartling.
Note the cut rafter
deliberately supported
by an apparently
original collar,
indicating the site of the
former vent in the roof.*

Figure 13.17
Rare photograph of 1854 showing the exceptionally large oasthouse at
Newhouse, Bodiam. Note the conical vent absent of cowl and the
stack of hop poles in the foreground. [183/34]

projecting 'chimney' - the only positively identified such representation todate.[24] So, although there is some evidence to suggest the occasional use of 'chimneys' in oasthouses during the 17th century, at present the cartographic and architectural evidence tends to agree with Cronk that the use of vents appears not to have become common until the early or mid 18th century.

The white painted rotating cowls which cap the vents and which are today considered the principal hallmark of an oasthouse did not make their appearance until the close of our study period. It is true that a few rare examples may have existed during the mid 18th century (certainly they were in use by 1782) though they were not widely adopted until the early 19th century.[25] It was probably during this period that the vent at Homestead Farm had a cowl added, struts being introduced in order to strengthen the collar upon which the central spindle rested. Some oasthouses did not possess cowls even in the mid 19th century, a point well illustrated by a photograph taken in 1854 of the late 18th-century oasthouse at Newhouse Farm, Bodiam (Figure 13.17).[26]

THE CHAMBER BESIDE THE DRYING FLOOR

In the later oasthouses the first-floor area or chamber beside the drying kiln was not only utilized as a

reception area for the crop as it was brought in from the fields, but also as an area where the dried crop could be laid to cool, thereby freeing the drying floor for the next load of harvested hops. In addition, it was here too that the dried and cooled hops were pocketed - that is, compressed within a long sack hanging from a circular hole in the floor.

With the phenomenal increase in the acreage dedicated to hops and the corresponding increase in the number of drying kilns, it can be seen why it was thought necessary to dedicate an area within the oasthouse for cooling. But in the early years the acreages were very low and a glance at Figures 13.6 and 13.7 will show that in some instances the area beside the drying floor was very small. Indeed, in most instances it was probably too small to have been used as a cooling area and the crop must have been allowed to cool upon the drying floor and then bagged before the next part of the crop could be dried. Indeed, this must have been the case in the oasthouses of types A and B where the drying floor was the only area at first-floor level. It must also have been the case at Little Bucksteep, Warbleton, shown in Figure 13.7, where most of the tiny area beside the drying floor was occupied by the stairs and treading hole.

A further indication of this is to be found in the type-C1 late 17th- or early 18th-century oasthouse at Wessons, Wadhurst. Although located within the High

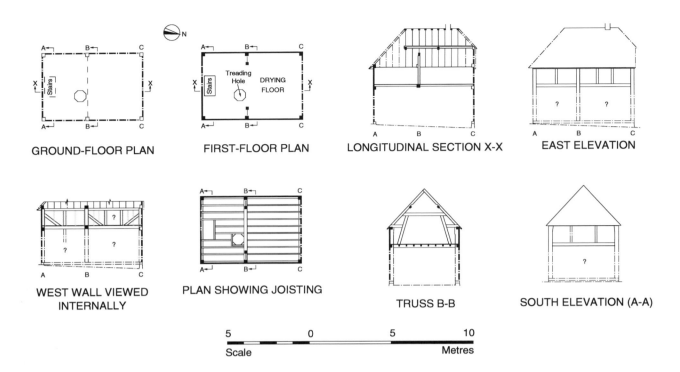

GROUND-FLOOR PLAN   FIRST-FLOOR PLAN   LONGITUDINAL SECTION X-X   EAST ELEVATION

WEST WALL VIEWED INTERNALLY   PLAN SHOWING JOISTING   TRUSS B-B   SOUTH ELEVATION (A-A)

Figure 13.18
Reconstruction details of oasthouse at Wessons, Wadhurst,
as built in the late 17th or early 18th centuries.

Figure 13.19 (left)
Treading hole cantilevered out
into the roof area of the lean-to
outshut within the oasthouse at
Beestons, Warbleton. [865/3]

Weald, this building is just outside the study area and is therefore excluded from the statistics quoted earlier. As Figure 13.18 illustrates, here not only is the area adjacent to the drying floor small, but in addition the treading hole is placed in what at first sight seems a very awkward position, in the opening immediately adjacent to the drying floor. Surely, this was to allow easy access to the hole direct from the drying floor.

In this respect, a point which needs to be considered is how the hops were pocketed within those type-A and -B buildings which possessed only a drying floor at first-floor level. Although there is at present no definitive answer to this question, one possible arrangement is that shown in Figure 13.19 at Beestons, Warbleton. Here, despite ample first-floor space, a cantilevered platform was built projecting out from the first floor into an open lean-to outshut. Similar cantilevered platforms could have been provided

Inventory Number (ESRO W/INV)	Description of Building	Month	Contents of Oasthouses									Inv. Ref. to	
			Charcoal	Oast Hair	Malt Mill/Quern [1]	Malt Tubs	Sundry Equipment [2]	Malt &/or Barley	Hops	Other Crops [3]	Husbandry Tackle	Barley or Malt	Hop Growing
19	Malthouse	April	-	✓	✓	-	✓	-	-	-	-	✓	✓
89	Malthouse	Oct	-	-	-	-	-	-	-	-	✓	-	-
331	Malthouse	Aug	✓	✓	-	-	-	-	-	-	-	✓	-
504	Malthouse	March	✓	-	-	-	-	✓	✓	-	-	✓	✓
532	Oasthouse	May	2	-	✓	-	-	-	-	-	-	✓	✓
753	Oasthouse	Feb	✓	✓	-	-	-	-	-	-	-	✓	-
788	Oasthouse	April	✓	✓	-	-	-	✓	-	✓	-	✓	✓
909	Not Named	Oct	✓	-	-	-	-	-	✓	-	-	✓	✓
935	Oasthouse	Jan	✓	-	-	-	-	-	✓	✓	-	✓	✓
1158	Oasthouse	Jan	✓	-	-	-	✓	-	-	-	-	✓	-
1178	Malthouse	Feb	✓	-	✓	-	-	✓	-	✓	-	✓	-
1446	Oasthouse	-	✓	-	-	-	-	-	-	✓	✓	✓	-
1476	Oasthouse	April	✓	-	-	✓	-	-	-	-	-	✓	✓
1499	Oasthouse	June	✓	-	-	-	-	✓	-	-	-	✓	✓
1515	Oasthouse	Oct	✓	-	-	-	-	-	✓	-	-	✓	-
1545	Oasthouse	Jan	✓	-	-	-	-	-	-	-	-	✓	-
1582	Oasthouse	May	✓	-	-	-	✓	-	-	-	-	✓	-
1623	Oasthouse	-	3	✓	-	-	-	-	-	-	-	✓	-
1703	Oasthouse	Oct	✓	-	✓	-	-	-	-	-	-	✓	✓
2124	Malthouse	Feb	-	-	-	-	-	-	-	-	✓	✓	✓
2221	Oasthouse	March	✓	-	✓	-	-	-	-	-	-	✓	✓
2383	Malthouse	Jan	-	-	-	-	-	✓	-	✓	-	-	✓
2430	Oasthouse	Sept	-	-	-	-	-	-	✓	-	-	✓	-
2433	Oasthouse	Sept	✓	✓	-	-	✓	-	✓	✓	-	✓	-
943	Malthouse [4]	Feb	-	-	✓	-	-	-	✓	✓	-	✓	✓
1155	Malthouse [4]	Jan	✓	-	✓	-	-	✓	✓	-	-	✓	✓
1208	Malthouse [5]	April	3	✓	-	-	✓	-	-	-	-	✓	-
1770	Malthouse [5]	May	3	✓	-	-	-	✓	-	✓	-	-	✓

Notes
1. 1 Horse Mill, 1 Steel Mill, 1 Malt Mill, 4 Malt Querns.
2. 1 Weights & Scales, 1 Sieve, 1 Shovel, 2 Sacks & Bags, 1 Bed
3. Wheat, Oats & peas
4. Two inventories of the same property dated 1717 & 1719
5. Ditto but dated 1720 & 1725.

Figure 13.20
The contents of oasthouses as indicated
in early 18th-century inventories.

projecting out from the drying floors of the type-A and -B oasts. Alternatively, perhaps a small section of the drying floor was sacrificed for the purpose.

CONTENTS AND ANCILLARY USES OF OASTHOUSES

Figure 13.20 lists the contents of 28 oasthouses as recorded in the early 18th-century probate inventories for an area in the northeast of Hastings rape. It should be borne in mind that the details given are not exhaustive. Many items, particularly if small or of little value, were covered by the blanket term 'and other small things'

invariably found at the end of each description. Most entries, however, list the oast hair, (a matting of horse hair laid over the slatted floor of the drying chamber) whilst the charcoal fuel, which by this date was used in lieu of wood, is also mentioned in several instances. Some form of malt mill or quern was present in a quarter of the buildings, though only one reference is made to a malt tub for steeping the barley or oats. In most instances the tub probably took the form of a fixture (as was the case at Robertsbridge Abbey in 1567) and would therefore not be appraised. In this respect it is worth noting that over half the inventories covered by Figure 13.20 give evidence of malt-making interests.[27]

Malt, barley, oats and hops are mentioned within the oasthouses in a little under half the sample, whilst eight of the buildings were also used for the storage of wheat and peas. These latter references imply that in some instances oasthouses were utilized as granaries, a logical function considering the short period during which an oasthouse would otherwise have been utilized each year. At Hayes, Northiam, and Great Sprays, Penhurst early/mid 18th-century extensions appear to have been made to the buildings for use as granaries: certainly in 1830 the first-floor chamber of the extension at Great Sprays was described as such. At that date the ground-floor area beneath it was utilized as an implement shed.[28] Husbandry tackle is mentioned within three of the early 18th-century oasthouses listed in Figure 13.20, whilst the wide ground-floor doorways at Staces, Dallington and Hampden Lodge, Mayfield suggest a similar use in these instances too. The doorway arrangement in the end wall of the early/mid 18th-century extension at Hayes Farm, Northiam, on the other hand, suggests that the ground-floor area was in that instance utilized as a stable, as was certainly the case on the ground-floor within the stowage range in the oasthouse at Homestead Farm, Brightling. Similar arrangements are to be found in the slightly later, but very similar oasthouses at Haselden Farm, Dallington and Church Farm, Penhurst.

At Great Sprays, Penhurst, a mid 18th-century lean-to outshut was in use as a charcoal store in 1830, and it was probably for this purpose that it was added.[29] The contemporary lean-to outshuts at Cross Cottage, Warbleton (period B) and Hayes Farm, Northiam (period A) were probably put to a similar use.

DETAILS OF CONSTRUCTION

Despite the fire risk, it is clear from both documentary and architectural sources that prior to *c*1800 most oasthouses were timber framed. Those built by Roberts upon his Boarzell Estate in Ticehurst in the 1660s and 1670s (*see* above) utilized this form of construction, as did that set up by John Everenden at

Sedlescombe in 1622.[30] The infill of Everenden's oast was later replaced by brick panels as part of a modernization scheme undertaken in 1655-6.[31] A late 17th-century plan of Silverhill Farm, Salehurst depicts the oasthouse on that farm with exposed timber framing.[32] This was also the case with the daub-infilled framing in fifteen (possibly sixteen) of the early examples which survive. For a selection *see* Figure 13.21 and 13.22. Another building, that at Copens, Ticehurst, had only the upper part of its timberwork exposed, the lower storey being weatherboarded, a feature found in many barns (*see* Chapter 7). At variance with the designs found in barn construction, most exposed framing within the surviving oasthouses was of small-panel type, the storey heights being divided at mid-height by horizontal rails.

Although originally daub infilled, to judge from a plan of 1717, by that date the framing at Great Sprays, Penhurst had already been clad with weatherboarding: certainly its mid 18th-century extension was designed to be weatherclad from the outset.[33] The mid 18th-century oasthouses at Wedds and Birchen Wood, both in Ticehurst, were also designed to be weatherboarded, as too were the timber-framed first-floor walls of the stowage bays at Homestead Farm, Brightling. The latter, a mid 18th-century building, is the only oasthouse included within this study to possess a kiln and drying chamber constructed in brick, a material also used for the ground-floor walls of the stowage range. The front wall of the oasthouse at Stunts Green, Wartling was rebuilt in brick, probably in *c*1727 when the present brick-fronted farm house was construction. Otherwise, the only oasthouse within the sample to incorporate brick walling is that at Hayes Farm, Northiam, where it was used in the construction of the early/mid 18th-century extension. Even as late as 1793 an 'almost new' oasthouse on Herrings Estate, Dallington possessed walls clad partly in 'clay' (daub) and partly with boarding, whilst the remaining three oasts

on that estate were also of timber construction. None incorporated brick.[34] A survey of Ashburnham Estate made in 1830, however, depicts well the revolution which had occurred in oasthouse construction in the interim, for of the 28 such buildings described in the survey only four were entirely of timber construction, whilst the remainder were either of brick or, in two cases, stone. Even so, many were still at least partially timber framed and weatherboarded on the upper storey.[35]

The obvious reason for the change was the ever present hazard of fire in such buildings, for, in contrast, most barns on the estate were still entirely constructed of timber framing. Similarly, many barns also possessed thatched roof coverings whereas, with two exceptions, the oasthouses were tiled. However, even at this date the roof of the oasthouses at Johns Cross, Mountfield and Herrings, Dallington were thatched, a feature which in earlier times appears not infrequently to have been the

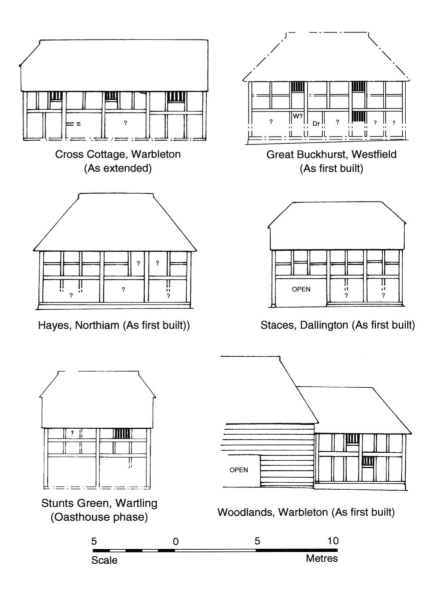

Cross Cottage, Warbleton
(As extended)

Great Buckhurst, Westfield
(As first built)

Hayes, Northiam (As first built))

Staces, Dallington (As first built)

Stunts Green, Wartling
(Oasthouse phase)

Woodlands, Warbleton (As first built)

Scale — 5 0 5 10 Metres

Figure 13.21 (right) External elevations of a selection of oasthouses.

*Figure 13.22 (right)
Mid 18th-century oasthouse
at Hampden Lodge,
Mayfield.* [284/10A]

Internal truss,
Woodlands, Warbleton

Internal truss,
Beechcroft, Herstmonceux

Truss within stowage area

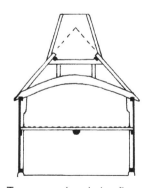

Truss crossing drying floor

Hampden Lodge, Mayfield

5   0   5

Scale   Metres

*Figure 13.23
Examples of open trusses
within oasthouses.*

case. In 1793, for instance, two of the four oasthouses on Herrings Estate were thatched, though admittedly one of these was also partially tiled. The 'malthouse' at Church Farm, Etchingham, possessed a thatched covering in 1597, as did that erected by John Everenden at Sedlescombe in 1622, though the latter was subsequently converted to tile as part of the refurbishments undertaken in 1655-6.[36] One of the three oasthouses built by Roberts on his Ticehurst estate in the 1660s and 1670s specifically mention that the building was to be sufficiently strong to bear tiling, though (by inference) the other two were to be thatched (*see* above).

Having due regard for the fire risk, it seems likely that, wherever possible, owners gave high priority to the tiling of their oasthouses. Even with their increased use of non-combustible materials, the oasthouses on the Ashburnham Estate in 1833 were excluded from fire insurance for the period during which the kilns were in use, a clear indication of the risk attached to such buildings at this time.[37]

At least where surviving buildings are concerned, during the 17th and early/mid 18th centuries roofs usually incorporated hipped terminals, though some half hips are known, as at Stunts Green, Wartling. Indeed, in some instances such terminals were a necessity due to the lowness of the first-floor side walls. For this reason too, the intermediate tiebeams at both Copens and Woodlands were entirely omitted, whilst at Beech Croft, Herstmonceux; Little Bucksteep and Cross Cottage (period B), both in Warbleton; Hayes Farm, Northiam; and Hampden Lodge, Mayfield; the tiebeams in the open trusses were trimmed by passing struts in order to allow greater freedom of movement to those working within the chambers (Figure 13.23). At Hampden Lodge the freestanding truss within the drying chamber itself is fitted with an acutely cambered tiebeam to give a somewhat similar effect, the trusses with truncated tiebeams being restricted to the stowage bays of this particular building. This was not always the case, however, for the truncated tiebeam at Cross Cottage (as extended) was located within the drying chamber, as too may have been the case at Hayes. Those open trusses in oasthouses which do incorporate full tiebeams are only very rarely braced.

Original windows survive in some of the buildings and are evidenced in the majority of the others. All were unglazed and most possessed timber mullions of diamond section. Those at Hampden Lodge are exceptional in that they utilize a series of very thin timber mullions.

Apart from the variations in structure noted above, the general details of construction found in oasthouses may be regarded as similar to those described for barns.

14   ANCILLARY FARM BUILDINGS

As discussed in Chapter 3, barns and oasthouses should not be regarded as the only agricultural buildings which once existed upon the farms. Given the small size of many of the farms, it should perhaps be no surprise that in the early years ancillary buildings were most frequently found on the larger holdings and were usually absent on small farms. They only became common on farms of all sizes during the late 18th and, more particularly, the early 19th centuries. Thus, the cluster of sundry farm buildings found in most farmsteads today only became the norm after the close of the period here under consideration.

With the exception of two stables and a sheephouse, all the known surviving ancillary buildings within the study area appear to post date c1700, and probably represent the better built examples of their types.[1] Even these are few in number and are unlikely to be fully representative of those which formerly existed.

STABLES AND STALLS

Detailed surveys of the Herrings and Ashburnham Estates made in 1793 and 1830 respectively indicate that 80-90% of farms by that date possessed some form of stabling.[2] In other respects the pictures painted by these two surveys differ markedly. For example, whereas in 1793 the stables on the Herrings Estate were of timber and were largely incorporated into barns (either as lofted ends or lean-to outshuts) by 1830 most of those on the Ashburnham Estate were constructed of brick and tile and over half were detached buildings - some were single storeyed, others lofted over. Most of those which were not freestanding were incorporated into either barns or oasthouses.

Although information of this type obtained from just two detailed surveys cannot be taken as proof, the implication is that during the period 1790 to 1830 stables were becoming both larger and better built. Indeed, having regard for the increase in the amount of land devoted to arable (and the resultant increase in the number of draught animals required) and bearing in mind the number of landlords with an eye to agricultural

Figure 14.1
Interior of the small early 17th-century stable at Toll, Warbleton. The roof has been rebuilt and the end lean-to outshut (extreme right) raised to the same height as the remainder of the walls within the building. [324/13]

improvement, this is precisely what one would expect to find.

To return to the period covered by this present study, it has already been demonstrated that both barns and, to a lesser extent, oasthouses sometimes incorporated stabling facilities (*see* Chapters 6 and 13). But how common were detached stables? Were they as scarce as the late 18th-century survey of Herrings Estate suggests?

To judge from the available information, this does indeed appear to have been the case. Five manorial surveys are known for the period 1567-1727 which give reliable details of all buildings upon the tenements. Although in total these surveys cover 76 separate farms, only 13 are recorded as possessing a detached stable. A further three farms are listed as incorporating detached stalls, though the precise definition of a stall at this period is uncertain. Perhaps significantly, all three references are in the Mountfield manorial survey of 1672, a survey which refers to one stable only, and that on a holding which also possessed a stall.[3] It may be that in the mind of this particular surveyor the term 'stall' signified a building housing draught oxen, whereas other surveyors merely used the term 'stable' regardless of whether it housed horses or draught oxen. If this was not the case, then it seems strange that stalls should only be found on Mountfield Manor. Furthermore, bearing in mind that in the High Weald oxen were the principal draught animals at the period under consideration, it seems surprising that in the other four surveys no detached buildings were constructed to house them.

Luckily, for the purposes of this article, such an argument is somewhat superfluous, for it is known from the stalls and stables incorporated into barns that, except in the finer details of their fittings, for all intents and purposes both were identical. In all the surviving known detached examples the fittings have been destroyed.

As with other ancillary buildings, the larger the farm the more likely it was to have included a detached stable/stall. This is well illustrated by an analysis of the 76 farms included in the five reliable mid 16th- to early 18th-century surveys.[4] Forty-four of the farms consisted of less than 50 acres, and of these only two possessed a detached stable or stall, whereas six of the 21 farms of 50-99 acres had such a building, as did seven of the 11 farms of over 100 acres.

Unfortunately very few stables survive. Only seven examples which pre-date *c*1770 are at present known within the rape, and two of these (at Byre House, Northiam and Old Vicarage, Salehurst) have never been associated with agriculture. Even so, as there is unlikely to have been any substantial variation between stables located on farms and those not, they have here been included.

The surviving examples range in size from the two-horse stable at Byre House, which measures 4.00 metres x 3.65 metres (13'2" x 12'0") up to the combined wagon/coach house and stables at Great Dixter, Northiam, which measures 21.40 metres x 6.45 metres (70'3" x 21'3"). This latter example is exceptional. With one, or possibly two exceptions, all possessed an upper loft and are therefore likely to represent the better constructed buildings of their type, a point to some extent borne out by the fact that those at Hill House, Crowhurst and Durrants, Warbleton are constructed of brick and are located upon the home farms of minor gentry.

Built during the first half of the 17th century, the stable at Toll, Warbleton (Figures 14.1 and 14.4) is the earliest confirmed surviving example. It has a relatively tall stable area which is open to the roof, adjacent to which was an end lean-to outshut (now adjusted) which was probably used either as a tackle room or hay store. Those at Byre House, Northiam and Durrants, Warbleton (Figure 14.4) are in many respects very similar to one another. However, at Byre House the two animals faced the end wall, whereas the three animals at Durrants faced

Figure 14.2
Small stable standing beside the road a little to one side of Durrants Farmhouse, Warbleton. The farmyard is located at the opposite end of the farmhouse. [290/2]

Figure 14.3
First-floor loft at Durrants, Warbleton. [290/5]

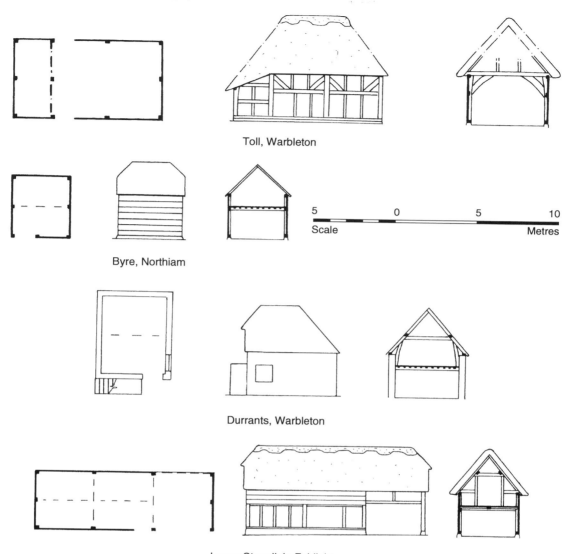

Toll, Warbleton

Byre, Northiam

Durrants, Warbleton

Lower Stonelink, Fairlight

Figure 14.4
A selection of stables and stalls

Figure 14.5
Trusses crossing hay loft over cattle stalls at
Lower Stonelink, Fairlight, viewed from
wagon house in end of building. [212/34A]

the side wall. In both instances the buildings measure approximately 3.75 metres (12'6") from the wall in front of the animal's nose to that behind its tail. The stalls at Byre House would have been approximately 1.75 metres (5'9") wide; those at Durrants approximately 1.65 metres (5'6"). Assuming the animals faced the side wall, Lower Stonelink, Fairlight (Figure 14.4) also shows similar dimensions - it measures 3.75 metres (12'6") in width and, if divided to house four animals, would have had stalls 1.80 metres (5'11") wide. In this instance, however, the building incorporates an extra bay attached to the side of the stable. Unlike the stable area (which is lofted over - *see* Figure 14.5) this third bay was never floored. A full-width opening in its east wall shows it to

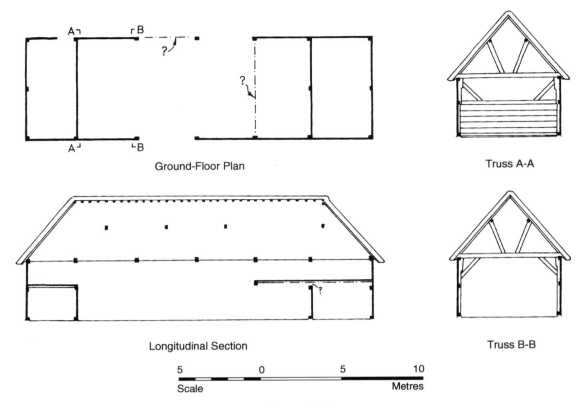

Ground-Floor Plan

Truss A-A

Longitudinal Section

Truss B-B

5   0   5   10
Scale   Metres

Figure 14.6
Probable combined stables and coach house (early 18th century),
Great Dixter, Northiam.

have been used as a wagon shed. A similar arrangement formerly existed in the brick stables of 1725 at Hill House, Crowhurst (not illustrated), and probably also at the Old Vicarage, Salehurst (not illustrated). In the latter two instances any such area was more likely to have housed a coach than a wagon, and this was probably also the case with the massive early 18th-century barn-like structure located in front of the mansion house at Great Dixter, Northiam (Figure 14.6).

OPEN-FRONTED SHELTER SHEDS

It appears not to have been until the late 18th or early 19th centuries that open-fronted cattle shelters and wagon lodges became commonplace. Judging from the survey of Herrings Estate, Dallington, made in 1793, some changes were already under way by that date, though the principal period of construction for such buildings appears to have been between *c*1790 and 1830. By 1830 virtually all the farms in excess of 100 acres, and roughly half those below that acreage on the extensive Ashburnham Estate possessed a wagon lodge and from one to as many as seven cattle shelters (excluding those incorporated into lean-to outshuts).[5] Some farms are included in both the 1793 and 1830

surveys, and these illustrate very clearly the major increase in such buildings which occurred between these two dates (*see* Figure 3.13).

Prior to the mid 18th century open-fronted shelters appear to have been very rare, none being mentioned on the 76 farms included within the five mid 16th- to early 18th-century surveys for which good building details are given. For that matter, no confirmed reference has as yet been found locally to an open-fronted cattle shelter prior to 1748, at which date such a shed (one of the four still known to survive) is depicted at Downoak Farm, Westfield (*see* below).[6] It is accepted that a few sundry references, such as that in 1643 when John Everenden of Sedlescombe set up a lodge for fattening oxen, could relate to this type of building.[7] References to wagon houses are a little more numerous, four being mentioned in the 89 early 18th-century inventories analysed covering ten parishes in the northeast of Hastings rape.[8] Of these, three were described as wain houses and a fourth as 'lodges' (in the plural). In addition, there are a few known casual references to such buildings. For instance, under the terms of a lease dated 1712 relating to the 96-acre Hobbs Farm, Beckley, the landlord was to improve the oasthouse and set up a wain lodge. At that date the holding already contained a farmhouse, barn and

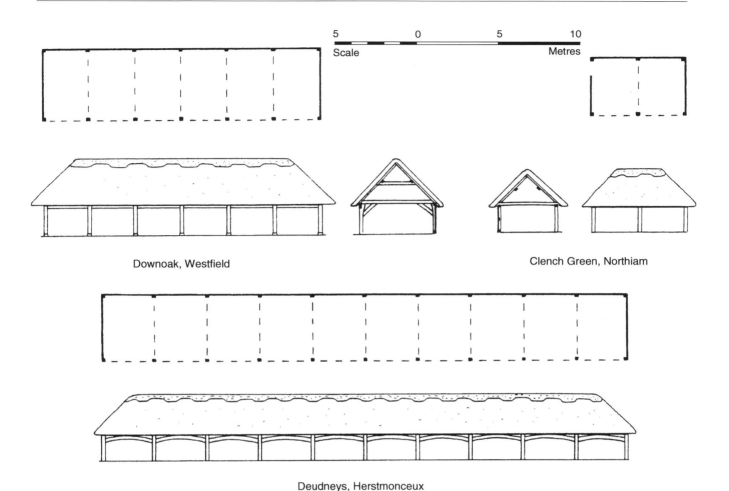

Downoak, Westfield

Clench Green, Northiam

Deudneys, Herstmonceux

Figure 14.7
A selection of open-fronted shelter sheds

Figure 14.8
Shelter shed cut down in width and reused as
a lean-to outshut, Coopers, Wartling. [322/14]

stable, in addition to the oasthouse.[9] Even so, it seems likely that wagon lodges were rare, even on large farms, prior to the late 17th century.

Although surviving late 18th- and 19th-century shelter sheds are common, only four early examples, together with a further three fragments, are currently known within the rape. One of the fragments, now cut down in width and added as a lean-to outshut to the barn at Coopers, Wartling, appears to be of 17th-century date (*see* Figure 14.8), though the remainder almost certainly belong to the mid 18th century. Details of the four complete examples are shown in Figures 14.7 and 14.9. Those at Downoak, Westfield; Deudneys, Herstmonceux; and Prinkle, Wartling, are timber framed in traditional style with jowled principal posts, arch bracing to the open trusses, and walls of weatherboarding fixed to regularly-spaced studs.

The shelter shed at Prinkle, Wartling is the most elaborate of the three, examples. It is double width and appears to have incorporated a central partition

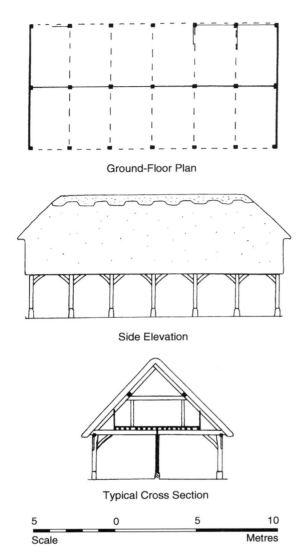

Ground-Floor Plan

Side Elevation

Typical Cross Section

5   0   5   10
Scale   Metres

Figure 14.9
Details of shelter shed with granary over,
Prinkle, Wartling.

Figure 14.10
Shelter shed at Prinkle, Wartling. [324/30]

Figure 14.11
Loft over shelter shed at Prinkle, Wartling. [324/24]

(Figure 14.9). Some of the posts contain round-ended mortices for rails, allowing the formation of pens, whilst the attic space above the shelter was utilized as a granary. The open arcades down the side of the building are arch braced in order to strengthen the wallplates. Additional timbers are incorporated immediately below the wallplates at Downoak for the same reason, a feature also found over the wagon doors of some barns (*see* Chapter 5). A similar effect is achieved at Deudneys by introducing a curved timber beneath the wallplate.

A fourth shelter shed, that at Clench Green, Northiam, is somewhat atypical in that its principal posts lack jowls and there is a complete absence of bracing. Furthermore, although the walls are boarded, the boards are butt edged and set vertically. Each plank is nailed to

Figure 14.12
Exterior of tiny shelter shed at
Clench Green, Northiam. [248/18A]

Figure 14.13
Clench Green, Northiam. Vertical board wall fixed
at mid height to a horizontal rail [248/18A]

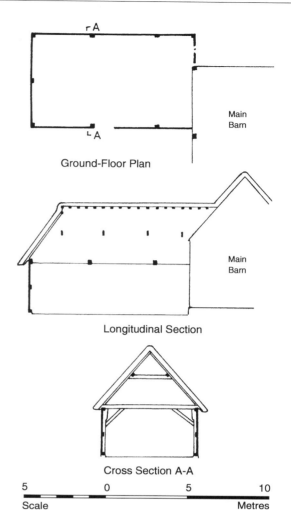

Figure 14.14
Cattle House at Little Bainden, Mayfield.

the face of the frame at top and bottom and strengthened at mid-height by a horizontal rail jointed into the principal posts. Most of the rails have been replaced, but where they survive they have rounded edges. At the northern end of the west wall is a contemporary doorway.

With the exception of the building at Prinkle (which makes use of staggered-butt-purlin construction with late-style windbraces and half-hipped terminals) the roofs are of clasped-side-purlin type with collar trusses and hipped ends. All were thatched. Deudneys incorporates plank windbraces nailed to the soffit of the rafters, a feature noticed in a few late barns (*see* Chapter 10).

OTHER TYPES OF BUILDINGS

Not all the ancillary buildings of the 16th, 17th and early 18th centuries complied to the types so far described, though these were the most common. The 1597 survey of the tenements held at the will of the lord of Etchingham Manor, for instance, mentions a 'little

house for calves' together with 'outhouses for the housing of cattle of five rooms' and 'one other little house boarded'.[10] An early 18th-century fully enclosed cattle house still exists attached to the barn at Little Bainden, Mayfield (Figures 14.14 and 14.15). Measuring 9.95 metres x 5.95 metres (32'8" x 19'6"), it is very barn-like in its general appearance, except that it possesses but one small, normal-width doorway. There are no indications of there having been permanent pens or stalls within the building. In terms of its general design it can be compared to the large, two-bay area divided off at the end of the early 18th-century barn at Cralle, Warbleton.

Another barn-like structure is the sheephouse which was built in the late 16th century upon the home farm of Brede Place (Figures 14.16 and 14.17). This isolated building is the only known example within the rape of a structure purposely constructed for the care of sheep. Its existence is probably explained by the large flocks which the farm ran upon its extensive marshlands adjacent to the River Brede. Except for its exceptionally

*Figure 14.15
Interior of cattle
house at
Little Bainden,
Mayfield,
showing loose
temporary pens
for the animals.
[283/15]*

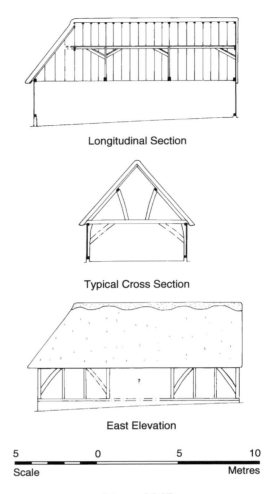

Longitudinal Section

Typical Cross Section

East Elevation

*Figure 14.17
Reconstruction drawing of Sheephouse,
Brede, as built in the late 16th century.*

*Figure 14.16
The Sheephouse, Brede, as in the 1920s or 1930s,
prior to its conversion into a dwelling. [440/6]*

low walls, the design of the building varies in no major way from that of a typical local barn. Indeed, tall wagon doors were later inserted into one of its side walls in order that it could be utilized for that purpose. It is now converted into a house.

Several other types of building which are known to have occasionally been built are not represented locally by surviving examples. For instance, apple mills used in the making of cider formerly existed at Rowley Farm, Ticehurst and Abbey Farm, Salehurst, whilst the 1567 Robertsbridge manorial survey also mentions the occasional hayloft.[11] Detached granaries also appear to have been built in the area, but only very occasionally. Two early 18th-century inventories appear to refer to such buildings upon farms in Udimore and Peasmarsh.[12] The only other known reference to such a building within the study area is an early/mid 19th-century painting of an unidentified farmstead, supposedly near Hastings, in which a small rectangular granary is shown set on staddle stones close to a barn.[13]

15   THE FARMHOUSE AND ITS ASSOCIATED OUTHOUSING

When considering agricultural buildings the farmhouse itself, together with any attendant outhousing, should not be overlooked, for the sharp divide which often exists today between workplace and home was far less apparent in past centuries. In addition to providing accommodation for the farmer and his family, the house on an agricultural holding also commonly incorporated a milkhouse used for the processing of dairy products, commercial meat processing areas, spaces dedicated to the storage of grain and other produce, and, in some instances, malt manufacture and hop drying. In all these respects the farmhouse varied markedly from those houses not associated with agriculture.

GRAIN AND FRUIT STORAGE

Although in some instances during the early 18th century threshed grain was stored within the floored ends of barns or within oasthouses, or (perhaps very occasionally) in a purpose-built granary, the probate inventories indicate that it was normal within the High Weald to use part of the farmhouse for this purpose. Most houses by this date possessed a garret area, and, within the average-size farmhouse, it was this space which was normally used as the granary and produce store. In smaller houses in which the upper chambers still remained open to the roof, or which incorporated either flimsy or high-set ceilings, one of the first-floor chambers was normally utilized. Likewise, those large houses which incorporated rear wings sometimes used first-floor chambers within these rear parts of the house for this purpose.[1] Where first-floor storage was adopted within a small house one of the chambers above the service rooms was normally chosen. In almost all instances neither the storage chambers nor the garrets contained beds: even beds of low value are absent.

Four of the forty early 18th-century inventories examined as part of this study recorded crops stored in both the garret and within one of the service chambers, though in two of these the service chamber and garret were described together, suggesting that they were in some way linked.[2] It may be that these buildings embodied a similar design to that found at Roadend Farmhouse, Udimore and Rose Bank, Robertsbridge, where the service chamber not only remained open to the roof in 1981, but was then still used for storage purposes and had direct access to the garret space above the other chambers, with no partition between the chamber and garret.

In another example (Partridges, Iden, *see* Figure 15.1) the garret was reached through the service chamber, in this instance called the 'old mill room'. Neither space was linked by doorways to the first-floor bed chambers, but were instead reached by a separate

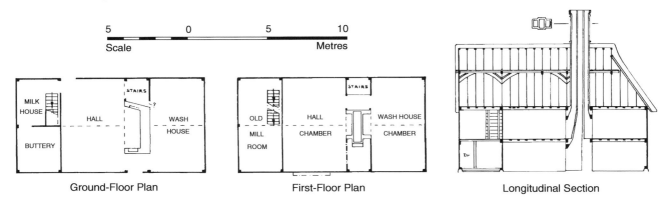

Figure 15.1
Partridges, Iden. Details as in the early 18th century.

stair, as had been the case since the house was built in the third quarter of the 16th century. This was a 30 acre holding which in 1730 was occupied by Steven Spilstead who, in addition to farming the property, carried on a business as a joiner. Like many other small farmers at this time, he was a dual-economist, being supported both by his meagre agricultural income and that earned as a craftsman. Within his garret in November 1730 were housed a load of wheat, 11 sacks, some apples and 'other things', whilst the old mill room housed a quern (hence 'mill room') a chest, some peas and oats and 'other things'.[3]

A variation on this theme existed in 1712 at Forstal Farm, within the same parish. Thomas Cadwell who occupied it was one of the largest farmers in the parish, being tenant not only of this 125-acre holding, but also of a nearby, but separately owned barn and 86 acres called 'Parklands'. At his death in 1712 the house at Forstal was only 10 years old. It still survives and is of 'T' plan, with the principal rooms located within the head of the 'T', behind which is a much lower rear range (Figure 15.2). A reconstruction of its form in 1712 is shown in Figure 15.3. In this instance the extensive storage garrets above the principal bed chambers in the main range were reached through the independently accessed farm servants' lodgings within the loft-like first-floor chamber in the rear range. This chamber was still open to the roof and still housed the garret stairs in 1977 (Figure 15.4). When Cadwell's inventory was appraised in October 1712 the garrets had within them about seven seams of wheat, four bushels of malt, a malt mill and some old iron. The servant's chamber (or 'wash house chamber' as it was called in the inventory) through which the garrets were reached had within it three beds, but, apparently, no other furniture, and no stored goods worth specifying.[4]

Numerous other examples could be cited, but

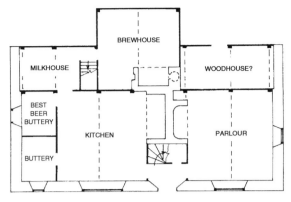

Ground-Floor Plan

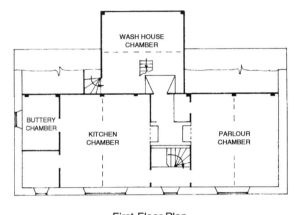

First-Floor Plan

Figure 15.3
Forstal, Iden, as built in 1692 and as existing
at the death of Thomas Cadwell in 1712.

Figure 15.2
Rear of Forstal, Iden, showing low
brewhouse/wash house range projecting
at right angles from the main range. [202/29]

Figure 15.4
Forstal, Iden. Interior of 'wash house chamber'
which in 1977 remained open to its roof and still
contained the stair rising to the storage garrets
over the chambers in the main range. [202/19]

those given above will suffice to indicate the kinds of arrangements found at this period. The situation as described for the early 18th century is known to have applied to the mid 17th century also, and almost certainly dates back to the introduction of ceilings into chambers, which occurred commonly from the late 16th century onwards.[5] But what of the period before?

Prior to the existence of garrets it would be logical to suggest that one of the first-floor chambers within the farmhouse would have been used for storing threshed crops and other farm produce, as was indeed the case in those later houses which lacked garrets. In some areas of England the chamber over a formerly open hall was utilized for this purpose, but this appears not to have been the case in eastern Sussex. In the Weald the hall chamber was usually the first to be improved by the insertion of a ceiling. Furthermore, it was commonly heated from the outset by the only first-floor fireplace.[6] Even so, there is good evidence from the medieval/post-medieval transition to suggest that one of the chambers was indeed utilized for storage. It was not that over the hall, but that located over the service rooms. The evidence comes from a number of houses built between 1500 and 1540.[7] From the outset these buildings possessed floored-over halls and contemporary chimneys (either timber framed or brick) but did not initially incorporate an interconnecting doorway between the hall chamber and service chamber. Thus, although both the hall chamber and parlour chamber were interconnected and were accessible via a single staircase at the parlour end of the house, the service chamber was reached via its own dedicated stairs.

Because of the nature of the alterations it is more difficult to pick up similar arrangements within the modifications of this period made to medieval houses. Despite this, occasional examples can be observed. At Parkhill, Burwash a chamber was inserted into the lower end of a medieval open hall early in the 16th century, leaving the upper bay of the hall open to the roof. No doorway was cut through to interconnect the new chamber with the adjacent service chamber; it was instead supplied with its own stairs rising through the hall ceiling.[8] The implication of this is that the existing function of the service chamber was quite different from that intended for the new chamber over the lower hall bay, and thus no interconnection was required (or indeed desirable) between these two chambers.

It is true that this segregation of the service chamber from the remainder of the house need not imply a storage function, though at 25/27 High Street, Robertsbridge this was the only chamber to lack a contemporary ceiling, implying a lowly use. At Parkhill, Burwash (mentioned above) this low-status use for the service chamber can be traced back to medieval times, for even when first built the windows within this chamber were not fitted with sliding shutters, whereas those within the parlour chamber were.

Even when ceilings were finally inserted into the upper chambers the service chamber was often left open to the roof until a late date, an indication of its continued lowly status.[9] These factors, together with the known later preference for the use of service chambers for storage in houses where garret storage was not an option, must make a strong case for their normal use from an early date for storage purposes. Indeed, as both the 'parlour' and its room above are known during the medieval and transitional periods to have been utilized as bed/sitting chambers, at this period there was no alternative place available within the house for crop storage (but *see* below with regards to larger farms).[10]

The configuration described above has considerable logic. The private apartments (parlour and associated room over) were located at the 'high end' of the hall, away from the main external doorways, and were usually divided from the hall by a single doorway serving both spaces. In contrast, the work rooms (services) and the chamber above them were situated at the 'low end' of the hall, near the entrances and were each independently accessed from the hall. It was only the introduction of garrets into the roof spaces during the later years of the 16th century that allowed the transfer of the processed crops up into the garrets, freeing the entire first floor for use as bed chambers. This in turn, freed the parlour of beds, allowing it to become truly a withdrawing or 'best' room.

THE MILKHOUSE

The documentary sources indicate that during the 17th and early 18th centuries a milkhouse was considered essential upon all working farms. Even where a farmhouse inventory mentions two service rooms or less, the milkhouse is invariably present, though in such circumstances its contents show it to have doubled as either a pantry and/or buttery.[11] It was here, on fixed benches, that the butter and cheese was manufactured. The cheese press, being a large piece of equipment, was often housed elsewhere. Likewise, it was not unusual to store the ripening cheeses in another part of the building, though it will be no surprise to learn that few followed the example of Thomas Cadwell of Forstal Farm, Iden, who, in 1712, was storing his 39 cheeses within his parlour.[12] Perhaps he did not entertain his neighbours very often!

Whether the milkhouse had always been a feature of the farmhouses of eastern Sussex is not clear. An isolated inventory of a farm in Hooe dated 1455 mentions a hall, chamber, storeroom, and kitchen (the latter perhaps detached) but there is no mention of a milkhouse. Furthermore, the kitchen was the only room mentioned which housed utensils which may have been used in association with butter and cheese-making.[13]

HOP DRYING AND MALT MANUFACTURE WITHIN FARMHOUSES

It may seen unusual to associate hop-drying activities with farmhouses, yet in 1574 Reynold Scot records that 'some use to dry their hops in a garret, or upon the floor of a loft or chamber' and he goes on to say that 'if you have no oste, dry them in a loft as open to the air as may be'. He advises such people to ensure that the loft is thoroughly clean before laying the hops 'not half a foot thick' and suggests that they 'turn them once a day at least, by the space of two or three weeks. This being done, sweep them into a corner of your loft, and there let them lye as long more, for yet there remaineth peril in packing them'.[14]

How long such makeshift drying methods persisted, or how common they were can only be guessed, for they would leave no architectural evidence. In this respect it may be no coincidence that purpose-built oasthouses appear to have been uncommon until the mid 17th century, perhaps suggesting that prior to that date most hop acreages were too small to warrant investment in dedicated structures (*see* Chapter 13). However, it is equally possible that in these early days the low acreages dedicated to hops only warranted the construction of a small drying kiln or 'oast' which could be accommodated within the corner of a room within the house. An oast of this type may have been incorporated within the exceptionally large attached service range at Church House, Northiam in 1628, for the 'oasthouse' and 'oast chamber' of John Frewen are described in his inventory sandwiched between the buttery and garret of his house. As the 'oast chamber' included two beds and other furnishings, the 'oast' may have been a fixture within a ground-floor service room, with a normal chamber above it (*ie* the oast chamber was so called because of its location above the room incorporating the oast, rather than reflecting the chamber's use in connection with hop drying or malt manufacture).[15] In this respect the oast may have taken a similar form to that which existed within the detached kitchen at Great Worge, Brightling, in 1567 (*see* below).

AGRICULTURAL ACTIVITIES UNDERTAKEN WITHIN AN OUTHOUSE ASSOCIATED WITH THE FARMHOUSE

The preceding section indicates that indoor farming-related activities (both storage and processing) were not confined to dedicated buildings located within the farmstead. They could (and often were) carried on within what we would today consider domestic space. In

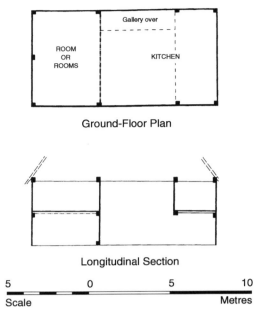

Ground-Floor Plan

Longitudinal Section

Figure 15.5
Detached 'kitchen' at Beestons, Warbleton.

this respect it is worth bearing in mind that during the 15th and 16th centuries a number of households - especially those associated with large acreages - may have opted for an alternative solution.

It is known that during this period in addition to a house and barn a surprisingly high percentage of properties within the High Weald possessed a detached service building, called in the documents a '*coquina*' or 'kitchen'. Few of these buildings survive, but those which do are often relatively large, multi-roomed structures of two storeys. Typically they have two or three ground-floor rooms (of which the principal room - the 'kitchen' proper - was partially open from ground to roof) and incorporated one or more first-floor chambers. The example illustrated in Figure 15.5 is that at Beestons Farm, Warbleton, which, after having apparently been used as a house for a short time in the early 17th century, was subsequently converted into an oasthouse.[16]

The agricultural processing activities described above as often carried out within the farmhouse were all capable of being undertaken equally well within a detached 'kitchen', thereby removing them from the domestic environment. That this was indeed sometimes (if not commonly) the case is indicated by a description made in 1567 of a detached kitchen at Great Worge, Brightling. It was a multi-roomed, two-storeyed building, apparently of the type which most commonly survives today. It measured 30 foot by 16½ foot (9.15 metres x 5.00 metres) internally and included, on the ground floor, what sounds like a purely domestic bakehouse. An oven is listed within the main room - the 'kitchen' proper - so the 'bakehouse' was most likely used solely for the preparation of items for baking. In addition to the oven, the main room also included an 'oast to dry malt', indicating that it incorporated the function of an oasthouse. The principal purpose of this room, however, was described as the 'dressing of meat' (*ie* the cutting up of carcases into joints). A third ground-floor room was in use as a 'milkhouse', so in this instance the dairying too was undertaken within the 'kitchen'

Figure 15.6 (above)
One of the upper chambers within the mid/late 16th century 'kitchen' at Wardsbrook, Ticehurst. The first-floor chambers within late medieval and early post-medieval houses (and, indeed, within some barns) would have been very similar to this in both size and appearance. [284/33A]

Figure 15.7 (right)
Longitudinal section through Combe Manor, Wadhurst showing a 'kitchen' building added onto the end of the farmhouse during the middle years of the 16th century.

building rather than within the farmhouse.[17] Although this particular kitchen no longer survives, the house does. It is of 'Wealden' design and incorporates the usual pair of service rooms, which presumably in this instance were used in textbook fashion as buttery and pantry (rather than buttery and milkhouse).

Of the agricultural functions described earlier as commonly undertaken within the farmhouse, the only element missing from the kitchen at Great Worge was that of grain and fruit storage. The 1567 description makes clear that upper chambers were present, and these were probably similar in both appearance and size to those in the extant 'kitchen' buildings, an example of which is illustrated in Figure 15.6. What the 1567 description does not indicate is the uses to which these first-floor spaces were put. Grain and fruit storage must be likely contenders for at least one of the chambers. In this respect it may be no coincidence that the service chamber within the farmhouse at Great Worge is abnormally well finished. It incorporates an open truss and seems to have been intended as a principal chamber rather than for the storage of produce.

With one possible exception - Comphurst, Wartling - all the large rural multi-roomed detached 'kitchens' which survive within the study area are located upon what were, by local East Sussex standards, exceptionally large holdings. Even the owner of Comphurst is known to have leased an undefined acreage of demesne and thus, despite owning less than 50 acres, he too may have run a substantial farming enterprise. None of the other holdings was less than 100 acres in extent, and four exceeded 200 acres. Great Worge was of similar large size.[18]

As the 16th century progressed detached 'kitchens' fell increasingly from favour. Perhaps significantly, during this same period attached service ranges of similar layout were sometimes incorporated either at one end or, more often, at the rear of farmhouses on large-acreage holdings. Typical examples from Combe Manor,

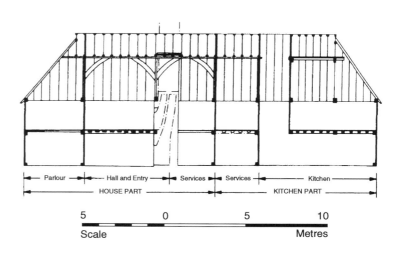

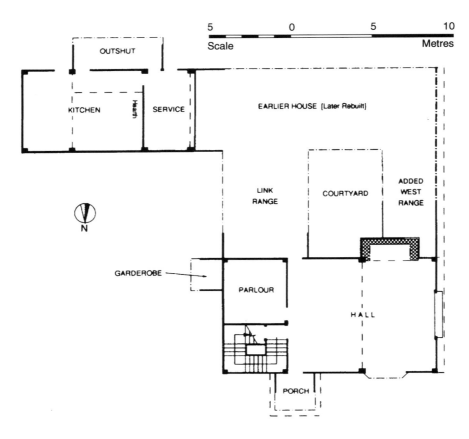

Figure 15.8
Ground-floor plan of Wardsbrook, Ticehurst in the mid 16th century
following the construction of the attached 'kitchen' range extending
eastwards from the rear of the house. The house was sized down in c1700
at which date the 'kitchen' range became a detached oasthouse (see Figure 15.10)

Wadhurst; Bugsell, Salehurst; and Wardsbrook, Ticehurst are shown in Figures 15.7 to 15.9.

It was almost certainly the norm for average local households to have consisted of a nuclear, or, at most, a three-generation family. But given the exceptionally large acreages of the farms which incorporated these detached and attached multi-roomed kitchens, is that assumption valid in these cases? Unfortunately there is little evidence to help answer this question. Live-in farm servants appear to have been rare in the Weald of East Sussex, but, despite this, by the early 18th century they were usual on large farms (*see* Chapter 2). Whether the same household structure existed in the 16th century is unclear. However, given the large size of the holdings upon which these multi-roomed 'kitchens' are located, it is certainly possible that these buildings were being used in part to accommodate resident farm workers. Furthermore, sufficient is known regarding the farming practices of the region to be certain that, in general terms, the smaller the holding the more it tended towards subsistence farming, whilst the larger holdings were

usually run as profit-making businesses. These large holdings are precisely the type which would have required large storage areas for processing grain and pulses. The Great Worge description mentions malting, an operation which could be classed as either domestic or agricultural/industrial, depending upon the scale of the operation. Some of the fruit and vegetables would have required processing and, if grown on a commercial scale, both the processing and subsequent storage may have required considerable space.

The above addresses crop processing and storage only. But it should be remembered that the Weald was primarily a cattle fatstock region. Could the same logic apply to meat? Prior to the over-wintering of most animals, the autumn cull is likely to have produced a not inconsiderable number of carcases, some of which might have been smoked, other salted. The Great Worge description makes it clear that one of the uses of the principal room within that kitchen was dressing carcases. This and the associated preservation process required space. If the carcases were smoked, this would explain

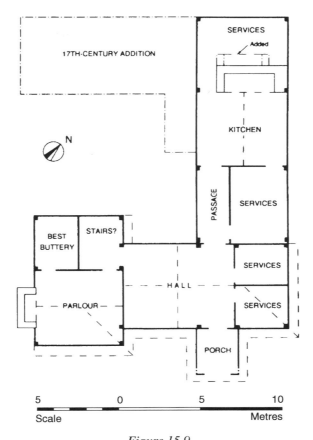

Figure 15.9
Ground-floor plan of Bugsell, Salehurst showing attached 'kitchen' range extending back from the main range. Note how in the early 17th century the house was again extended, converting it into 'U' plan with additional service and storage rooms within the added range.

Figure 15.10
'Kitchen' range at Wardsbrook, Ticehurst. It was detached from the house when the latter was sized down in c1700. The oast roundels were added in the 19th century. [284/25A]

the continued inclusion of an area open to the rafters within kitchen buildings, and indeed kitchen ranges on larger farms, long after the demise of the open hall. Could it in part also explain the galleries which crossed most of these rooms? Regardless of whether cured or salted, the processed carcases would require storage, and this is likely to have been considerable on these large-acreage farms where meat was produced for the market as well as household requirements.

Even if the operator of a small family farm wished to fully segregate his farming activities from this living space, it is unlikely that the scale of his operations, or indeed the profitability of his activities would have made this possible. The high number of detached kitchens present, even on small farms during the 16th century may have meant that some of the more smelly and obnoxious processes could be segregated, but for such men domestic grain storage and dairying would, no doubt, have mostly been undertaken within the farmhouse. But, on those few large-acreage holdings the farmer - be he owner or tenant - had the opportunity to process and store the commercial products of his farm, and to lodge his agricultural servants away from his living areas. Whether these spaces should be classified as domestic or agricultural is another matter. Indeed, to attempt such a classification risks forming artificial barriers which our ancestors would not have recognized. They lived and worked from home.

16   CONCLUSIONS

All currently available evidence suggests that during the 15th century and the first half of the 16th century Wealden agriculture was in depression. However, the number of surviving hall houses of the period must indicate that for some of the local population a relatively high standard of living was attainable. Perhaps significantly, the highest concentrations of such buildings are found in the towns of Battle, Hastings, Rye and Winchelsea and in the much more rural nucleated trading settlements of Burwash, Robertsbridge and Sedlescombe, centres where agriculture played but a secondary role. Very few barns survive locally from before the mid 16th century, whilst those which do appear in no way to be typical.

It is known from documentary sources that during the mid 16th century virtually all holdings in excess of 15 acres (and a few below that acreage) possessed a barn. At this time about half the farms were of no more than 15-50 acres in extent. In the mid 15th century the number of small farms is likely to have been greater. It must be significant that almost all the surviving barns of this period appear to have been located upon farms in excess of 50 acres. Furthermore, having due regard for the low level of Wealden rents at this time, and bearing in mind the general state of local agriculture, it seems fair to suggest that those barns which survive were constructed by the more wealthy owner-occupiers or, to a lesser extent, by the owners of major estates with large, well maintained farms capable of attracting good tenants. This point is further emphasized by the general high quality of construction to be seen within the extant examples. For example, the timbers of all the surviving barns of this period are of ample scantling and good quality. The external walls of most originally incorporated at least some weatherboarding which was accommodated into the frame using either neatly-cut grooves or rebates - an expensive and totally unnecessary detail.

It can be argued, therefore, that these early barns are of little use in ascertaining the nature of an 'average' barn at this period. The economic circumstances of the region at that time were probably sufficient to discourage heavy investment in building stock by all but the more successful of owner-occupiers and rentiers. The very fact that none of the 'average' buildings have survived, even in an extended form, or as reused material incorporated into later buildings, must surely suggest that they were in some way considered inferior to their successors. They were probably both cheap and easy to erect and were, perhaps, built using small-section timbers (not exclusively, indeed perhaps rarely of oak) which were considered not worth reusing - or able to be reused - when the buildings were reconstructed.

Demographic pressures, which occurred in tandem with an increase in economic activity during the reign of Elizabeth heralded a time of change for Wealden agriculture. This change, it is argued, was sufficiently marked to be classed as revolutionary, albeit that it was relatively minor in nature in comparison to that experienced in later times. For many years it has been known that an upsurge in the reconstruction and modification of local dwellings occurred during this period. It should, therefore, not be too surprising to discover that a major rebuild of barns also occurred during the same period. The causes are not difficult to detect. Since the 1510s inflation had gradually been taking hold, though due to the depressed state of local agriculture, it was not until the 1550s that Wealden rents began to reflect this. A noticeable, though slight increase in the construction of barns during the mid 16th century can be interpreted as a response to rising wheat prices by the more progressive of the larger owner-occupiers. However, not until the 1580s and 90s is widespread evidence found of major improvements in Wealden agriculture. Local rents were by this date rising far more steeply than inflation, a likely reaction to increasing population, which stimulated demand for land. High wheat prices encouraged an increase in the arable acreage which in turn necessitated an increase in crop storage capacity. Greatly improved rents encouraged many landowners to respond positively to their tenants' requests for improved storage facilities, especially if this gave an excuse for increasing rents still further.

Even the barns on small farms commonly survive for this period, though not surprisingly their survival rate appears to have been half that for barns on farms of 50-150 acres, and a quarter that on farms in excess of 150 acres. However, in common with the barns on larger farms, they are invariably well built. They use purpose-cut, neatly-squared timbers with little inclusion of waney edges. The carpentry techniques adopted are as sophisticated as those found in dwellings of the period, whilst their constructional design reflects little or no financial restraint.

The vast majority of barns within the study area which survive from this time are relatively small. Roughly half incorporate either one or two storage bays only. Considering the size of the farming units and the regional bias towards cattle-rearing and fattening (as opposed to arable farming) this should not be surprising. Equally expected is the high proportion of barns which incorporate within them either animal-shelters or other specialized functions. However, the discovery of regional variations within the rape, both as regards the distribution of barns incorporating ancillary functions and the method by which they were accommodated, was entirely unexpected. For example, in the north of the rape roughly two-thirds of the surviving barns of this period incorporate ancillary functions, compared with only a third in the southern coastal region. Furthermore, in the north the ancillary functions were at this date principally accommodated within lofted bays, whereas along the coastal area lean-to outshuts were utilized almost exclusively. Likewise, in the coastal region aisled barns are more common that unaisled examples, whilst in the north aisles are very rarely encountered.

It is perhaps worth observing that both lean-to outshuts and aisles are similar to one another in their general external appearance. In terms of their construction they vary only in as much as aisles incorporate an open arcade between them and the main body of the barn, whereas a lean-to is divided from the barn proper by a wall. Whether the regional differences noted above were caused by an as yet undetected subtle variation in the agriculture of the two areas, or whether it represents a hang-over from an earlier tradition rooted, say, in the initial settlement pattern of the region is as yet unclear. Until detailed work is undertaken in the neighbouring areas it is not even known whether the variations noted above form part of an overall pattern, or merely an isolated local phenomenon.

Although barns are effectively the only agricultural buildings to survive from the period before the mid 17th century, they were not the only structures present. Admittedly other buildings were not common. The existence of more than one farm building (in addition to the farmhouse and barn) was at this time rare on all but the larger farms. At this date small farms of

between 15 and 50 acres accounted for roughly half the total number of agricultural holdings. Few of these possessed anything more than a house and barn. No wonder so many barns incorporated ancillary functions! Most of the additional buildings which then existed were devoted to the shelter of cattle and/or horses.

Local rents and wheat prices continued to rise during the early 17th century, wheat prices reaching a peak during the 1640s. Up to this time the reconstruction of barns doubtlessly continued, though with greater stability of both rents and arable acreages, the rate of rebuilding was no doubt slowing down. The second half of the 17th century actually saw a reduction in wheat prices which, coupled with stable rents and only very slight inflation, gave little incentive for the construction of new barns. Falling rents and a slump in wheat prices during the early 18th century must have had very much the same effect. This theoretical period of reduced building actively is reflected well by a very marked drop in the number of surviving barns datable to this period.

Furthermore, when compared with those of the 'rebuild', in many cases the barns which were constructed during this period show distinct signs of economic restraint. Timber scantlings were reduced, waney-edged timber, large quantities of sapwood, and reused material all became commonplace. Surplus braces were omitted, and roof forms became increasingly basic in their construction. It is not that the buildings were being under-designed, merely that the conspicuous waste of the 'rebuild' period was being pared away. Even so, it must be admitted that in many instances the quality of the workmanship had dropped, especially where finish was concerned. In some respects, however, the new buildings were superior to their predecessors, for weatherboarding was used with increased regularity at all social levels. By the end of the period the use of daub infill in surviving buildings was all but unheard of.

Probably the most important change to occur regarding agricultural buildings during this period was the widespread introduction of oasthouses. Such buildings had existed in small numbers during the 'rebuild' era and, where used solely for malt manufacture, even before that date. But it was during the mid/late 17th century that these buildings became common on all but the small-acreage farms. Towards the end of the period open-fronted shelter sheds (for both animals and wagons) also began to become more frequent on both medium-sized and large farms.

After a century of relatively stability, rents, wheat prices, and the cost of living were by *c*1740 all rising once again, albeit slowly at first. Increasing local population throughout the second half of the 18th century, followed by a very marked rise in wheat prices during the 1800s and 1810s resulted in a phenomenal increase in the amount of local land devoted to arable, and a major burst of farm amalgamations. Inevitably this caused a spate of barn reconstructions and extension works, on a par with, if not more marked than that which had occurred during the late 16th- and early 17th-century 'rebuild'. In common with the period preceding the 'rebuild', the larger, more progressive farmers appear to have taken advantage of rising wheat prices as soon as they occurred, for already by the 1740s some men in this group were either rebuilding or enlarging their barns. But these men were the exception. There appears to have been a relatively slow build up towards the peak in rebuilds which occurred during the closing years of the 18th century and the first half of the 19th century - the period often labelled 'The Agricultural Revolution'.

With so much of the land devoted to arable, cattle appear to have been housed either within doors or in pens and yards in greater numbers and for longer periods than ever before. Shelter sheds serving outdoor pens and yards were already present on many farms by *c*1770. The major period for the construction of such buildings, however, appears to have occurred between 1770 and 1830. In marked contrast to earlier periods, by the mid 19th century it was exceptional to find a farm without at least one open-fronted cattle shelter. Many possessed several such buildings. The same period saw the introduction of wagon sheds as a norm and a major burst of oasthouse reconstructions brought about by a radical increase in hop acreages and major improvements in drying techniques.

The 20th century saw the virtual demise of the small working farm, with many farmyards standing derelict or, in latter years converted to domestic use. Upon those farms which remain active, the traditional buildings are in most instances considered grossly inadequate for modern agriculture and are being swept aside to make way for yet another generation of farm buildings. In both design and appearance these differ totally from their predecessors.

17   NOTES AND REFERENCES

ABBREVIATIONS

BL	British Library.
CKS	Centre for Kentish Studies, Maidstone.
ESRO	East Sussex Record Office, Lewes.
HBES	Historic Buildings in Eastern Sussex.
HMAG	Hastings Museum and Art Gallery.
PRO	Public Record Office.
ROHAS	Rape of Hastings Architectural Survey.
SAC	Sussex Archaeological Collections.
SRS	Sussex Record Society.
UCLFAU	University College London Field Archaeology Unit.
VCH	Victoria County Histories of England, The County of Sussex.
WSRO	West Sussex Record Office, Chichester.

NOTES AND REFERENCES

1   INTRODUCTION

1. L Caffyn, A Study of Farm Buildings in Selected Parishes of East Susses, in *SAC* **121** (1983), 149-172. The three chapters on barns in J. Warren (ed.). *Wealden Buildings: studies in Kent, Sussex and Surrey* (1990) are, D. Martin and B. J. Martin, Farm buildings in the Eastern Weald; K. Coutin and M. Holt, Barns of the High Weald; R. Dales, Warnham Barns: a parish study in the Western Weald.
2. Jones and Bell 1992.
3. D. Martin, *A Study of the pre-1750 barns within the Rape of Hastings to ascertain their current survival and usage* (UCLFAU, unpublished report (January 1992).

2   THE AGRICULTURAL SCENE

1. For further details regarding geology *see* Institute of Geological Sciences 1"-1 mile and 1:25,000 detailed geological maps; R. W. Gallois, *British Regional Geology: The Wealden District* (4th Edition 1965, based on previous editions by the late F. H. Edmunds MA).
2. Brent 1976, 48.
3. Brent 1976, 39.
4. Brent 1976, 43.

5. ESRO ELT. The figures have been calculated by dividing the total rental assessment of the parish (less assessments for woodland, tithes, stock *etc*) by the total acreage of the parish (less principal tracts of woodland). In those parishes where the rental value of woodland is not stated this information has had to be calculated.
6. *Ministry of Agriculture, Fisheries and Food 4"-1 mile map of land classification and usage* (1964).
7. Searle 1974, 331. *See also* Searle 1974, 331 footnote 33.
8. Searle 1974, 376-383.
9. ESRO BAT 42, 81-88.
10. As an example, parts of Battle Abbey's farm of Marley were converted into copyholds during this period.
11. Brent 1976, 48; HMAG RAY Box 2, 1597 Survey of Udimore Manor.
12. *HBES* Vol. 1 (1977-80), 6-12.   Many additional references to wayside cottages have come to light since the above article was written.
13. Ashburnham, Brightling, Burwash, Dallington, Etchingham, Penhurst and Warbleton.
14. *VCH* **2** (1909), 279.
15. ESRO RAF, Pebsham Rental.
16. ESRO FRE 520.
17. Cornwall 1954, 70 and 79.
18. Sample of parishes as given in note 13 above.
19. ESRO FRE 7487.
20. Cornwall 1954, 67-92; Brent 1976, 38-48; Chalklin 1965, 73-109.
21. *Compare* CKS U1475 M 242-3 with *SRS* **47** (1944, 1-124. *See also* Searle 1974, 351-383; F. Aldsworth and D. Freke, *Historic Towns in Sussex An Archaeological Survey* (1976), 65.
22. Searle 1974, 359-60.
23. C. Platt, *Medieval England.   A Social History and Archaeology from the Conquest to 1600 AD* (1978), 129-131.
24. Searle 1974, 368-9.
25. *VCH* **9** (1937), 117 and 134.
26. Searle 1974, 376-383.
27. Searle 1974, 368-9.
28. Searle 1974, 368-9.
29. Brandon 1971, 75.
30. Pelham 1937, 209.
31. *SRS* **47** (Robertsbridge Manor, 1567); ESRO AMS 4892 (Playden Manor, 1567); CKS U47/42 M12 (Methersham Farm, Beckley, 1567); CKS U 269 E 341 (Demesne of

the manors of Ore, The Winde, Gensing, Frenchcourt, Lankhurst and Guestling 1559/60).

32. CKS U 269 E 341.
33. Brent 1976, 41.
34. Brent 1976, 47.
35. Kerridge, *Agricultural Revolution.* 26, 246-8.
36. ESRO D 165/11/pt.
37. ESRO RAF. Uncatalogued.
38. Chalklin 1965, 76. The arable amounts to 34.6% of woodland is ignored.
39. ESRO SAS/HC.
40. Chalklin 1965, 76-7.
41. ESRO SAS/FB/116; ESRO AMS 5788.
42. G. Jones, 'Report on Sempstead Farm Documents' *Recologea Papers* Vol. 5 No. 5 (1977), 75.
43. Henderson 1951-2, 52.
44. ESRO Tithe Award Schedules.
45. *VCH* 2 (1909), 275.
46. ESRO T 132 (Burghurst manor, 1540); *SRS* 47 (Robertsbridge manor, 1567).
47. *SRS* 47, 38 tenement 105; 47, tenement 124; 93, tenement 214.
48. Short 1975, 160-161.
49. Tenantry lands of Hammerden manor in 1618 (ESRO SAS/Co/b/157); tenantry and demesne lands of Crowham manor early 17th century (ESRO RAF Uncatalogued) and the farms on the Tufton estate *c*1705 (ESRO DAP 1/3).
50. ESRO W/INV 19, 55, 55, 532, 794, 1242, 1499, 1770 and 2483.
51. In the late 18th and early 19th century the massive increase in arable was geared primarily to the production of additional wheat. *cf* Henderson 1951-2, 52. Writing in the early 19th century Arthur Young lamented the irrational attachment of Weald farmers to the cultivation of wheat *cf* Brent 1976, 40-41.
52. Searle 1974, 460.
53. Brent 1976, 40; Chalklin 1965, 77-9.
54. Chalklin 1965, 78.
55. Brent 1976, 41; Chalklin 1965, 79.
56. ESRO - W/INV 91 and 794.
57. *HBES* 1 (1977-80), 97.
58. Brent 1976, 41.
59. Brent 1976, 40.
60. *HBES* 1 (1977-80), 100.
61. ESRO SAS/Co/b/157 (1618), 77% of farms; ESRO AMS 4440 (*c*1645), 52% of farms; ESRO D 386 (1672), 44% f farms. *See also* Brent 1976, 41.
62. Brent 1976, 41.
63. *SRS* 47 (1944), 126.
64. ESRO SAS/Co/b/157.
65. Cronk 1978, 101.
66. Brent 1976, 41.
67. *SRS* 53 (1953), 175. The building survives as 21-21b Northbridge Street.
68. Mayhew 1987, 163, 239. Regarding imports into Rye and subsequent exports from the same town *see* R. F. Dell, (ed), Rye Shipping Records 1566-1590, *SRS* 64 (1965-6), 92-142. There are other references to shipments into Rye in the 1560s and 1570s. *See also* Brent 1976, 45.
69. Brent 1976, 45.
70. Brent 1976, 41.

71. ESRO PAR 477; Young 1813, 129-137; ESRO PAR 377/6/1/1.
72. As a sample *see* ESRO ASH 4382 and 4396; ESRO AMS 4854; ESRO ACC 2452. *See also* references in ESRO PAR 477/6, and Chalklin 1965, 95.
73. Chalklin 1965, 93-4.
74. *HBES* 1 (1977-80), 99.
75. Chalklin 1965, 93; Fussell 1951-2, 81.
76. Brent 1976, 44.
77. Chalklin 1965, 105.
78. Brent 1976, 44.
79. ESRO SAS/Co/b/157 (1618), 60% of farms, a figure typical of other surveys.
80. Chalklin 1965, 89.
81. For an example *see* ESRO ACC 2452/1.
82. ESRO RAF Box 25 (1590); ESRO BAT 42 *fo.* 57 (1569); BL ADD CH 30928 (1573).
83. ESRO W/INV 164, 524, 914, 1043, 2090 and 2297. The small size of the farms is indicated by the land tax rentable values. No. 524 is non-typical, having a herd of five cows and three young beasts.
84. *HBES* 1 (1977-80), 94 and 111-113.
85. The sample is taken from the parishes of Beckley, Brede, Iden, Northiam, Peasmarsh, Playden and Udimore. The approximate acreages are based on the ratable value given in the land tax returns for the years in which the inventories were taken:
    • *Farms of c15-49 acres* - ESRO W/INV 4, 126, 162, 512, 799, 817, 857, 1094, 1197, 1242, 1331, 1406, 1440, 1467, 1703, 1791, 2026, 2218, 2281, 2318, 2430, 2573, 2500, 2608, 2655 (Total = 25).
    • *Farms of c50-99 acres* - ESRO W/INV 28, 276, 278, 661, 972, 1157, 1158, 1178, 1208, 1446, 1770, 2124, 2307, 2308, 2362, 2383, 2572 (Total = 17).
    • *Farms of c100-199 acres* - ESRO W/INV 574, 753, 826, 909, 943, 1155, 1306, 1314, 1422, 1476, 1499, 2221, 2352, 2433, 2444, 2483, 2593, 2628 (Total = 18).
    • *Farms of over c200 acres* - ESRO W/INV 353, 794, 963, 1803 (Total = 4).
88. Cornwall 1954, 73.
89. Fussell 1951-2, 63.
88. Cornwall 1954, 72.
89. Cornwall 1954, 75.
90. Cornwall 1954, 73.
91. Cornwall 1954, 73-4.
92. ESRO W/INV 353 and 1803.
93. Brent 1976, 42 and 47.
94. Cornwall 1954, 73.
95. Brent 1976, 46-7.
96. ESRO W/INV 55, 1152, 1791 and 2308. Number 2308 mentions a timber tug used for hauling timber.
97. Brent 1976, 42.
98. ESRO W/INV 374 is an example of this.
99. *HBES* 1 (1977-80), 95.
100. *HBES* 1 (1977-80), 96.
101. ESRO W/INV 794 and 2628.
102. R. Machin (ed), *Probate Inventories and Manorial Excepts of Chetnol, Leigh and Yetminster* (1976), 16.
103. ESRO W/INV 963.
104. Chalklin 1965, 100.
105. Chalklin 1965, 100; Brent 1976, 43.

106. Searle and Ross 1967, 111, 128 and 149; ESRO FRE 520, 75; ESRO PAR 477/6.
107. Rev. W. D. Parish, *A Dictionary of the Sussex Dialect and Collection of Provincialisms in use in the County Of Sussex* (originally published by Farncombe & Co., Lewes 1875; Republished by Gardner's of Bexhill Ltd. Expanded, augmented and illustrated by Helena Hall 1957), 52.
108. Fussell 1951-2, 62.
109. Searle and Ross 1967, 99.
110. *HBES* **1** (1977-80), 100-103.
111. ESRO W/INV 1703. .
112. Two hives and three hog troughs, together with hop poles *etc* have been omitted from the list, not being husbandry tackle.
113. The inventories are as given in footnote 101, with the exclusion of the following which do not give detailed descriptions of husbandry tackle- ESRO W/INV 276, 574, 661, 857, 963, 1208, 1314, 1422, 1803, 2307, 2444, 2575 and 2593.
114. ESRO W/INV 1624.
115. Searle and Ross 1967, 116, 121, 125, 129, 135, 144, 150 and 159.
116. ESRO XA3/2 400.6.
117. Nine gentry estates are included in the analysis. These are Great Knelle (Shelley family); Brickwall and Brede Place (owned by the Frewens of Brickwall); Gatecourt (Piers family); Dixter (Gott family); Tufton Place (the Earls of Thanet); Robertsbridge (the Earls of Leicester); Great Sanders (Bishop family), Church House, Northiam (Frewens of Church House); Ewhurst and Mote estates (Powell family). The owner occupiers included are Frewen of Brickwall; Frewen of Church House; Bishop of Great Sanders.
118. Many court rolls contain details of leased out copyhold properties. As examples *see* ESRO SAS/Co/b/12-25 (Hammerden manor) and ESRO RAF Uncatalogued (Crowham manor).
119. *SRS* **47**; *Ibid* Vol. 53; ESRO SAS/FB/116.
120. Short 1975, 164.
121. Rents based on an analysis of local leases and surveys. Wheat prices and cost of living based on figures for Burnett 1969. The figures are calculated on ten year averages.
122. Burnett 1969, 60-62.
123. Searle 1974, 369.
124. ESRO A. 2496.
125. ESRO FRE 6952; ESRO GLY 1236.
126. *SRS* **47**, tenement 339, 345-72, 373-4, 382-3 and 385.
127. CKS U 269 E 341.
128. CKS U 269 E 341.
129. CKS U 47/42 M 12.
130. ESRO GLY 1237.
131. ESRO D 165/11/pt.
132. ESRO GLY 1238.
133. *SRS* **53**, Tenements 138, 140, 144 and 145.
134. ESRO AMS 5744/57; ESRO SAS/Co/C/127.
135. The figures reconstructed by Prof. E. H. Phelps Brown and Sheila V. Hopkins differ in detail from those of prof. D. Knoop and G. P. Jones, but both show the same trends. *cf* Burnett 1969.

136. ESRO AMS 5691.
137. Burnett 1969, 61; Chalklin 1965, 65.
138. Great Bainden, Mayfield, leased in 1651 at £60, and in 1695/6 at £50, though the rent had recovered by 1713 (ESRO GLY 1240, 1242 and 1244). Similarly, the rent of Broughtons Farm, Ewhurst fell from £15 in 1683 to £13 in 1707 (CKS U 991 E 3). These are typical examples.
139. *HBES* **1** (1977-80), 88-9.
140. Brent 1978, 41-49.
141. ESRO ELT, Ninfield parish. Figure 2.34 excludes Mr Abraham Onslow, who is listed in both the poll tax return and the land tax return for the same year, but of whom nothing is currently known. His assessment in the land tax return is not for land, but for 'his office', the rentable value of which is given at the high sum of £25. Both 'in dwellers' and 'out dwellers' are separately listed within the return, and Onslow is included amongst the 'in dwellers' (*ie* he was a resident of the parish).
142. ESRO FRE 520.
143. ESRO PAR 254/6/7.

3. THE FARMSTEAD

1. ESRO SAS/Co/d/1, Plots 366-376.
2. ESRO SAS/Co/b/157.
3. WSRO EP II/17/3 & 4.
4. In particular the surveyor John Stonestrete gives very clear details in his plans of the 1730s.
5. WSRO Ep II/17/3.
6. ESRO AMS 5788/1.
7. ESRO ASH 2364-6.
8. Based on areas of adjacent holdings in Hothligh and Stretfield boroughs in Robertsbridge manor 1567 (*SRS* **47**), the tenants at will on Etchingham manor 1597 (*SRS* **53**, Tenements 138-156), the tenements of Mountfield manor 1672 (ESRO D 386), Tufton estate *c*1705 (ESRO DAP Box 1) and Bivelham manor 1727 (ESRO GLY 1127).
9. *SRS* **47** (1944), 125-126.
10. ESRO RAF Box 25.
11. *SRS* **53** (1953), 200.
12. *SRS* **53** (1953), 201-202.
13. *SRS* **53** (1953), 203.
14. ESRO ASH 1173.
15. ESRO ASH 2364-6.

4. BARNS: SURVIVAL AND CONSTRUCTION DATES

1. As many late looking barns were checked internally during the field work undertaken up to 1982 as was feasible. In 1982 198 barns of pre *c*1750 date had been identified. In the 23 years since that date a further 18 buildings have been added. For a full list, with ESRO archive reference numbers to the individual architectural reports *see* the Appendix at the end of this volume.
2. Some barns were demolished between the initial commencement of field work in 1967 and completion in 1982. These buildings are counted as surviving. Many of

the buildings included in this study have been demolished since 1982.

3. D. Martin and B. J. Mastin, *An Architectural History of Robertsbridge* (1974), 8-9, 66-70.
4. ESRO SAS/Co/b/157.
5. ESRO BAT 42 and FRE 520 (ii).
6. ESRO BAT 42 and XA3/16.
7. The barns at High Holmstead, Parsonage Farm and Pebsham Farm have erection dates inscribed upon them, whilst those at Bunces, Marley and Trulilows have been dated from documentary sources.

5. BARNS: LAYOUT AND DESIGN
CROP STORAGE AND PROCESSING

1. *HBES* **1** (1977-1981), 98.
2. G. E. Evans, *The Farm and Village* (1969, paperback), 82.
3. ESRO W/INV 2021.
4. Lower Stonelink, Fairlight. The building has since been extended.
5. J. E. C. Peters, *Discovering Traditional Farm Buildings* (1981), 17-18.

6. BARNS: LAYOUT AND DESIGN
ANCILLARY USES

1. ESRO SAS/Co/b/16.
2. ESRO HBR 1/1047; 1/0440 (Rev.); 1/0083 (Rev.); 1/1422.
3. *SRS* **53** (1953), 201.
4. ESRO XA24/2.
5. ESRO RAF Box 25.
6. ESRO ASH 2364-6.
7. *SRS* **47** (1944), 125-126.
8. Henry Huntington Library BA 439, 440, 454, 458 - microfilm copy in ESRO, XA3/21
9. *SRS* **65** (1967), 80.
10. Unpublished papers delivered at Vernacular Architecture Group Winter Conference, 1977.
11. Unpublished papers delivered at Vernacular Architecture Group Winter Conference, 1977.

7. BARNS: DETAILS OF CONSTRUCTION.
WALLS AND CLADDING

1. ESRO PAR 441/1/1/2, fo. 55.
2. For further details and discussion relating to the use of braces in houses *see HBES* **5** (1989), 40-49.
3. ESRO SAS/Box 16. The entry relates only to the construction of the house, though the barn may be taken to be of this period. Until this date the property did not possess a barn.
4. *see HBES* **5** (1989), 40-49; 56-69.
5. The exception is Wenbans, Wadhurst, for which *see* Figure 6.6.
6. ESRO HBR 1/1240. A sample of the boards is held within the collections at the Weald and Downland Open

Air Museum.
7. ESRO HBR 1/1406.
8. *HBES* **5** (1989), 83; *See also HBES* **2** (1981), 40-44.

8. BARNS: DETAILS OF CONSTRUCTION.
TRUSSES, ARCADES AND INTERNAL
PARTITIONS

1. J. E. C. Peters, *Discovering Traditional Farm Buildings* (1981), 16.

9. BARNS: DETAILS OF CONSTRUCTION.
UPPER FLOORS

[No notes or references to this chapter.]

10. BARNS: DETAILS OF CONSTRUCTION.
ROOFS

1. L. F. Salzman, *Buildings in England Down to 1540 A Documentary History* (1952), 224.
2. ESRO ASH 1173.
3. *SRS* **53** (1953), 199-204.
4. *SRS* **47** (1944), 124-126.
5. Searle 1974, 268-269.
6. ESRO HBR 1/1269.
7. *HBES* **1** (1977-1980), 36-38.
8. ESRO AMS 5691/2; ESRO FRE 520, fos. 44, 57, 60, 65, 70, 71, 80.
9. ESRO ASH 2364-6.
10. ESRO HBR 1/1272.
11. The earliest dated example of a hip lacking a high-set collar is that in the crosswing of Chant Stream Farmhouse, Westfield, built in 1673, *see* ESRO HBR 1/0408.
12. R. E. Howard, Dr R. R. Laxton and Dr C. D. Litton, *Tree-ring analysis of timbers from Falmer Court Barn, Falmer, East Sussex*, Unpublished Nottingham University Tree-Ring Dating Laboratory report No. 42 (1998); For tree-ring dating relating to the barn from Cowfold *see* guidebook to the Weald and Downland Open Air Museum.
13. E. Roberts, *Hampshire Houses, 1250-1700: Their Dating & Development* (2003), 27-37; P. Grey, 'Dating Wealden Buildings', in J. Warren (ed), *Wealden Buildings* (1990), 47-60.
14. *See* Chapter 7, note 3.
15. A. Beckett, 'A Tornado in Sussex' *Sussex County Magazine*, **8** (1934), 291-8.

11. BARNS: SELECTED EXAMPLES.
THE MEDIEVAL PERIOD

1. Lease of the manor of Warbleton dated 29th Sept. 1640, contained within the archive of the charity of Henry Smith deposited at Surrey History Centre by Warren & Co, Solicitors, via East Sussex Record Office.

2. *SRS* **53** (1953), 144-146; ESRO SAU 296-326; ESRO TDE 127.
3. VCH **9** (1937), 273; *SAC* **52** (1909), 153-155.
4. ESRO D165/60; ESRO PAR 254/6/2 & 10; ESRO TDE 34.
5. *SRS* **53** (1953), 83-90
6. ESRO FRE 7983.

12. BARNS: SELECTED EXAMPLES. THE POST-MEDIEVAL PERIOD

1. ESRO SAS/Co/B/157, tenement 46, plots 366-376; ESRO TDE 2.
2. ESRO AMS 5744; ESRO TDE 157.
3. ESRO ELT, Burwash.
4. ESRO ASH 165-166, 736.
5. ESRO/SAS/HC 343.
6. *SRS* **53** (1953), 28-30; ESRO DUNN 42/1.
7. *SRS* **47** (1944), 54-55.
8. ESRO ELT, Northiam; ESRO TDE 96.
9. ESRO ASH 165; ASH 202; ESRO TDE 16.
10. VCH **9** (1937), 254. *See also* ESRO HBR 1/0723.
11. ESRO SAS/Co/D/12.ESRO SAS Box E2.
12. ESRO SAS Box E2.
13. ESRO RAF Unlisted - Crowhurst manorial records; ESRO RAF 23/5; ESRO ELT, Crowhurst.
14. *SRS* **47** (1944), 63; ESRO TDE 121, Whatlington.
15. ESRO D165/60 - Records of Brightling Prebendal Manor.
16. *Ibid.*
17. HMAG JER Box 2 - Records of Udimore Manor.
18. *SRS* **47** (1944), 111-112; ESRO RAF Box 25.
19. ESRO ASH L231-233, ASH L1924-1926, ASH B488.
20. *Ibid*; ESRO AMS 79.
21. *SRS* **47** (1944), 61.
22. ESRO SAS/ACC 801.

13. MALTHOUSES AND OASTHOUSES

1. R. Scot, *A Perfitte Platform of a Hoppe Garden* (1574, reprinted 1576, 1578, 1644).
2. D & B Martin, Detached Kitchens in Eastern Sussex; A re-assessment of the evidence' in *Vernacular Architecture* **28** (1997), 85-91; J. T. Smith, 'Detached Kitchens or Adjoining Houses' in *Vernacular Architecture* **32** (2001), 16-19; D. & B. Martin, 'Detached Kitchens or Adjoining Houses: A response' in *Vernacular Architecture* **32** (2001), 20-33; ESRO HBR 1/0021; ESRO HBR 1/0496.
3. *SRS* **47** (1944), 124-127.
4. *SRS* **53** (1953), 175.
5. ESRO D 386.
6. Jones and Bell 1992.
7. ESRO RAF 38/3.
8. *SRS* **47** (1944), 126.
9. For a full discussion regarding the drying process *see* Jones and Bell 1992, 3-9.
10. Cronk 1978, 102-103.
11. This building was wrongly described as a brewery in Martin, D, and Mastin, B, *An Architectural History of Robertsbridge* (1974), 36 and Figure 16.

12. Cronk 1978., 104.
13. ESRO DUNN 42/8. *See also* Jones and Bell 1992, 20.
14. ESRO DUNN 37/8. *See also* Jones and Bell 1992, 20-22. Jones and Bell considered the 'outlet' to be a form of vent or 'chimney' projecting through the roof in order to allow the hot air to escape. However, in our view the wording of the document makes this conclusion unlikely; the outlet is referred to amongst the details of the building's size and layout. Furthermore, the term is encountered in local documents in relation to buildings other than oasthouses. For instance, in April 1558 the court rolls of Hammerden Manor, Ticehurst, granted licence to William Oxenbridge to demolish the 'utlatt' [*ie* outlet] of a barn upon his holding at Limden - ESRO SAS/Co/B/17. The medieval barn at Limden survived long enough to be surveyed and showed clear evidence of having incorporated a lean-to cattle shelter at its northern end. Although the Oxford English Dictionary does not specifically give a lean-to outshut as one of the definitions for the word, one definition is close, '*a field, yard or other enclosure attached to a house*'. As an illustration the following quote is given, '*. . . . where the cows are tied up, and which is retained by the outgoing tenant as an outlet for his cattle*'. The wording could be taken to imply that the term was used to indicate an outshut attached to a building, but separately accessed from the exterior.
15. ESRO DUNN 37/8. *See also* Jones and Bell 1992, 22.
16. Jones and Bell 1992, 3-23.
17. Cronk 1978, 106.
18. ESRO ASH 1173.
19. Cronk 1978, 105.
20. Jones and Bell 1992, 20
21. ESRO RAF 38/3.
22. ESRO ASH 4382; HMAG MA 267.
23. ESRO DUN 44/4; ESRO DUNN 42/1; Acc 2452.
24. HMAG MA 8.
25. Cronk 1978, 107.
26. ESRO HBR 3/R183/35.
27. *SRS* **47** (1944), 126.
28. ESRO ASH 1173.
29. ESRO ASH 1173.
30. ESRO FRE 520, 27.
31. ESRO FRE 520, 82 and 84.
32. HMAG MA 267.
33. ESRO ASH 4382.
34. ESRO ASH 2364-6.
35. ESRO ASH 1173.
36. ESRO ASH 2364-6; *SRS* **53** (1953), 200; ESRO FRE 520, 74, 84.
37. ESRO ASH 1300 (pt).

14. ANCILLARY BUILDINGS

1. ESRO HBR 1/0574 (Toll, Warbleton), 1/876 (Stunts Green, Wartling), 1/918 (Sheephouse, Brede). The building at Stunts Green was in use as an oasthouse/ malthouse by 1697 (ESRO RAF 38/3).
2. ESRO ASH 1173 & 2364-6.
3. ESRO D386.

4. *See* Chapter 3, note 8 above.
5. ESRO ASH 1173 & 2364-6.
6. HMAG MA 8.
7. ESRO FRE 520 fo.133.
8. *HBES* **1** (1977-80), 103.
9. ESRO AMS 5822/25.
10. *SRS* **53** (1953), 199-204.
11. ESRO SAS/Co/b/157 fo 14; *SRS* **47** (1944), 124-126.
12. ESRO W/INV 2124 & 2628.
13. HMAG L.659.

15. THE FARMHOUSE AND ITS ASSOCIATED OUTHOUSING

1. *HBES* **1** (1977-80), 98-99.
2. ESRO W/INV 89 & 1770.
3. ESRO W/INV 2281.
4. ESRO W/INV 353.
5. PRO PROB 4. East Sussex Inventories.
6. Barley 1961, 67; ESRO HBR 1/0113, 1/0309, 1/0438 are typical examples.

7. ESRO HBR 1/0007, 1/0097, 1/0140, 1/0159, 1/0269. All possess crownposts and related roof types.
8. ESRO HBR 1/0047 (Rev.)
9. ESRO HBR 1/0138, 1/0226, 1/0692 are typical examples.
10. Barley 1961, 43-44.
11. *HBES* **1** (1977-80), 111-113. *Also* PRO PROB 4 - East Sussex Inventories.
12. ESRO W/INV 353
13. ESRO XA3/2 400.6.
14. Cronk 1978, 102.
15. ESRO FRE 166; ESRO HBR1/0313.
16. For discussions relating to detached kitchen in East Sussex *see* D & B Martin, Detached Kitchens in Eastern Sussex; A re-assessment of the evidence' in *Vernacular Architecture* **28** (1997), 85-91; J. T. Smith, 'Detached Kitchens or Adjoining Houses' in *Vernacular Architecture* **32** (2001), 16-19; D. & B. Martin, 'Detached Kitchens or Adjoining Houses: A response' in *Vernacular Architecture* **32** (2001), 20-33. For Beestons Farm, Warbleton *see* ESRO HBR 1/0496 (Rev.).
17. BL ADD MSS 45194. *See also* ESRO HBR 1/0919.
18. *See* note 16.

18   BIBLIOGRAPHY

Barley, M.W. 1961.   *The English Farmhouse and Cottage* (1961),

Brandon, P. F. 1971. Agriculture and the Effect of Floods and Weather at Barnhorne, Sussex, During the Late Middle Ages, in *SAC* **109**, 69-93.

Brent, C. 1976. Rural Employment and Population in Sussex between 1550 and 1640, Pt. 1, in *SAC.* **114**, 27-48.

Brent, C. 1978. Rural Employment and Population in Sussex between 1550 and 1640 Pt. 2, in *SAC* **116**, 41-56.

Burnett, J. 1969. *A History of the Cost of Living.*

Chalklin, C.W. 1965. *Seventeenth Century Kent, A Social and Economic History.*

Cornwall, J. 1954. Farming in Sussex 1560-1640, in *SAC* **92**, 48-92.

Cronk, A. 1978. Oasts in Kent and East Sussex Pt. 1, in *Archaeologia Cantiana* **94**, 99-110.

Fussell, G. E. 1951-2. Four Centuries of Farming Systems in Sussex 1500-1900, in *SAC* **90**, 60-102.

Jones, G and Bell, J. 1992. *Oasthouses in Sussex and Kent: Their history and development.*

Henderson, H. C. K. 1951-52. The 1801 Crop Returns for Sussex', in *SAC* **90**, 51-59.

Ingram, W. F. 1909. Agriculture, in *VCH* **2**, 273-290.

Mayhew, G. 1987. *Tudor Rye.*

Pelham, R. A. 1937. 'The Agricultural Geography of the Chichester Estates in 1388, in *SAC* **78**, 195-210.

Searle, E. 1974. *Lordship and Community, Battle Abbey and its Banlieu 1066-1538.*

Searle, E and Ross, B (eds). 1967. The Cellarers' Rolls of Battle Abbey 1275-1513, *SRS* **65**.

Short, B. 1975. The Turnover of Tenants on the Ashburnham Estate, 1830-1850, in *SAC* **113**, 157-174.

Young, Rev. A. 1813. *General View of the Agriculture of the County of Sussex.* 2nd Edition.

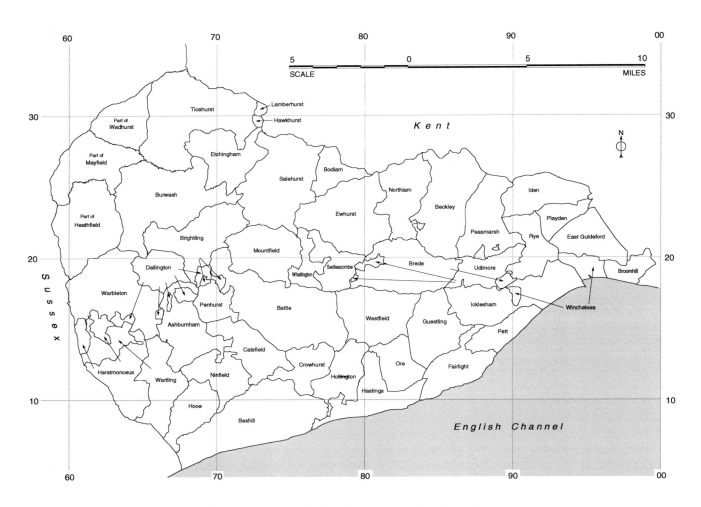

Plan showing the historical parishes within the Rape of Hastings
prior to boundary changes made in 1894

166

APPENDIX
LIST OF FARM BUILDINGS WITHIN THE RAPE OF HASTINGS
USED WITHIN THIS STUDY

BARNS INCLUDED IN THE ORIGINAL ANALYSIS [Chapters 4-10]

Historical Parish	Farm Name	National Grid Reference	Archive Ref. ESRO HBR/1/****	Date of Construction	Date of Extension
Ashburnham	Brigden Hill Farm	TQ 6669 1562	0566	?	-
	Brownbread Street	TQ 6762 1493	0565	E17th C	-
	Lattendens	TQ 6647 1654	0772	E17th C	L17th C
	Reedlands Farm	TQ 6777 1572	0564	E17th C	M18th C
	Thornden	TQ 6733 1685	0770	E18th C	-
Battle	Marley Farm	TQ 7665 1653	0429	E18th C	-
	Nortons Farm	TQ 7843 1563	0177	L17th C	E18th C
Beckley	Church Farm	TQ 8441 2367	0538	E16th C	-
	Glasseye	TQ 8384 2148	0754	L17th C	-
	Great Conster	TQ 8440 2085	0753	E17th C	M17th C
	Great Knelle	TQ 8530 2581	0445	E18th C	-
	Kings Bank Farm	TQ 8543 2345	0536	Medieval	L17th C
	Little Harmers Farm	TQ 8529 2280	0537	M16th C	-
	Oxenbridge Farm	TQ 8701 2551	0449	E17th C	-
	Roadend Farm	TQ 8403 2346	0539	E18th C	-
	Stockherds Farm	TQ 8480 2299	0444	L17th C	-
	Tilebarn	TQ 8427 2216	0755	?	-
Bexhill	Highwoods	TQ 7255 0921	0136	M18th C	
	Lower Worsham	TQ 7590 0943	0556	E17th C	E18th C
	Pebsham Farm	TQ 7649 0892	0112	M16th C	M18th C
Brede	Conster Manor	TQ 8270 2084	0340	M16th C	-
	Pickdick	TQ 8461 1833	0752	E16th C	E18th C
	Shearfold Farm	TQ 8274 1837	0546	L17th C	-
Brightling	Brightling Place	TQ 6920 2163	0016	M18th C	-
	Coldharbour Farm	TQ 6803 1926	0467	M17th C	-
	Glebe Farm	TQ 6865 2107	0769	M18th C	-
	Little Sprays Farm	TQ 6955 1833	0464	E17th C	-
	Little Worge	TQ 6579 2136	0468	M18th C	-
Burwash	Bowmans	TQ 6810 2297	0768	M16th C	18th C
	Great Tott Farm	TQ 6867 2526	0578	M16th C	-
	Holmshurst	TQ 6436 2540	0761	E/M16th C	E17th C
	Mount House	TQ 6756 2471	0650	E17th C	-
	Parkhill Farm	TQ 6478 2248	0250	Medieval	-
	Square Farm	TQ 6776 2503	0015	E17th C	-
	Woodknowle	TQ 6532 2605	0162	Medieval	L16th C
Catsfield	Hophouse Farm	TQ 7143 1302	0560	E18th C	-

Historical Parish	*Farm Name*	*National Grid Reference*	*Archive Ref. ESRO HBR/1/*****	*Date of Construction*	*Date of Extension*
Crowhurst	Court Lodge	TQ 7589 1226	0558	E18th C	-
	Crouchers Farm	TQ 7628 2230	0693	E17th C	-
	Hill House Farm	TQ 7513 1198	0557	E18th C	-
Dallington	Claytons Farm	TQ 6666 1871	0466	L16th C	L17th C
	Giffords Farm	TQ 6876 1902	0009	M17th C	-
	Newcastle Farm	TQ 6480 1886	0423	?	-
	Northfleet Farm	TQ 6472 1900	0406	M17th C	-
	Prinkle Farm	TQ 6567 1916	0474	E17th C	-
	Redpale Farm	TQ 6588 1625	0687	E17th C	M18th C
	Stream Farm	TQ 6551 1854	0472	?	-
	Thorneyfold Farm	TQ 6437 1594	0422	L17th C	-
Ewhurst	Boyces Farm	TQ 7960 2244	0353	E17th C	M18th C
	Miles Farm	TQ 7878 2138	0540	L17th C	-
Fairlight	Lower Stonelink Farm	TQ 8731 1285	0281	M17th C	E18th C
Guestling	Broomham	TQ 8518 1513	0748	E18th C	-
	Copshall Farm	TQ 8489 1550	0462	E17th C	E17th C
	Lidham Hill Farm	TQ 8394 1665	0459	E17th C	-
	Lower Lidham Hill Farm	TQ 8424 1676	0460	L17th C	-
	Lower Snailham Farm	TQ 8515 1718	0461	E18th C	-
	Old Coghurst, Major Barn	TQ 8331 1385	0296	E18th C	M18th C
	Old Coghurst, Minor Barn	TQ 8333 1385	0295	Medieval	-
Heathfield	Great Bigknowle	TQ 6228 2443	0760	L16th C	-
	Great Stonehurst	TQ 6119 2476	0759	E17th C	-
	Kingsdown Farm	TQ 6345 2286	0606	E17th C	E18th C
	Little Pigstrood	TQ 6071 2474	0758	E17th C	-
	Manor Farm	TQ 6006 2036	0174	Medieval	-
	Pigstrood	TQ 6041 2504	0757	M18th C	-
Herstmonceux	Cherry Croft	TQ 6393 1079	0766	M16th C	E17th C
	Deudneys Farm	TQ 6166 1199	0567	E17th C	-
	Gingers Green Farm	TQ 6229 1262	0569	L16th C	-
	Lower Stunts Green Farm	TQ 6263 1297	0570	L17th C	-
Hooe	Court Lodge, Minor Barn	TQ 6843 0876	0434	L17th C	-
	Dewburys Farm	TQ 6920 1047	0431	E17th C	-
	Longdown Farm	TQ 6976 1015	0555	M16th C	-
	Nutbrowns Farm	TQ 6776 0928	0433	M18th C	-
	Parsonage Farm	TQ 6779 0952	0432	M16th C	-
Icklesham	Manor Farm	TQ 8821 1632	0587	E17th C	M17th C
Iden	Rafters	TQ 9175 2346	0534	M17th C	-
	Randolphs Farm	TQ 9158 2324	0535	E18th C	-
Mayfield	Bivelham Forge Farm	TQ 6401 2670	0291	L17th C	-
	Froghole	TQ 6213 2576	0763	E17th C	-
	Gillhope Farm	TQ 6108 2607	0235	E17th C	L17th C
	Golds Farm	TQ 6300 2686	0532	E17th C	-
	Great Bainden	TQ 5969 2633	0454	E17th C	L17th C
	Little Bainden	TQ 6058 2631	0452	E17th C	-
	Piccadilly	TQ 5946 2644	0455	E17th C	-
	Rolfs Farm	TQ 6144 2709	0533	Medieval	E17th C
Mountfield	Baldwins Farm	TQ 7207 2086	0271	?	^
	Crowhurst Farm	TQ 7287 1903	0520	L17th C	-
	Mountfield Park Farm	TQ 7136 2185	0279	E17th C	-
Ninfield	Akehurst Farm	TQ 6996 1065	0554	?	-

Historical Parish	Farm Name	National Grid Reference	Archive Ref. ESRO HBR/1/****	Date of Construction	Date of Extension
Ninfield *cont.*	Ingrams Farm	TQ 7108 1206	0430	L16th C	-
	Farmhouse Farm	TQ 6942 1210	0563	E17th C	L17th C
Northiam	Crockers	TQ 8261 2596	0439	L17th C	-
	Church House	TQ 8310 2456	0358	E17th C	-
	Clench Green Farm	TQ 8264 2497	0361	L16th C	-
	Common Woods Farm	TQ 8210 2284	0443	E17th C	-
	Goatley Manor	TQ 8334 2481	0442	?	-
	Major Barn, Great Dixter	TQ 8196 2516	0440	Medieval	-
	Hayes Farm	TQ 8303 2443	0447	L17th C	-
	Tanhouse Farm	TQ 8223 2181	0286	M16th C	-
	Wildings	TQ 8306 2503	0446	E17th C	-
	Yewtree Farm	TQ 8206 2267	0684	Medieval	Medieval
Peasmarsh	Barline Farm	TQ 8727 2124	0463	E17th C	-
	Grove Farm	TQ 8674 2128	0275	M17th C	-
Penhurst	Bunces Farm	TQ 6891 1777	0465	E18th C	-
	Hill Farm	TQ 7010 1639	0320	L16th C	-
Pett	Elms Farm	TQ 8776 1412	0155	L16th C	-
	Lunsford Farm	TQ 8834 1382	0121	E18th C	-
Salehurst	Goodgrooms	TQ 7494 2412	0019	?	L17th C
	Great Wigsell, Jacks Barn	TQ 7589 2746	0081	Medieval	-
	Great Wigsell, Lower Barn	TQ 7663 2747	0067	?	-
	Grove Farm	TQ 7388 2344	0074	E18th C	-
	Haislemans Farm	TQ 7544 2529	0057	L17th C	-
	Merriments Farm	TQ 7498 2828	0383	E17th C	L17th C
	Mill Cottage	TQ 7423 2570	0083	Medieval	-
	Moat Farm	TQ 7575 2438	0087	Medieval	L17th C
	Nether Ockham	TQ 7350 2514	0479	E17th C	-
	Old Peans	TQ 7240 2344	0068	M16th C	-
	Park Farm, South Barn	TQ 7500 2316	0090	E17th C	-
	Parsonage Farm	TQ 7498 2434	0022	M16th C	-
	Walters Farm	TQ 7444 2236	0088	L16th C	-
Sedlescombe	Swailes Green Farm	TQ 7714 2101	0541	E18th C	-
Ticehurst	Bines Farm	TQ 6713 2793	0050	L16th C	-
	Boarders Farm	TQ 6810 3131	0428	?	-
	Chessons Farm	TQ 6667 3192	0247	E18th C	-
	Copens Farm	TQ 6782 3201	0092	Medieval	E17th C
	Hammerden Farm	TQ 6623 2713	0349	M16th C	E18th C
	Limden Farm	TQ 6713 2918	0203	Medieval	-
	Lower Tolhurst	TQ 6744 3103	0531	L17th C?	E18th C
	Maplesden Farm	TQ 6529 2895	0240	Medieval	-
	Norwoods	TQ 6901 3168	0762	E17th C	-
	Quedley Farm	TQ 7090 3071	0530	M18th C	-
	Wardsbrook Major	TQ 6878 2910	0017	E17th C	-
	Wardsbrook Minor	TQ 6876 2911	0018	Medieval	-
Udimore	Lower Float Farm	TQ 8817 1809	0480	L16th C	L17th C
	Roadend Farm	TQ 8878 1831	0544	L16th C	E18th C
	Stocks Farm	TQ 8704 1891	0543	E17th C	-
	Wick Farm	TQ 8863 1956	0545	E17th C	-
Wadhurst	Chittinghurst	TQ 6154 2910	0456	Medieval	Medieval
	Wenbans	TQ 6339 2976	0374	L16th C	-
Warbleton	Attwoods Farm	TQ 6467 1518	0407	E17th C	M17th C

Historical Parish	Farm Name	National Grid Reference	Archive Ref. ESRO HBR/1/****	Date of Construction	Date of Extension
Warbleton *cont.*	Batsford Farm	TQ 6305 1609	9415	Medieval	-
	Beestons Farm	TQ 6025 1649	0513	M16th C	M18th C
	Combe Ash	TQ 6440 1695	0421	E17th C	M17th C
	Court Lodge	TQ 6087 1813	0471	E17th C	-
	Cralle Place	TQ 6079 1604	0413	E18th C	-
	Deans Farm	TQ 6421 1760	0427	L16th C	-
	Durrants Farm	TQ 6218 1698	0476	L16th C	E18th C
	Grovelye Farm	TQ 6454 1814	0420	L17th C	-
	High Holmstead	TQ 6252 2015	0469	E18th C	-
	Hodges	TQ 6557 1541	0519	?	-
	Homelands	TQ 6260 1800	0575	M17th C	-
	Huntons Farm	TQ 6190 1780	0412	L17th C	E18th C
	Iwood Place Farm	TQ 6329 1677	0414	E17th C	-
	Kingsley Hill	TQ 6158 1800	0655	L16th C	-
	Little Rabbits Farm	TQ 6610 1736	0424	L16th C	-
	Little Redpale Farm	TQ 6597 1696	0425	?	-
	Stonelands Farm	TQ 6354 1588	0417	E18th C	-
	Summertree Farm	TQ 6410 1621	0475	E18th C	-
	Thorrington	TQ 6173 1873	0470	M18th C	-
	Tilement Farm	TQ 6090 1728	0419	L16th C	-
	Toll Farm	TQ 6516 1439	0573	Medieval	E18th C
	Woodlands Farm	TQ 6593 1625	0426	E17th C	-
Wartling	Boreham Farm	TQ 6671 1126	0561	?	-
	Conquorers	TQ 6201 1330	0767	L17th C	E18th C
	Coopers Farm	TQ 6555 0957	0562	M17th C	-
	Court Lodge	TQ 6580 0914	0764	E18th C	-
	Manor Pound	TQ 6526 1204	0572	E18th C	-
	Prinkle Farm	TQ 6556 1415	0576	L16th C	M17th C
	Stunts Green Farm	TQ 6264 1309	0571	L16th C	E17th C
	Trulilows	TQ 6303 1484	0418	E16th C	-
Westfield	Church Place Farm	TQ 8096 1508	0551	E17th C	-
	Downoak, North Barn	TQ 8184 1594	0548	L17th C	-
	Downoak, South Barn	TQ 8179 1576	0549	L17th C	-
	Gotways	TQ 7847 1611	0559	L17th C	M18th C
	Luffs Farm	TQ 7831 1741	0450	M17th C	-
	Southings Farm	TQ 8190 1609	0547	M16th C	-
	Westbrook Farm	TQ 8089 1626	0458	M17th C	-
Whatlington	Hancox	TQ 7666 1905	0146	E18th C	-
	Lea Bank	TQ 7578 2161	0542	E17th C	-

BARNS SURVEYED SINCE 1982 [Chapters 4-10]

[These barns are not included in the stastistics quoted within this volume]

Historical Parish	Farm Name	National Grid Reference	Archive Ref. ESRO HBR/1/****	Date of Construction	Date of Extension
Ashburnham	Court Lodge	TQ 6824 1644	0911	17th C	-
Brede	Brooks Lodge	TQ 8057 1832	1514	E18th C	-
Catsfield	Old Farm Place	TQ 7328 1228	0775	E18th C	-
Etchingham	Burgham	TQ 7022 2791	1047	Medieval	-
Fairlight	Cherry Garden	TQ 8618 1271	1116	L17th C	-
Guestling	Great Maxfield	TQ 8334 1528	1012	L17th C	-
	Rocks	TQ 8405 1337	1051	E18th C	-
Heathfield	Pottens Mill	TQ 6135 2420	1120	16th C	-
Herstmonceux	Elms	TQ 6379 1256	0981	M/L17th C	-
Hollington	Mayfield	TQ 7776 1099	0843	*c*1600	-
Icklesham	Ashes	TQ 8891 1582	0814	E17th C	-
Mayfield	Broadhurst	TQ 6290 2503	1131	Medieval?	-
Peasmarsh	Pelsham	TQ 8778 2072	1272	*c*1700	-
Pett	Gatehurst	TQ 8777 1387	1159	*c*1700	-
Sedlescombe	Durhamford	TQ 7727 1886	1276	*c*1600	-
	Little Swales Green	TQ 7723 2101	1140	16th or17th C	
Udimore	Vine	TQ 8676 1899	0846	17th C	-
Westfield	Great Buckhurst	TQ 7940 1590	1421	Medieval	-

OASTHOUSES [Chapter 13]

Historical Parish	Farm Name	National Grid Reference	Archive Ref. ESRO HBR/1/****	Date of Construction	Date of Extension
Brede	Pipers Green	TQ 82271878	0970	M/L17th C	
Brightling	Homestead Farm	TQ 7030 1875	0366	M18th C	
Burwash	Hoppers Croft	TQ 6752 2478	0921	17th C	E18th C
	Platts Farm	TQ 6878 2356	1253	(?use)	M18th C
Catsfield	Henleys Down Farm	TQ 7332 1243	0777	17th C	
Dallington	Staces Farm	TQ 6624 1956	0474	E/M18th C	
Guestling	Church Farm	TQ 8556 1450	0718	E/M18th C	
Herstmonceux	Beechcoft	TQ 6211 1458	1226	*c.*1680	
Mayfield	Hampden Lodge	TQ 6206 2683	0457	M18th C	
	Little Bainden	TQ 6050 2629	1429	M18th C	
Northiam	Hayes Farm	TQ 8304 2446	0448	17th C	E18th C
	Silverden	TQ 8318 2481	0883	(? use)	*c*1700
	Tanhouse	TQ 8223 2181	0286	(Barn)	E18thC
Penhurst	Great Sprays	TQ 6963 1763	0139	L17th C	
Salehurst	Langham Cottage	TQ 7372 2355	0002	*c*1700	
Ticehurst	Birchen Wood Farm	TQ 7032 2970	0387	*c*1700	
	Copens	TQ 6797 3200	0201	17th C	
	Wedds Farm	TQ 6792 2918	0579	M18th C	
Warbleton	Cross Cottage	TQ 6266 1850	0527	17th C	*c*1700
	Little Bucksteep	TQ 6488 1739	0784	*c*1700	
	Woodlands Farm	TQ 6594 1625	0435	L17th C	
Wartling	Stunts Green	TQ 6265 1303	0876	(Stable)	*c*1727
Westfield	Great Buckhurst	TQ 7942 1586	1422	M18th C	

OASTHOUSES CONVERTED FROM 'DETACHED KITCHENS' [Chapter 13]

Historical Parish	Farm Name	National Grid Reference	Archive Ref. ESRO HBR/1/****	Date of Construction	Date of Extension
Ticehurst	Wardsbrook Farm	TQ 6874 2909	0021	M16th C	17th C
Warbleton	Beestons Farm	TQ 6025 1654	0496	15th C	c1800

ANCILLARY FARM BUILDINGS [Chapter 14]

Historical Parish	Farm Name	Building Type	National Grid Reference	Archive Ref. ESRO HBR/1/****	Date of Construction
Ashburnham	Court Lodge	Stable	TQ 6818 1640	0913	18th C
Brede	Sheephouse	Sheephouse	TQ 8378 1800	0918	L16th C
Fairlight	Lower Stonelink	Cattle House	TQ 8729 1284	0282	c1700
Herstmonceux	Deudneys Farm	Shelter Shed	TQ 6167 1201	0568	M18th C
	Moetes	?	TQ 6202 1553	0882	M18th C
Mayfield	Little Bainden	Cattle house	TQ 6058 2630	0453	c1700
Northiam	Byre House	Stable	TQ 8286 2450	0678	18th C
	Clench Green	Shelter Shed	TQ 8264 2498	0362	18th C
	Great Dixter	Coach House	TQ 8199 2517	0441	E18th C
	Tufton Place	Stables	TQ 8146 2375	0947	L17th C
Salehurst	Vicarage	Stables	TQ 7488 2433	0104	18th C
Warbleton	Durrants	Stable	TQ 6214 1691	0477	c1700
	Toll Farm	Stables	TQ 6514 1429	0574	E17th C
Wartling	Prinkle	Granary	TQ 6559 1412	0577	E/M18th C
	Stunts Green	Stable?	TQ 6265 1303	0876	c1600
Westfield	Downoak	Shelter Shed	TQ 8176 1576	0550	c1700

INDEX

The following index excludes endnotes. Illustrations are listed under the page number upon which they occur and are not separately identified. All farms and farm buildings are referred to by the ancient parish in which they are located and are indexed both by name and parish.